Trust, Tourism Development and Planning

The dynamics of trust and distrust are central to understanding modern society, social relations and development processes. However, numerous studies suggest that societal trust and citizens' trust in government and its institutions are on the decline, challenging the legitimacy of government and leading to an undemocratic and unsustainable form of development. Recognizing its importance, the authors for the first time situate trust within the context of tourism development and planning.

This volume discusses trust in tourism from different yet intrinsically connected perspectives. Chapters review how diminishing societal trust may have adversely affected tourism planning systems, the role of trust in good tourism governance and sustainable tourism, how trust can be used as a facilitator of participatory tourism planning, political trust in tourism institutions, and how tourism development can be a basis for trust creation among society members. In addition, a final section on 'Researching Trust in Tourism Development' means that readers are provided not only with a thorough theoretical understanding of trust and of its importance in sustainable tourism and good governance of the sector, but also on the methodological aspects of researching trust in the context of tourism development and planning.

This significant volume is valuable reading for students, academics and researchers interested in tourism development and planning.

Robin Nunkoo, Ph.D, is Senior Lecturer in Management at the University of Mauritius and a Visiting Senior Research Fellow at the Faculty of Management, University of Johannesburg, South Africa.

Stephen L. J. Smith, Ph.D, is Professor at the University of Guelph, Canada.

Contemporary Geographies of Leisure, Tourism and Mobility

Series Editor: C. Michael Hall, *Professor at the Department of Management, College of Business and Economics, University of Canterbury, Christchurch, New Zealand*

The aim of this series is to explore and communicate the intersections and relationships between leisure, tourism and human mobility within the social sciences.

It will incorporate both traditional and new perspectives on leisure and tourism from contemporary geography, e.g. notions of identity, representation and culture, while also providing for perspectives from cognate areas such as anthropology, cultural studies, gastronomy and food studies, marketing, policy studies and political economy, regional and urban planning and sociology, within the development of an integrated field of leisure and tourism studies.

Also, increasingly, tourism and leisure are regarded as steps in a continuum of human mobility. Inclusion of mobility in the series offers the prospect to examine the relationship between tourism and migration, the sojourner, educational travel and second home and retirement travel phenomena.

The series comprises two strands:

Contemporary Geographies of Leisure, Tourism and Mobility aims to address the needs of students and academics, and the titles will be published in hardback and paperback. Titles include:

Routledge Studies in Contemporary Geographies of Leisure, Tourism and Mobility is a forum for innovative new research intended for research students and academics, and the titles will be available in hardback only. Titles include:

Trust, Tourism Development and Planning

Edited by Robin Nunkoo and
Stephen L. J. Smith

Routledge
Taylor & Francis Group

LONDON AND NEW YORK

First published 2015
by Routledge
2 Park Square, Milton Park, Abingdon, Oxon OX14 4RN

and by Routledge
711 Third Avenue, New York, NY 10017

Routledge is an imprint of the Taylor & Francis Group, an informa business

British Library Cataloguing in Publication Data
A catalogue record for this book is available from the British Library

Library of Congress Cataloging-in-Publication Data
A catalog record for this book has been requested

ISBN: 978-0-415-82601-3 (hbk)
ISBN: 978-0-203-53781-7 (ebk)

Typeset in Times New Roman
by Apex CoVantage, LLC

Printed and bound by CPI Group (UK) Ltd, Croydon, CR0 4YY

Contents

Illustrations

Figures

Tables

Contributors

Bill Bramwell, PhD, is Professor of International Tourism Studies at Sheffield Hallam University, UK. He is co-editor of the *Journal of Sustainable Tourism*, and he has edited books on tourism's relationships with partnerships, sustainability in Europe, rural development, governance and policymaking and coastal areas in Southern Europe. His research interests include tourism policy and planning, tourism and environmental politics, governance in tourism, tourism development and society in China and political economy and tourism development.

Osman Culha is a PhD candidate at Adnan Menderes University, Tourism Management Department, and he has been working as a lecturer in Didim Vocational School. He graduated from Commercial and Tourism Education Faculty of Gazi University and obtained an MSc in Tourism Management at Dokuz Eylul University. His research interests include tourism management, human resources management and education and training in tourism.

Peter Edwards, PhD, is an adjunct researcher at the Department of Forest Products, Swedish University of Agricultural Sciences in Uppsala, Sweden. While his current research involves international relations and forest policy, he has a background in political sociology, specializing in participatory processes and trust in urban planning.

Berrin Güzel, PhD, is Assistant Professor at the University of Adnan Menderes, Turkey. She has several articles and book chapters on HRM, tourism and organizational behavior. Her research interests include organizational behavior, human resource management, management and organization, and tourism.

C. Michael Hall, PhD, is a Professor in the Department of Management, Marketing and Entrepreneurship, University of Canterbury, New Zealand; Docent in the Department of Geography, University of Oulu, Finland; and Visiting Professor, Linnaeus University School of Business and Economics, Kalmar, Sweden. He is a co-editor of Current Issues in Tourism and has published widely on tourism, regional development, environmental change and history, and gastronomy.

Ceren İşçi is a PhD candidate in the Tourism Management Department at Adnan Menderes University, Turkey. She is a lecturer at the Mugla Sıtkı Kocman

University in the Department of Travel Management. Her research interests are in e-Tourism, tourism marketing and destination branding.

Fergus Lyon, PhD, is Professor of Enterprise and Organizations in the Centre for Enterprise and Economic Development Research, Middlesex University, UK. His research interests include trust and cooperation in networks and clusters, enterprise behavior, social enterprise and entrepreneurship, market institutions, social enterprise and economic development policy. Professor Lyon has published widely including papers in *Organization Studies, International Small Business Journal, Cambridge Journal of Economics, Society and Space, World Development* and *Human Organization*. He has carried out research in the UK, Ghana, Nigeria, India, Pakistan and Nepal. Recent work involves trust in business science relationships and the concept of social enterprise.

Heather L. Mair, PhD, is an Associate Professor in the Department of Recreation and Leisure Studies at the University of Waterloo in Ontario, Canada. Her interests include investigations of community development in the context of leisure, sport and tourism; critical approaches to tourism and leisure research; and critical pedagogies.

Guido Möllering, PhD, is Associate Professor of Organization and Management and holds the EWE Chair of Economic Organization and Trust at the School of Humanities & Social Sciences, Jacobs University Bremen, Germany. He earned his PhD in Management at the University of Cambridge, UK, and his Habilitation (postdoctoral degree, venia legendi) in Business Administration at Freie Universität Berlin, Germany. His main areas of research are interorganizational relationships, organizational fields, and trust. Professor Möllering has published several books and many articles in leading journals such as *Organization Science, Organization Studies* and *Journal of International Business Studies*. He is a senior editor of *Organization Studies* and associate editor of the *Journal of Trust Research*.

Gianna Moscardo, PhD, is Professor in the School of Business at James Cook University. Prior to joining JCU, Gianna was the Tourism Research project leader for the CRC Reef Research for eight years. Her research interests include evaluating tourism as a sustainable development strategy with an emphasis on understanding the relationships between characteristics of tourism development and dimensions of destination community well-being. She is also interested in understanding tourist behavior and experiences and the effectiveness of tourist interpretation.

Robin Nunkoo obtained his PhD from the University of Waterloo, Canada. Robin is the Associate Editor of *Journal of Hospitality Marketing and Management*, a Resource Editor for *Annals of Tourism Research*, and an editorial board member of several leading journals. He has research interests in political trust, sustainable tourism, structural equation modeling, and theoretical and methodological issues in social science research. His articles appear in such leading journals as *Annals of Tourism Research, Tourism Management, Journal of*

Travel Research, Journal of Sustainable Tourism, and *Journal of Hospitality and Tourism Research.*

Mark N. K. Saunders, PhD, is Professor of Business Research Methods in the Surrey Business School at the University of Surrey, Guildford, UK. His research interests include human resource aspects of the management of change, in particular trust within and between organizations; small and medium-sized enterprise success and research methods, in particular methods for understanding organizational relationships and online methods. He has coauthored and edited a range of books including *Research Methods for Business Students* (currently in its sixth edition), *Organizational Trust: A Cultural Perspective* and, with Fergus Lyon and Guido Möllering, the *Handbook of Research Methods on Trust.* Professor Saunders's research has been published widely in journals including *Employee Relations, Field Methods, Journal of Personnel Psychology, Journal of Small Business Management* and *Management Learning.*

Stephen L. J. Smith holds a PhD from Texas A&M. His research interests focus on tourism economics, policy, and destination marketing and management. He is the author of numerous articles in scholarly journals as well as several books. He is past-Chair of the Canadian Tourism Commission's Research Committee, past-Chair of the Canadian Tourism Human Resources Council's Research Committee. Stephen consults with various government and not-for-profit agencies. He is an Elected Fellow of the International Statistical Institute, past-Chair of their Committee on Statistics in Travel and Tourism, and an Elected Fellow of the International Academy for the Study of Tourism.

Atila Yüksel, PhD, is Professor of Marketing at the University of Adnan Menderes, Turkey. He serves on the editorial board of ten international scientific journals, and he is the co-founding editor of *Journal of Travel and Hospitality Management* and the editor of *Journal of Travel and Tourism Research.* He has published, both independently and in co-authorship in *Tourism Management, Journal of Hospitality and Tourism Research, Journal of Travel and Tourism Marketing, Cornell Hospitality Quarterly, Annals of Tourism Research, Journal of Quality Assurance in Tourism and Hospitality* and *Journal of Vacation Marketing.* He has co-authored four books and he is the editor of *Tourist Satisfaction and Complaining Behavior: Measurement and Management Issues in the Hospitality and Tourism industry.* Professor Yüksel's research interests are in tourism planning, destination management, services marketing and customer relationship management.

Fisun Yüksel, PhD, is Associate Professor of Marketing at the University of Adnan Menderes, Turkey. She has published in *Tourism Management, Journal of Hospitality and Tourism Research, Journal of Travel and Tourism Marketing, Annals of Tourism Research* and *Journal of Vacation Marketing.* She has co-authored one book and several book chapters. Her research interests are in tourism planning, services marketing and destination branding.

1 Trust, tourism development, and planning

Robin Nunkoo and Stephen L. J. Smith

Trust is a complex construct that is difficult to define and operationalize (Simpson, 2007) because there are so many different ways of conceptualizing and defining it. Seppanen *et al.* (2007) catalogued more than 70 definitions. This does not stop social scientists from offering definitions; it is just that there are numerous and sometimes conflicting conceptualizations of trust. Consequently, it has remained an elusive term in the social science literature and has often been used in different and not always compatible ways. However, despite such divergences, it is universally accepted that trust is a psychological condition defined as "a psychological state comprising the intention to accept vulnerability based upon positive expectations of the intentions or behavior of another" (Rousseau *et al.*, 1998, p. 395). The psychological dimensions of trust are embedded in the majority of definitions put forward by researchers from different social science disciples. For example, Garfinkel (1963) and Luhmann (1988) considered trust as a general attitude or expectancy about other people and the social systems in which they are embedded. Other researchers suggest that trust is a more complex and multidimensional construct comprising affective and motivational components (Bromiley and Cummings, 1996). However, some social scientists argue that psychological definitions of trust are insufficient in explaining trust because they are narrowly too cognitive and ignore the emotional and social influences on trust decisions (Kramer, 1999). Consequently, these researchers suggest that it is important to conceptualize trust in terms of individuals' choice behavior in various trust dilemma situations (Miller, 1992). March (1994) argued that an advantage of conceptualizing trust as a choice behavior relates to the fact that decisions become observable behaviors and noted that such a conceptualization of trust fits well with existing conceptual frameworks useful for empirical testing and theoretical development.

Studies on trust in the social science literature can be grouped into two categories. Early work on the subject adopted a dispositional (person-centered) view to trust and considered trust as general beliefs and attitudes about the degree to which other people are likely to be reliable, cooperative, or helpful in daily life contexts (Rotter, 1971). The second category of studies on trust (which emerged in the early 1980s) conceptualized and measured trust in specific partners and relationships (interpersonal trust) (Holmes and Rempel, 1989). From this perspective, trust is defined as a psychological state or orientation of an actor (the trustor) toward a specific partner (the trustee) with whom the actor is in some way interdependent to attain valued outcomes or resources. From this perspective, trust stimulates cooperation among actors (Moorman *et al.*, 1992), creates goodwill that preserves the relationship (Kumar, 1996), decreases fear and greed (Hwang and Willem, 1997), reduces risk in the transaction (Morgan and Hunt, 1994), and enhances the partners' satisfaction with and commitment to the exchange (Anderson and Narus, 1990; Morgan and Hunt, 1994). Thus, trust is not only about a set of positive expectations, but it also includes the willingness to act on those beliefs (Luhmann, 1979). These trust beliefs shape attitudes and behaviors of the actors in social exchanges (Sheppard and Sherman, 1998).

Trust, tourism development, and planning

Trust is essential for effective planning and development, as Laurian (2009, p. 369) noted:

> Trust is a central element of planning practice because the profession is positioned at the nexus of public and private interests, has a crucial role in the contested management of space, and seeks to promote democratic governance and public participation in local decision making.

Trust as a fundamental ingredient is the basis on which planning agencies and other stakeholders' rely as it creates the necessary conditions on the basis of which successful partnerships and collaboration take place in development planning (Connick and Innes, 2003; Höppner, 2009; Kumar and Paddison, 2000; O'Riordan and Ward, 1997). Thus, trust highly influences the success or failure of planning and development processes.

In the tourism sector, especially in democratic societies, trust helps governments pass legislation, make tourism plans, invest in public and public–private partnerships, and have reasonably smooth relationships among governmental organizations and, indeed, different governments, and between government and citizens. For example, trust in tourism institutions has been found to influence public support for tourism development in developing countries (e.g. Nunkoo *et al.*, 2012; Nunkoo and Ramkissoon, 2012) as well as developed ones (e.g. Nunkoo and Smith, 2013). The existence of a reasonable level of trust among key tourism players and between those players and the society in which they operate significantly affects the nature and magnitude of environmental, social, and economic impacts and other strategies developed to minimize negative consequences. Empirical evidence suggests a recursive relationship between trust and public perceptions of tourism development. While in some contexts public trust has been found to shape residents' perceptions of the benefits and costs of tourism development (e.g. Nunkoo and Ramkissoon, 2011), perceptions of tourism are influenced by public trust in tourism institutions in other situations (e.g. Nunkoo *et al.*, 2012; Nunkoo and Ramkissoon, 2012; Nunkoo and Smith, 2013).

At a more commercial level, for customers and tourism businesses, trust facilitates business decisions that involve consumer relations, contracts and interactions with suppliers, partnerships, licensing, and long-term business dealings. Trust also shapes employer–employee relationships, facilitates the hiring and retention of employees, promote investments, and supports partnerships among businesses and between businesses and government/nongovernmental agencies in the tourism sector. It is not that where there is little trust these activities cannot happen, but where there is little trust these activities are much more difficult and time-consuming – and less likely to be successful. Nevertheless, a two-way relationship between trust and tourism development can be established. While successful and sustainable tourism development and planning requires that tourism stakeholders trust each other because "trust lubricates cooperation," tourism networks also foster trust among development participants (Putnam *et al.*, 1993, p. 171).

The study of trust has evolved over time, from an early focus on the origins of an individual's willingness (or lack of willingness) to trust to a stronger emphasis on interpersonal dynamics and the social/organizational determinants in the support (or destruction) of trust. However, despite such developments, the importance of trust and the number of authors who write about trust, there is very little empirical research on the role of trust in tourism planning and development. This book explores the phenomenon of trust in a variety of contexts by a number of international experts. The main body of the book begins with a discussion (Chapter 2, by Edwards and Nunkoo) on the need and importance of trust in tourism planning and development. In this chapter, Edwards and Nunkoo contextualize and define the concept of trust and discuss the various dimensions of trust relevant to tourism planning and development. Edwards and Nunkoo provide a useful classification of trust, including one based on the formation of trust, such as a rational calculation of benefits and costs associated with tourism development. The contributors discuss the need for trust in tourism planning from the perspectives of community and social life, stakeholders' power in tourism, good governance, and democratic legitimacy. Edwards and Nunkoo further explore the necessity for trust in tourism development by exploring the crisis of trust that has developed as a result of a risk, pluralistic, right-based, and liberal society.

In Chapter 3, Bramwell explores the relationships among trust, governance, and sustainable tourism. As he notes, politics is never far beneath the surface of the formation and implementation of policies and practices that determine to a significant degree whether tourism in a jurisdiction – from city to multinational bloc – is sustainable. Bramwell discusses the nature of tourism governance and sustainable tourism, and, like Edwards and Nunkoo, he argues that there is consideration of the specific character of trust within tourism governance, including its relations with political legitimacy. Bramwell elaborates on various contextual relationships between sustainable tourism and trust. He argues that questions of trust and mistrust are highly dependent on context and that the relationships among trust, governance, and sustainable tourism are far more complex than is sometimes assumed.

Mair, in Chapter 4, explores the nature of participatory tourism planning. She is interested in what constitutes a "community" and how community members are able to participate in the planning process. She explores the nature of planning and the importance of involving community members in planning endeavours, and concludes by asking whether "sustainable tourism" is more about sustaining a community or sustaining the sector. She looks at the various approaches to tourism planning and highlights the fact that collaborative planning, or participatory planning in her vocabulary, is predicated on citizens and denizens having trust in planners and decision makers as well as planners and decision makers trusting "ordinary" residents. Mair discusses how participatory planning fosters trust among stakeholders.

Moscardo considers the complex relationship among tourism development, social capital, and trust. In Chapter 5, she argues that there are forms of capital beyond economic and financial such as human and natural. However, she also acknowledges that the idea of extending the concept of capital to economic and financial realms is controversial. In this context, she describes three approaches to deciding the determinants of "a good life": (1) individual freedom of choice, (2) a subjective quality-of-life model, and (3) the "good society" model, which situates a good life in the context of a healthy, stable society. She reviews literature on social capital, and her discussion highlights the need to be more careful in defining what social capital is, how it is generated, how it is used, and what it is used for. Within this discussion, she recognizes trust as an important factor contributing to the development of social capital. After conceptualizing trust in the context of social capital development, she notes that trust which is often considered as part of social capital is, in fact, distinct from the latter. In this chapter, Moscardo articulates a framework linking tourism development to trust and social capital, and notes the importance of stakeholders developing a shared understanding of what values and goals are fundamental to a destination.

In Chapter 6, Hall addresses the topic of human security in tourism with specific reference to climate change. While concern over security is often associated with issues such as criminal activity, war, and terrorism, he adds climate change and environmental disasters to this list of challenges. In this chapter, Hall argues that trust in the context of environmental change is even more significant than in other tourism planning contexts. Like other authors in this volume, Hall asserts that the role of tourism planning is not to maximize benefits for the sector but to secure the interests of destination communities. The combination of environmental change with the challenges imposed by poverty make planning all the more urgent, from local to international scales, and from the individual to the community. His discussion of security is explored in the context of different forms of governance, including possible planning interventions at different scales of planning. Adaptation to and mitigation of environmental change require appropriate policy, technological, and behavioral innovations that, in turn, require trust for success. And with Moscardo, Hall emphasizes the need for shared values and reciprocal or cooperative actions, and, more importantly, trust.

Distrust in the impartiality and fairness of decision makers in a destination can result in the withdrawal of residents from offering support for tourism development or participating in planning initiatives. This issue is examined by Yüksel, Yüksel, Culha, Güzel, and İşçi in Chapter 7. The contributors examine people who for whatever reason are excluded from tourism development planning. The authors focus on planning in developing countries, with a particular look at clientelism – a form of social organization in which a powerful "patron" promises benefits to relatively powerless "clients" in exchange for loyalty and votes and corruption. They propose a series of propositions describing the forces to which local residents will become involved and supportive of tourism development – or oppose it. Fundamental to these propositions are elements of trust, reliability, transparency, accountability, and accessibility to institutions that make decisions.

In the penultimate chapter, Nunkoo extends the concept of trust to a political context. Given undisputable role of government in tourism development and planning as political economy approach suggests, Nunkoo argues that a democratic and sustainable form of tourism requires that residents' trust government institutions involved in tourism policy making. He studies the notion of trust in the context of an exchange relationship between government and citizens. Using social exchange theory, institutional theory of political trust, and cultural theory of political trust, Nunkoo develops a conceptual framework that examines political trust in tourism and the relationship between the latter and community support for tourism development. He pays special attention to the correlates of political trust and considers which aspects of institutions and societal culture are likely to have a determining impact on the levels of citizens' and denizens' trust in government in tourism development. He offers several propositions that deserve empirical attention. Nunkoo concludes that the concept of political trust in tourism offers several opportunities for research and argues that it can be better understood if studied from different, often conflicting, theoretical perspectives.

The final chapter, by Saunders, Lyon, and Möllering, provides insights into methodological issues and concepts related to researching trust in the context of tourism. The authors note that the diversity of methods and concepts poses challenges for researchers, but the diversity provides the opportunity to draw from different traditions and experiences. They offer an overview of the leading empirical (quantitative) and subjective (qualitative) methods as well as mixed research designs. The choice of methods is influenced by the researcher's assumptions and preferred epistemology. Further, the focus of research may be on the trustors' intentions, the trustworthiness of the person/agency being trusted, the act of trusting, or the process of developing trust.

The perspectives taken by our various authors reflect the diversity of approaches and foci related to trust scholarship. To start, there is the topic of not just defining trust but offering classifications of trust – what types, how are they formed, and so on. Several authors offer classifications of trust such as trust based on a rational process, a function of personal experience, or a dynamic based on formal control mechanisms. Other authors couch research on trust in the framework of social exchange theory. In other words, they look at trust as the result of a process involving mutual agreements, understandings, and a *quid pro quo* dynamic. Some authors reflect on a number of contemporary social trends that make the granting of trust increasingly problematic, such as growing awareness of negative effects of tourism and the rise of a right-based and pluralistic society. Further, many societies in Europe and the West are increasingly multicultural, with a concomitant decline in shared values and ambitions. Such a lack of consensus that glues a society together eventually permits seeds of discord and suspicion to take root and grow. With a decreasing sense of commonality, social values decline, accompanied with an emphasis on individual rights, trust is further compromised. Another face of this trend is the growth in what is usually called "neoliberalism," an emphasis on a free-market economy, less government intervention, and greater emphasis on technocratic problem solving and worldviews.

The authors in this book examine not only the types of trust and from where they arise but some of the impediments to the creation or nurturing of trust and their implications for tourism development and planning. To use Edwards and Nunkoo's words, they perceive "a crisis of trust" in tourism development and planning, although not acknowledged as such by researchers and scholars. Some authors note that trust scholarship has yet to adequately address challenges associated with managing threats, whether human or natural, and to develop mechanisms for minimizing or mitigating threats. In particular, more attention needs to be given to governance structures that can promote adaptation and mitigation strategies for emerging threats.

All authors in this volume reflect the fact that trust occurs in a social context and that the development of tourism plans and policies involves some form of cooperation and, in principle, consultation among people and organizations. However, our contributors are also aware that there are community members who are excluded from planning and decision making. Greater, more inclusive involvement by the whole community should, in principle, permit more productive, successful, and enriching tourism projects – or, at a minimum, reduce conflicts and negative impacts in the community. Using the notion of trust, several of the authors offer strategies and perspectives that have the potential to optimize the outcomes of tourism planning and development. Research on trust also reflects the ontologies and preferred epistemologies of the scholars who explore the topics. This book provides an overview of many – although not all – of these approaches and worldviews.

Although our contributors approached the topic of trust from different yet related perspectives, they highlight an urgent need for tourism planners, scholars, and researchers to consider more seriously the role of trust in tourism development. Failure to do so is likely to distort tourism planning, where consensus becomes theoretically difficult, if not impossible. It is hoped that this book provides a basis for further research on trust and expands the lines of enquiry raised here. Multiple methods, concepts, perspective, questions, and data sources will be – as they have become – the norm for studying tourism and trust. Trust scholarship is becoming one of the most innovative and critical lines of research in tourism, development, and political economy.

References

Anderson, J. C., and Narus, J. A. (1990). A model of distributor firm and manufacturer firm working partnerships. *Journal of Marketing Research, 54*, 42–58.

Bromiley, P., and Cummings, L. L. (1996). Transaction costs in organization with trust. In R. Bies, R. Lewicki, and B. Sheppard (Eds.), *Research on Negotiation in Organizations* (pp. 219–247). Greenwich, CT: JAI Press.

Connick, S., and Innes, J. E. (2003). Outcomes of collaborative water policy making: Applying complexity thinking to evaluation. *Journal of Environmental Planning and Management, 46*(2), 177–197.

Garfinkel, H. (1963). A conception of, and experiments with, trust as a condition of stable concerted actions. In O. J. Harvey (Ed.), *Motivation and social interaction: Cognitive determinants* (pp. 81–93). New York: Ronald.

Holmes, J. G., and Rempel, J. K. (1989). Trust in close relationships. In C. Hendrick (Ed.), *Close relationships* (pp. 187–220). Newbury Park, CA: Sage.

Höppner, C. (2009). Trust – A monolithic panacea in land use planning? *Land Use Policy, 26*(4), 1046–1054.

Hwang, P., and Willem, B. (1997). Properties of trust: An analytical view. *Organizational Behavior and Human Decision Processes, 69*, 67–73.

Kramer, R. (1999). Trust and distrust in organizations: Emerging perspectives, enduring questions. *Annual Review of Psychology, 50*, 569–598.

Kumar, N. (1996). The power of trust in manufacturer–retailer relationships. *Harvard Business Review, 74*, 92–105.

Kumar, A., and Paddison, R. (2000). Trust and collaborative planning theory: The case of the Scottish planning system. *International Planning Studies, 5*(2), 205–223.

Laurian, L. (2009). Trust in planning: Theoretical and practical considerations for participatory and deliberative planning. *Planning Theory & Practice, 10*(3), 369–391.

Luhmann, N. (1979). *Trust and power*. New York: John Wiley.

Luhmann, N. (1988). Trust: Making and breaking cooperative relations. In D. Gambetta (Ed.), *Familiarity, Confidence, Trust: Problems and Alternative* (pp. 94–107). New York: Basil Blackwell.

March, J. G. (1994). *A primer on decision making*. New York: Free Press.

Miller, G. J. (1992). *Managerial dilemmas: The political economy of hierarchies*. New York: Cambridge University Press.

Moorman, C., Zaltman, G., and Deshpande, R. (1992). Relationships between providers and users of marketing research: The dynamics of trust within and between organizations. *Journal of Marketing Research, 29*, 312–314.

Morgan, R., and Hunt, S. D. (1994). The commitment-trust theory of relationship marketing. *Journal of Marketing, 58*, 20–38.

Nunkoo, R., and Ramkissoon, H. (2011). Developing a community support model for tourism. *Annals of Tourism Research, 38*(3), 964–988.

Nunkoo, R., and Ramkissoon, H. (2012). Power, trust, social exchange, and community support. *Annals of Tourism Research, 39*, 997–1023.

Nunkoo, R., Ramkissoon, H., and Gursoy, D. (2012). Public trust in tourism institutions. *Annals of Tourism Research, 39*(3), 1538–1564.

Nunkoo, R., and Smith, S. L. (2013). Political economy of tourism: Trust in government actors, political support, and their determinants. *Tourism Management, 36*, 120–132.

O'Riordan, T., and Ward, R. (1997). Building trust in shoreline management: Creating participatory consultation in shoreline management plans. *Land Use Policy, 14*(4), 257–276.

Putnam, R. D., Leonardi, R. and Nanetti, R. Y. (1993). *Making democracy work: Civic traditions of modern Italy*. Princeton, NJ: Princeton University Press.

Rotter, J. B. (1971). Generalized expectancies of interpersonal trust. *American Psychologist, 26*, 443–452.

Rousseau, D. M., Sitkin, S. B., Burt, R. S., and Camerer, C. (1998). Not so different after all: A cross-discipline view of trust. *Academy of Management Review, 23*(3), 393–404.

Seppanen, R., Blomqvist, K., and Sundqvist, S. 2007. Measuring inter-organizational trust: A critical review of the empirical research: 1990–2003. *Industrial Marketing Management, 36,* 249–265.

Sheppard, B. H., and Sherman, D. M. (1998). The grammars of trust: A model and general implications. *Academy of Management Review, 23*(3), 422–437.

Simpson, J. A. (2007). Psychological foundations of trust. *Current Directions in Psychological Science, 16*(5), 264–268.

2 The need for and crisis of trust in tourism planning and development

Peter Edwards and Robin Nunkoo

Introduction

We hear reports in the media that pollsters and others find that trust in politicians, government, media, and various professionals is decreasing or already at an all-time low. The media and some academics have seized this phenomenon and suggest that we may (or may not) be facing or experiencing a crisis of trust, in this case in the planning profession. The crisis of trust may be more acute in tourism planning due to the combined, heavy involvement of politicians, government and planners and a plethora of already mistrusted organizations, professions and individuals. If society in general is losing trust in politicians, government and planning professionals, what does this mean for tourism planning and development?

Conversely, we might ask whether there is really a crisis of trust or whether it is, as O'Neill (2002) claims, a distorted view of reality or more of a rising culture of suspicion. Perhaps the crisis of trust and/or a culture of suspicion do exist, particularly among the general public, politicians and the media, but are not as widespread as the media and others would have us believe. It may be a more localized or contextual problem. Whether or not the crisis exists, trust is a necessary component of all aspects of functioning in our daily lives and society in general – everyone must place trust in someone else (interpersonal trust), and we need to trust that our political and decision-making systems will provide us with just, fair and legitimate institutions (institutional trust). There is good evidence that we in society say we trust less, but this does not automatically translate into showing less trust – it may simply be a matter of what we tell pollsters in response to vague or general questions rather than an active refusal to trust (O'Neill, 2002).

Contextualizing and defining trust

Trust is a crucial aspect of our society and underlies the functioning of all institutions. In this chapter, we take the view that institutions are made up of norms, conventions and habits that are established over time and shape how we live and interact with society. Cook and Gronke (2005) found that while people have confidence in institutions, the latter may not necessarily be seen as trustworthy. Trust and confidence, while related, are not the same thing; neither does trustworthiness, often mentioned, equate to trust. At an individual level, trust is contextual because it depends on specific personal experiences – I may trust a particular doctor but not another based on my individual experiences with them. Trust is also contextualized in many disciplines, including the fields of psychology, sociology, political science, economics and mass media (Kasperson *et al.*, 1992). Each of these fields comprises a variety of more specific, contextualized meanings. This chapter brings together a number of broad concepts that are widely accepted and used in both political science and in planning and development contexts.

A number of authors have broadly defined trust as a psychological state comprising the intention to accept vulnerability based upon positive expectations of the intentions or behavior of another (Bijlsma-Frankema and Costa, 2005; Connell and Mannion, 2006; Möllering, 2005a; Rousseau *et al.*, 1998). This definition covers some of the major dimensions of trust and starts to situate it as a component of social and interpersonal phenomena, where one party, who is 'doing' the trusting, (the trustor) is taking a risk or making a leap of faith or going beyond what one would normally do (Bijlsma-Frankema and Costa, 2005: 261) with another party, who is being trusted, (the trustee) with the future expectation that they will fulfil their end of the transaction (Kasperson *et al.*, 1992). In essence, the trustor needs to be able to believe that the information that he or she is receiving from the trustee is true, cutting directly to the integrity of the trustee, be that an individual, organization or institution (Hosmer, 1995). This is linked with O'Neill's (2002) conception of trustworthiness. Trustworthiness involves the following elements:

Mutual meeting of expectations: Even this 'requirement' of the positive meeting of expectations may not be completely necessary. O'Neill (2002) notes that we may actually still trust others every day, all the while knowing that we face possible disappointment of not having our expectations met.

Interpersonal and institutional trust: Interpersonal trust is the trust that can be created between individual human beings, and comes from our early life (parents and upbringing), but is constantly adjusted and refined as we gain experiences throughout life (Mishler and Rose, 1997; Uslaner, 2004). This is one level of trust; the other level is institutional trust. Within each of these levels, one can find three types of trust (calculus-based, knowledge-based, and active trust). By considering interpersonal and institutional trust two distinct levels, we mean that interpersonal trust is created through tangible relationships – one can actually see, feel or communicate with the other party in the relationship. Institutional trust is on an intangible level – we know that particular laws, norms or customs exist; they may not be visible to us, but we are still able to form a relationship with them. However, this can be through different means than a tangible relationship. Individuals develop institutional trust through the relationships and interactions they have with individuals who are the human face of these institutions and the organizations that represent them.

Types of trust

Each of what we have called 'types of trust' encompasses a variety of names given to each by various authors (Edwards, 2009). These types of trust are also indicative of the relative strength or thickness of the trust they represent, in this case from weak to strong types of trust.

Calculus-based trust

Calculus-based trust (CBT) can be considered the most basic type of trust and is based upon a trustor's ongoing calculation of the trustee's predictability, one of the key dimensions of trust. In CBT, all the costs and benefits involved in the relationship are constantly calculated and evaluated by the trustor (Maguire *et al.*, 2001). In addition to calculating the costs and benefits, all the trustor's knowledge and information from previous interactions as well as expectations from future interactions are integrated to determine whether to trust (Möllering, 2005a; Neu, 1991). CBT is created, maintained, damaged or destroyed based on the outcomes of these calculations. These calculations also include consideration of incentives, rewards and punishments for creating, maintaining or damaging the trust relationship (Maguire *et al.*, 2001). In other words, coercion or remunerative control (forms of power) is a major sociological component of calculus-based trust, akin to a form of contracting (Lewicki and Benedict Bunker, 1995). Some recent work has investigated specifically the role that contracts may play in building trust in planning and development. However, the overall consensus is that where contracts have been involved in a successful trusting relationship, it may not have been the contracts, but the management of relationships around the contracts, that contributed most to trust. This can be seen as a market-oriented, rationalist economic calculation of the trust relationship; individuals are opportunistic and self-interested (Doney *et al.*, 1998) and will only trust if it is in their self-interest.

Swain and Tait (2007) have found that this type of trust is 'thin' and can break down easily. Questions have arisen about whether CBT can really be considered as trust. Lewicki and Benedict Bunker (1995) state that CBT is often the starting point for trust relationships, and that these relationships can develop professionally and sequentially, moving from CBT into knowledge-based trust (KBT), the next 'level' of trust when moving toward the pinnacle. One of the major differences between CBT and KBT is that KBT is generally free from the use of control or coercion. There may, however, be other, more subtle forms of power operating in KBT.

Knowledge-based trust

Knowledge-based trust, like CBT, relies heavily on the predictability of the trustee (Maguire *et al.*, 2001). There is, however, a progression from reliance on incentives and punishments to an increased reliance on information in KBT (Lewicki and Benedict Bunker, 1995). This increased reliance on information comes from the trustor's own observational and experiential 'data' over time, and particularly from a consistent pattern of behavior on the part of the trustee (Maguire *et al.*, 2001; Uslaner, 2002). With incentives and punishments eliminated and an increased knowledge of the trustee, this may partially eliminate self-interest and opportunism, opening up space for goodwill, a second key dimension of trust. Lewicki and Benedict Bunker (1995) go further by stating that regular communication needs to be present, in addition to consistent behavior and experiences. KBT therefore cannot be generated spontaneously or instantly; it emerges naturally over time through the increasing interaction and experience of stakeholders engaging in trusting relationships (Maguire *et al.*, 2001).

Because we have more interaction and experience with people or groups we already know, KBT has been closely linked to trust in people who we already know, or who are a part of our own group, culture or social group (Neu, 1991; Uslaner, 2002; Uslaner and Conley, 2003; Uslaner, 2004; Uslaner and Brown, 2005). Möllering (2005b) further suggests that this trust also may be due to similarities between various actors and stakeholders. Lewis and Weigert (1995) and Connell and Mannion (2006) propose that trust also involves previous knowledge of an actor or an institution as well as the situation or context surrounding the trust action.

Active trust

Active trust can be considered something of a pinnacle in trust and public participation processes, community engagement and the policy and planning realm, because it is a very strong and robust type of trust (Maguire *et al.*, 2001). Active trust breaks down barriers between sectors or interests by building new and creative collaborations, reducing risk and opening up opportunities (Banks *et al.*, 2000). Active trust is thus a social construction that is gradually and actively created and built up by the actors or stakeholders involved through processes of continuous communication and reflexive familiarization (Child and Möllering, 2003; Möllering, 2005a; 2005b; 2006). This suggests that there is a substantial amount of work and effort involved on the part of actors to ensure that this strong type of trust is energetically built and sustained. Active trust as a way to mitigate the crisis of trust is outlined later in this chapter.

The need for trust in tourism planning and development

Community and social life

Irrespective of its type, trust is required to build institutions, fora and decisions and community (Stein and Harper, 2003). Foucault (1984) considered that truth is the construct of political and economic forces within the societal web. He identified the creation of truth in contemporary society along the following traits: the centring of truth on scientific discourse; the accountability of truth to economic and political forces; the diffusion and consumption of truth via societal apparatuses; and the control of the distribution of truth by political and economic apparatuses. He went on to argue that truth arises from political debate and social confrontation. Foucault (1984) further suggested that each society has its regime of truth, its "general politics" of truth (p. 131). For Foucault (1984, 1980), truth should be understood as a system of ordered procedures for the production, regulation, distribution and operation of statements.

Wittgenstein concluded that trust, not power, underpins human and social life (Edwards, 1982) and, in particular, communication, understanding, knowledge and learning (Stein and Harper, 2003). Trust is needed by everyone because we need to rely on others acting as they say they will and need others to accept that we will act as we say we will (O'Neill, 2002). In other words, we need to meet others' expectations while others meet ours. Tourism development is characterized by social and network relationships among various stakeholders, each of whom is highly dependent on the other. Such relationships are typically based on commitment which is established through trust (Gulati and Sytch, 2007; Mavondo and Rodrigo, 2001). Further to the idea that trust is the glue of all social life, without trust we would have "total paralysis of action" (O'Neill, 2001: 12). Möllering (2001) goes even further, relating a situation where a total lack of trust has deteriorated into one of terror. Terror and terrorism further undermine trust through the spread of fear, corroding our ability to place trust (O'Neill, 2002). This is opposed to a situation where there is mistrust. Mistrust is a form of negative trust and can still be used to shape government and society.

Dominance of power

Despite the centrality of trust for the development of a modern and democratic society and in social relations, literature on tourism development and planning has traditionally been dominated by the concept of power (e.g. Altinay and Bowen, 2006; Beritelli and Laesser, 2011; Bramwell, 2006; Bramwell and Meyer, 2007; Cheong and Miller, 2000; Doorne, 1998; Ford *et al.*, 2012; Hall, 1994, 2003, 2010; Hannam, 2002; Macleod and Carrier, 2010; Moscardo, 2011; Obenour and Cooper, 2010; Reed, 1997), and little attention has been devoted to trust as an important ingredient of tourism planning and development. Michel Foucault's notion that truth is omnipresent in all aspects of a society is reinforced by Stein and Harper (2003) who argued that social discourses should not be understood only in terms of power, but they should also be viewed as comprising of trust among social actors. The researchers further asserted that a theoretical privileging of the concept of power only may blind researchers and scholars to other realities and could bring despair and suspicions among social actors, undermining their trust. They noted that an acute awareness of power may also induce paralysis and create a feeling of disempowerment for those who already see themselves as less powerful in the development process. An over focus on power may also be dangerous to planning theories as it may mean that everything is interpreted within a reductionist framework of power. Trust is useful in reducing conflicts and promoting effective collaboration and partnerships in planning and development (Beierle and Konisky, 2000; Laurian, 2009; Swain and Tait, 2007). For these reasons, Stein and Harper (2003) urged researchers to pay equal attention to the vocabulary of trust in social relations.

From government to governance

The need for trust considerations in tourism development is reinforced because of the shift in approach in tourism policy making from the notion of 'government' to that of 'governance' (Beaumont and Dredge, 2010; Hall, 2011), which is another key aspect in political economy (Bramwell, 2011). "Governance involves the processes for the regulation and mobilization of social action and for producing social order" (Bramwell and Lane, 2011: 412). Governance within a destination includes the arrangements and character of institutions, rules and processes through which tourism policy decisions are made and authority is exercised that affect that destination (Bevir, 2009). Good governance is necessary for destinations to achieve sustainable tourism, and it cannot be understood without taking into account the state's relationship with society (Bramwell, 2010; Bramwell and Lane, 2011). Several studies suggest that stakeholders' trust in institutions is important for achieving good governance and a democratic planning process (e.g. Bouckaert and van de Walle, 2003; Park and Blenkinsopp, 2011). Discussing the importance of trust in government for a democratic society, Nye *et al.* (1997) noted that:

> If people believe that government is incompetent and cannot be trusted, they are less likely to provide [critical] resources. Without critical resources, government cannot perform well, and if government cannot perform, people will become more dissatisfied and distrustful of it. Such a cumulative downward spiral could erode support for democracy as a form of governance.
>
> (p. 4)

Democratic legitimacy

Trust is the central pillar in politics and enhances people's ability to cooperate (Misztal, 1996). Legitimacy itself does not rely only on trust, but on an individual's sense of duty to obey a proper authority. Trust, therefore, may be an indicator of legitimacy in that people who trust that political power is appropriately exercised have good grounds for compliance with tourism policies and plans (Misztal, 1996). When there is minimal trust in the economic and political institutions of today and doubts about the type of rationality employed by these institutions, these institutions lack legitimacy (Misztal, 1996). Opening up the policy and planning process and including community stakeholders, who are then able to see and experience the rationality involved, normally increases trust and legitimacy in the process. Habermas also claims that any crisis in legitimacy can be traced to the lack of transparency in socio-political processes (Misztal, 1996). The participatory nature of tourism planning processes is also key to both trust and legitimacy, through, as Misztal (1996) claims, promoting a viable 'civil religion' of participation, cooperation and democratic accountability. Openness, transparency and accountability are considered key components of the legitimacy of not only the process but the frameworks behind them (Lawrence, 2004). However, institutional legitimacy is said to rest largely on actors, stakeholders and the general public having trust in them (Beck, 1999). So legitimacy requires openness, transparency, accountability and trust.

Stein and Harper (2003: 125) note that planning "is intended to be a fair and legitimate process, aiming to produce environments that are better places for living decent and healthy lives." This is particularly true of tourism planning, where this idea is applied to not only residents but 'transient' employees and tourists alike. To open up spaces to accommodate these different 'cultures', a radical paradigm shift is not needed, but rather trust, built up through a steady expansion from the current state (Stein and Harper, 2003). However, this is not always the case in tourism development and planning. Simmons (1994) notes that local communities are key stakeholders in tourism, but they are also often the least powerful in development, and consequently, they bear the majority of the negative consequences of tourism development. Their powerlessness and vulnerability to the adverse impacts of tourism development undermine their trust in tourism planning and development (Nunkoo and Smith, 2013). Tourism development should therefore become more participatory based at the community level. The concept of participatory democracy is important for the (democratic) legitimacy of tourism planning decisions (Beetham, 1991). However, only passive participation of communities does not provide all that is needed for legitimacy. Often, while community members and local organizations are able to participate in the planning process, they are excluded from the decision-making phase (Edwards, 2009; Kayat, 2002). Local communities must be part of both the planning and decision making for trust to develop – that is, they must actively participate in the tourism development process.

Crisis of trust

The crisis of trust discussed by a number of authors (O'Neill 2001; 2002; Swain and Tait, 2007) also highlights the need for trust in tourism planning and development. The Oxford dictionary (2003: 254) defines a crisis as "A time of intense difficulty or danger." Thus, we can infer that a crisis of trust exists when and where the general public and communities have lost trust in politicians, professionals and the media, for example. Swain and Tait (2007) describe four pillars that may contribute to building a crisis of trust in tourism planning and development. These pillars could also be considered red flags, highlighting the need for trust in tourism.

Rise of the risk society

The first pillar of the crisis of trust is the rise of the risk society. Beck (1992) describes the risk society as a way of dealing with hazards and uncertainties emerging from modernization (our modern society or industrial civilization). These hazards and uncertainties, related to tourism, can include local environmental degradation, pollution, crime, and climate change. Caplan (2000) notes that risks in modernity are distributed unequally, most often in an inverse relationship to wealth – less wealthy areas suffer proportionally more from increased risks than wealthy areas. Swain and Tait (2007) link the crisis of trust with reflexivity in the risk society, noting that reflexivity allows actors to think of, highlight or anticipate new areas and higher levels of risk. This, in turn, erodes the foundations of trust. Second, Swain and Tait (2007) note that as we become aware of the risks that we face, we transfer trust from being something that is founded upon personal experience to a reliance on expert systems and professionals.

The risk society may have a wider-ranging impact on trust in tourism planning and development than in other contexts. Not only are there risks affecting tourism planners and developers, local communities and governments involved, there are also the risks perceived by potential tourists. For example, Africa has perceived risks of cultural and linguistic barriers, primitive conditions, and unfounded myths and rumors (Lepp *et al.*, 2011). Ferreira and Harmse (2000) found that risk alters the demand patterns of tourists and can have a large impact on their behavior. In a world that already has increased uncertainty and risk from crime, terrorism, geopolitical tensions, and environmental disasters (Yeoman *et al.*, 2006), the risk society has a significant potential to contribute to a crisis of trust, with additional actors that are involved beyond those directly involved in tourism planning and the local communities.

Although this chapter does address the idea of trust in the face of 'outside' risks, some risks are also inherent in the process of building trust. This distinction between a known or unknown entity brings up the idea of trust needing the trustor to involve herself or himself in a certain degree of risk or uncertainty (Gilson, 2006). While trust is usually associated with decreasing risk or uncertainty (Lewicki and Benedict Bunker, 1995), the trustor needs to weigh the risk that he or she is trying to mitigate with the amount of risk or uncertainty involved in trusting someone to reduce the risk in the first place. Trust is not a response to certainty about others' future actions; it is needed precisely because we lack certainty about others' future behaviors. If people could be absolutely certain about the future actions of others, there would be no need for trust. Trust, through each of its types, is about reducing the risk we may face from the actions of others.

The rise of the pluralistic society

The second pillar of the crisis of trust is the rise of the pluralistic society in tourism development. Society today is fragmented – fragmented interests and loyalties, with power shared among many groups (Swain and Tait, 2007). The competition among these fragmented groups affects trust – those that do not have the same interests are not trusted (Uslaner, 2004). For example, as demonstrated by Gu and Ryan (2008), as tourists increased in a Beijing neighbourhood, an increasing polarization of opinions and perceptions of tourists and tourism development appeared, threatening the sense of community. The researchers concluded that this polarization could be a generational difference, with younger people more open to changes (through tourism) and older residents more resistant to change. In other situations, trust is compromised because state's activities increasingly happen through arm's-length relationships, with a growing role for agencies and public–private sector partnerships. Such a pluralistic tourism planning environment compromises trust among stakeholders, particular public trust in government and tourism-related institutions (Bramwell, 2011).

With the many interests in our fragmented society, even professionals, such as planners, who are supposed to work for the public good, are no longer able to figure out what the public good really is among all of the competing interests. Swain and Tait (2007) further contend that if the motivations behind planning are questioned, there is then a double crisis of trust in planning. These threaten legitimacy of government institutions and create political and social instability, making it difficult for the government to sustain economic activities (Bramwell, 2011). Participation, particularly through deliberative processes, can be seen as a way to bring a pluralistic community closer together and build trust. In the pluralistic society, tourism planners, among others, must contend with changing expectations, views and opinions.

The rise of the pluralistic society can be seen as both a challenge to and facilitator of building trust. In facilitating trust, the pluralistic society can be linked to KBT, particularly through Uslaner's (2002) and others' conception of us trusting people we already know or are familiar with. However, this promotes trust within potentially highly isolated groups and not throughout society more generally. The pluralistic society has a much stronger argument as a challenge to the building of trust as there is an increasing variety of interpretations of institutions, norms, customs and values due to a greater number of personal or group interests. Society then avoids trusting those individuals or groups that do not have the same specific interests as it does (Swain and Tait, 2007). This tendency of actors to stick with and trust similar actors implies that they may not be willing to take on the potentially increased risks involved with trusting strangers (Uslaner and Conley, 2003). At the level of KBT, then, trust can still be considered a closed affair, where trust remains within a particular group with like interests or values and does not extend to communities or society more broadly. This closeness could be considered a mechanism to protect actors from the exercise of power, as 'others' may not share the same values and may attempt to exploit a particular group of actors for their own ends (the exercise of power, in a variety of forms) (Uslaner and Conley, 2003). This is the way in which KBT shares characteristics with CBT, in that people will still act in their own self-interest, not increasing the amount of risk they may potentially face.

The rise of advanced liberalism

Another pillar of the crisis of trust as noted by Swain and Tait (2007) is the rise of advanced liberalism (also neoliberalism). This political ideology stresses a free-market economy and enterprise and is characterized by less government intervention where decisions are not made on behalf of an 'ethical man' but rather on behalf on an 'economic man' (Swain and Tait, 2007: 240). In liberal economies, the market is paramount and a free market is best in terms of organizing and distributing tourism resources and wealth among society members. Before the substantive rise of advanced liberalism, governments played a much greater role in tourism development (Schlicher, 2007). Neoliberal public-sector reforms that began in the 1980s resulted in the state becoming less involved in tourism policy and planning (Bevir, 2009; Dredge and Jenkins, 2007; Shone and Ali Memon, 2008). Such reforms have also meant that government's roles have changed from a public administration body that involved implementation of tourism policies geared toward provisions and management of public goods to a more corporatist model that emphasizes investment returns, efficiency and relationships with private tourism stakeholders (Hall, 1999). Hall further asserts that this has meant an increasing focus on individualism through achievements of self-interests, accompanied by a decline in legitimacy of government as perceived by its citizens. A case in point can be found in Turkey, where tourism planning and development has been 'privatized' in the form of a company called Betujab (Yüksel *et al.*, 2005). This company lacks any legal basis for planning and development, but is still able to act as a de facto public authority through its political and financial ties (Yüksel *et al.*, 2005). Having as its main objective to increase shareholders' value, the company fails to respond to the needs of local communities, creating an environment of mistrust in tourism planning and development.

Where communities could previously expect government to ensure some benefit or equitable sharing of benefits from tourism, some studies have shown that the neoliberal trickle-down economics have failed in tourism (Schlicher, 2007). While tourism planning and development should bring economic benefits to communities, Schlicher (2007) notes that neoliberal environments make it difficult for communities to benefit from tourism development in competition with multinational enterprises. Economic outcomes in liberal economies enable certain individuals to attain more wealth than others, resulting in inequality and monopolistic tendencies that favor tourism businesses at the expense of local people (Webster *et al.*, 2011). Inequalities in development and the marginalization of communities create distrust between local residents and tourism planners and developers. In this way, government has transformed itself from a 'public interest protector' to a 'protector of commercial interests', and, as in the third pillar, a rise in accountability and auditing (particularly financial) occurs. Trust has therefore shifted from the trust we have held in professionals to one of vertical calculation (Swain and Tait, 2007).

The rise of the rights-based society

The fourth pillar of the crisis of trust is the rise of the rights-based society. According to Swain and Tait (2007), this idea posits that the rights of individuals or groups are more important than their duties or obligations to society. The planning phase of tourism development usually includes political deliberation among various participants and consists of public discussion and internal reflection (Goodin and Niemeyer, 2006). During the public discussion phase, we see traits of the pluralistic and rights-based societies, where multiple tourism actors put forward potentially widely varying and conflicting views and positions and may feel entitled to certain benefits or concessions from others based on their perceived rights. This phase serves to inform actors who then go on to 'deliberate from within', potentially changing their views or attitudes (Goodin and Niemeyer, 2006) and creating new similarities (Bijlsma-Frankema and Costa, 2005) or new identities (Maguire *et al.*, 2001). KBT and active trust may be formed in this situation.

The neoliberal and pluralistic society have also provided the impetus for a rights-based society. For instance, in their analysis of tourism policies in Athens, Greece, Pastras and Bramwell (2013: 391) note that "the tendency for neoliberalism to overlook the well-being of certain groups of actors, however, was itself a stimulus to interest groups to request to be more fully involved in policy making." In the Pendjari National Park, Benin, one can broadly see how the rise of a pluralistic society contributed to mistrust. At a certain point in time, local park employees began to feel that their interests and rights to greater compensation were more important than the collective interests. Consequently, they began to engage in poaching and other illegal activities, leading to conflict between park management and villages and between villages, and in an ultimate loss of trust (Idrissou *et al.*, 2013).

Some, particularly legislators, suggest that to keep our rights and maintain trust, transparency and accountability in all transactions are important (Swain and Tait, 2007). This contributes to the rise of audit measures to ensure this accountability, transparency and openness. Legislators and decision makers have attempted to prevent this mistrust that has arisen out of the rights-based society through the introduction of further and stronger human rights, more information, comparisons, complaint systems, contracts, professional codes, audits, examinations and new technologies (O'Neill, 2002). Although they claim that more accountability and transparency is the way to solve the crisis of trust and to ostensibly to preserve or create trust, such actions, at best, create a very weak form of trust, what Edwards (2009) categorized as calculus-based trust and at the other end of the spectrum becomes control.

Control is a modality of power that often has negative connotations and is closely associated with trust. However, control goes beyond the idea of being mere power and has negative possibilities when associated with trust. Under the idea of a substitution relationship, formal control can be thought of as replacing trust. With formal institutions in place, these could have the effect of reducing uncertainty and vulnerability to such a low level that trust is no longer needed. While this is speculation on a most extreme case, Bijlsma-Frankema and Costa (2005) do claim that in economic terms, where there is more formal control, there is a subsequent decrease in trust. The converse could also be true: where there is less formal control, there is more room for trust to play a role. This way of thinking involves the more traditional thought of trust and control as a dualism, where these two notions belong together but are present as distinct concepts (Möllering, 2005c).

While trust and control have been studied extensively, the mechanisms at play between the two of them are not well understood (Möllering, 2005c). In the three types of trust (CBT, KBT, and active trust), we can start to see the different ways that control plays a role in each of them. CBT is often based on written contracts between the trustor and the trustee. This is one obvious form of formal control. It can be taken further with monitoring and enforcement of the contract or contracts, which involves control, leaving very little, if any, room for trust to be created.

Conversely, this monitoring and enforcement aspect can be left as an uncertainty, requiring a leap of faith on the part of the trustor that the trustee will comply with the contract. When this happens, a state of positive expectation is reached, and trust is formed.

With the increasing demand for accountability actions, an additional issue arising from trust relates to the truthfulness and validity of the information being provided under these auditing schemes. O'Neill (2002) states that we need good information to make our judgments as to whether to trust or not. If the information that we receive is not 'good', this will affect our judgment around trust. Sometimes this information is purposefully not good or deceptive (manipulation) – as society increases the number of checks and balances on people and organizations in the name of transparency and accountability, there will always be those who will attempt to, and who will successfully, circumvent the checks and balances and deceive others, leading to distrust. O'Neill (2002) sums this up by stating that transparency does not reduce deception, but may actually increase it through building a culture of suspicion, lowered morale and greater mistrust.

Nature of tourism planning

Burns (2004) claims that tourism planning is usually based on a master planning approach, where plans are driven not by the social and economic needs of the community but by the structure of technical and economic assistance. The researcher claims that such an approach has four fundamental flaws: it involves too many technical and financial resources, with projects often not realized; homogeneous/reductionist approaches are encouraged, leading to unrealistic and unachievable expectations; approaches are undemocratic and nonparticipatory; and plans are often constrained by national borders, setting up competition. The first three of Burns's (2004) flaws can be directly related or contributory to a crisis of trust in tourism planning. If plans are proposed through 'user-friendly' reductionist approaches that keep things simple where there is a tendency to use a single measurable indicator, dimension, scale of analysis, objective or time horizon (Gasparatos *et al.*, 2008), producing unrealistic expectations among the local community and future workforce, where expectations are not met by planners or developers, the community experiences a loss of trust. Where this turn of events happens on a more widespread temporal or spatial scale, over time, it contributes to a crisis of trust in tourism planning.

Conclusion

This chapter discusses some fundamental issues that raise an urgent need for planners, researchers and scholars to pay more attention to the vocabulary of trust in tourism planning and development given the paucity of research on this topic in tourism studies. Where trust has been analyzed, it has been considered from only one perspective – generally, the perspective of the community toward government authorities or politicians through social exchange theory (e.g. Nunkoo and

Ramkissoon, 2012; Nunkoo and Smith, 2013). Although social exchange theory works well for analyzing trust at a basic level, there is much more to it. As noted earlier by O'Neill (2001) and Möllering (2001), we cannot live without placing trust. O'Neill (2002) notes that proponents of the idea of the crisis of trust claim that mistrust can be found throughout all of society and at various levels. Much emphasis has been placed on the perception of others as being trustworthy rather than the actual process of placing trust, including its demands and benefits (O'Neill, 2001). What is the basis of trust when goodwill does not enter the picture? Because an individual or institution has proven reliable – they have previously met our expectations; however, this prior knowledge about the individual or institution and his or her positive meeting of our expectations does not explain our own actions in their entirety. Trust is a very complex phenomenon, intimately linked to power, individual values, faith and the context in which we find ourselves. One may trust social policies of government, but not tourism development ones; or one may trust certain tourism policies of government, but not others.

There exists a high potential for a crisis of trust to develop in autocratic and developing countries, manifested in all pillars of the crisis. For example, in terms of the risk society, there are increased risks to the local environment through the potential increased numbers of people that will be visiting an area. There is also increased risk on the side of the tourists themselves. Is a potentially difficult-to-reach location with no or limited democratic safeguards worth the risk to visit? In the case of autocratic and developing countries, a divergence of interests exists between the ruling class and much of the rest of the population. Each of these 'factions' (or others, as the case may be) have their own interests and act autonomously in their own interest, further building distrust. What about trust among the other actors and the tourists themselves, particularly in light of the risk society? Is there a crisis of trust in tourism development and planning, or is it actually a problem of selective mistrust? What are the implications of trust (or lack of trust) for tourism planning and development?

These questions have so far remained unanswered by tourism researchers and scholars, and tourism planning research has not assessed the role that trust plays in contributing to democracy and legitimacy of tourism development. There are a number of avenues for further research in this area. Each of the pillars highlighted above may not be enough to cause a crisis of trust; each pillar actually highlights the need for trust in tourism planning. Do all actors, including the tourists themselves, feel that risks have been mitigated or diminished so that their varied expectations of the tourism development are met? As tourism communities become increasingly pluralistic and focused on their 'rights', do they have confidence that their expectations, or a compromise of them, will be met? Research needs to look at the processes that tourism planners actually employ to hear the stories and expectations of all actors involved or impacted by tourism development and how the ensuing plans are developed and implemented to positively meet the greatest number of actor expectations, a key component of building trust.

Tourism planning and development may not be the only factor involved in the complex dynamic of trust creation. Such issues as population dynamics, power, other planning issues, political and financial factors or even long-standing mistrust that stems from colonial pasts may contribute to the creation of trust or mistrust in tourist communities. Trust may be present initially, but the ongoing management of tourism infrastructure and services also involves an ongoing dialogue between all actors to ensure that changing expectations can be met to ensure continued trust.

References

Altinay, L., and Bowen, D. (2006). Politics and tourism interface: The case of Cyprus. *Annals of Tourism Research*, 33:4, 939–956.

Banks, M., Lovatt, A., O'Connor, J. and Raffo, C. (2000) Risk and trust in the cultural industries. *Geoforum*, 31, 453–464.

Beaumont, N., and Dredge, D. (2010). Local tourism governance: A comparison of three network approaches. *Journal of Sustainable Tourism*, 18, 7–28.

Beck, U. (1992) *Risk Society*. London: Sage.

Beck, U. (1999) *World Risk Society*. Cambridge, UK: Polity.

Beetham, D. (1991) *The Legitimation of Power*. London: Macmillan.

Beierle, T. C., and Konisky, D. M. (2000). Values, conflict, and trust in participatory environmental planning. *Journal of Policy Analysis and Management*, 19:4, 587–602.

Beritelli, P., and Laesser, C. (2011). Power dimensions and influence reputation in tourist destination: Empirical evidence from a network of actors and stakeholders. *Tourism Management*, 32:6, 1299–1309.

Bevir, M. (2009). *Key Concepts in Governance*. London: Sage.

Bijlsma-Frankema, K., and Costa, A. (2005) Understanding the trust-control nexus. *International Sociology*, 20, 259–282.

Bouckaert, G., and van de Walle, S. (2003). Comparing measures of citizen trust and user satisfaction as indicators of 'good governance': Difficulties in linking trust and satisfaction indicators. *International Review of Administrative Sciences*, 69:3, 329–343.

Bramwell, B. (2006). Actors, power, and discourses of growth limits. *Annals of Tourism Research*, 33:4, 957–978.

Bramwell, B. (2010). Participative planning and governance for sustainable tourism. *Tourism Recreation Research*, 35:3, 239–249.

Bramwell, B. (2011). Governance, the state and sustainable tourism: A political economy approach. *Journal of Sustainable Tourism*, 19:4/5, 459–477.

Bramwell, B., and Lane, B. (2011). Critical research on the governance of tourism and sustainability. *Journal of Sustainable Tourism*, 19:4/5, 411–421.

Bramwell, B., and Meyer, D. (2007). Power and tourism policy relations in transition. *Annals of Tourism Research*, 34:3, 766–788.

Burns, P. M. (2004) Tourism planning – A third way? *Annals of Tourism Research*, 31: 24–43.

Caplan, P. (2000) Introduction: Risk revisited. In P. Caplan (Ed.), *Risk Revisited*. London: Pluto Press.

Cheong, S. M., and Miller, M. L. (2000). Power and tourism: A Foucauldian observation. *Annals of Tourism Research*, 27:2, 371–390.

Child, J., and Möllering, G. (2003) Contextual confidence and active trust development in the Chinese business environment. *Organization Science*, 14, 69–80.

Connell, N., and Mannion, R. (2006) Conceptualisations of trust in the organizational literature: Some indicators from a complementary perspective. *Journal of Health Organization and Management*, 20, 417–433.

Cook, T., and Gronke, P. (2005) The sceptical American: Revisiting the meanings of trust in government and confidence in institutions. *Journal of Politics*, 67, 784–803.

Doney, P., Cannon, J. and Mullen, M. (1998) Understanding the influence of national culture on the development of trust. *Academy of Management Review*, 23, 601–620.

Doorne, S. (1998). Power, participation and perception: An insider's perspective on the politics of the Wellington waterfront redevelopment. *Current Issues in Tourism*, 1:2, 129–166.

Dredge, D., and Jenkins, J. (2007). *Tourism Planning and Policy*. Milton: John Wiley.

Edwards, J. (1982) *Ethics without Philosophy: Wittgenstein and the Moral Life*. Gainesville: University Presses of Florida.

Edwards, P. (2009) *Trust: Power and Planning – Participatory Water Planning on the Gold Coast, Australia*. PhD Thesis, School of Environment. Brisbane: Griffith University.

Ferreira, S., and Harmse, C. (2000) Crime and tourism in South Africa: International tourists perception and risk. *South African Geographical Journal*, 82:2, 80–85.

Ford, R. C., Wang, Y., and Vestal, A. (2012). Power asymmetries in tourism distribution networks. *Tourism Management*, 39:2, 755–779.

Foucault, M. (1980). Trust and power. In C. Gordon (Ed.), *Power/Knowledge: Selected Interview and Other Writing 1972–1977* (pp. 109–133). New York: Pantheon Books.

Foucault, M. (1984). *The Foucault Reader*. P. Rabinow (Ed.). New York: Random House-Pantheon.

Gasparatos, A., El-Haram, M. and Horner, M. (2008) A critical review of reductionist approaches for assessing the progress towards sustainability. *Environmental Impact Assessment Review*, 28, 286–311.

Gilson, L. (2006) Trust in health care: Theoretical perspectives and research needs. *Journal of Health Organization and Management*, 20, 359–375.

Goodin, R., and Niemeyer, S. (2006) When does deliberation begin? Internal reflection versus public discussion in deliberative democracy. *Political Studies*, 51:4, 627–649.

Gu, H., and Ryan, C. (2008) Place attachment, identity and community impacts of tourism – the case of a Beijing hutong. *Tourism Management*, 29:4, 637–647.

Gulati, R. and Sytch, M. (2007). Dependence asymmetry and joint dependence in interorganizational relationships: Effects of embeddedness on exchange performance. *Administrative Sciences Quarterly*, 52, 32–69.

Hall, C. M. (1994). *Tourism and Politics: Policy, Power and Place*. Chichester, UK: John Wiley.

Hall, C. M. (1999). Rethinking collaboration and partnership: A public policy perspective. *Journal of Sustainable Tourism*, 7:3, 274–289.

Hall, C. M. (2003). Politics and place: An analysis of power in destination communities. In S. Sing, D. J. Timothy, and R. K. Dowling (Eds), *Tourism in Destination Communities* (pp. 99–113). Oxon, UK: CABI.

Hall, C. M. (2010). Power in tourism: Tourism in power. In D.V.L. Macleod and J. G. Carrier (Eds), *Tourism, Power and Culture: Anthropological Insights* (pp. 199–213). Bristol, UK: Channel View.

Hall, C. M. (2011). A typology of governance and its implications for tourism policy analysis. *Journal of Sustainable Tourism*, 19:4/5, 437–457.

Hannam, K. (2002). Tourism and development I: Globalization and power. *Progress in Development Studies*, 2, 227–234.

Hosmer, L. (1995) Trust: The connecting link between organizational theory and philosophical ethics. *Academy of Management Review*, 20, 379–403.

Idrissou, L., van Paassen, A., Aarts, N., Voudouhè, S. and Leeuwis, C. (2013) Trust and hidden conflict in participatory natural resource management: The case of the Pendjari national park in Benin. *Forest Policy and Economics*, 27: 65–74.

Kasperson, R., Golding, D. and Tuler, S. (1992) Social distrust as a factor in siting hazardous facilities and communicating risks. *Journal of Social Issues*, 48, 161–187.

Kayat, K. (2002) Power, social exchanges and tourism in Langkawi: Rethinking resident perceptions. *International Journal of Tourism Research*, 4:3, 171–191.

Laurian, L. (2009). Trust in planning: Theoretical and practical considerations for participatory and deliberative planning. *Planning Theory and Practice*, 10:3, 369–391.

Lawrence, G. (2004) Promoting sustainable development: The question of governance. Plenary address. *XI World Congress of Rural Sociology.* Trondheim, Norway. Available at: www.irsa-world.org/prior/XI/program/Lawrence.pdf

Lepp, A., Gibson, H. and Lane, C. (2011) Image and perceived risk: A study of Uganda and its official tourism website. *Tourism Management*, 32:3, 675–684.

Lewicki, R., and Benedict Bunker, B. (1995) Trust in relationships: A model of development and decline. In B. Benedict Bunker and J. Rubin (Eds), *Conflict, Cooperation, and Justice: Essays Inspired by the Work of Morton Deutsch.* San Francisco: Jossey-Bass.

Lewis, J., and Weigert, A. (1985) Trust as a social reality. *Social Forces*, 63, 967–985.

Macleod, D. V. L., and Carrier, J. G. (2010). *Tourism, Power and Culture: Anthropological Insights.* Bristol, UK: Channel View.

Maguire, S., Phillips, N. and Hardy, C. (2001) When 'silence = death', keep talking: Trust, control and the discursive construction of identity in the Canadian HIV/AIDS treatment domain. *Organization Studies*, 22, 285–310.

Mavondo, F. and Rodrigo, E. (2001). The effect of relationship dimensions on interpersonal and interorganizational commitment in organizations conducting business between Australia and China. *Journal of Business Research*, 52, 111–121.

Mishler, W. and Rose, R. (1997) Trust, distrust and scepticism: Popular evaluations of civil and political institutions in post-communist societies. *Journal of Politics*, 59, 418–451.

Misztal, B. (1996). *Trust in Modern Societies – The Search for the Bases of Social Order.* Cambridge, UK: Polity.

Möllering, G. (2001) Terror and trust (unpublished manuscript), Berlin.

Möllering, G. (2005a) Rational, institutional and active trust: Just do it!? In K. Bijlsma-Frankema and R. Woolthuis (Eds), *Trust under Pressure: Empirical Investigations of Trust and Trust Building in Uncertain Circumstances.* Cheltenham, UK: Edward Elgar.

Möllering, G. (2005b) Understanding trust from the perspective of sociological neoinstitutionalism: The interplay of institutions and agency. *MPIfG Discussion Papers.* Cologne, Germany: Max Planck Institute for the Study of Societies.

Möllering, G. (2005c) The trust/control duality – An integrative perspective on positive expectations of others. *International Sociology*, 20, 283–305.

Möllering, G. (2006) *Trust: Reason, Routine, Reflexivity.* Oxford: Elsevier.

Moscardo, G. (2011). Exploring social representations of tourism planning: Issues for governance. *Journal of Sustainable Tourism*, 19:4:, 423–436.

Neu, D. (1991) Trust, contracting and the prospectus process. *Accounting, Organizations and Society*, 16, 243–256.

Nunkoo, R., and Ramkissoon, H. (2012). Power, trust, social exchange and community support. *Annals of Tourism Research*, 39:2:, 997–1023.

Nunkoo, R., and Smith, S. L. (2013). Political economy of tourism: Trust in government actors, political support, and their determinants. *Tourism Management*, 36, 120–132.

Nye, J. S., Zelikow, P. D. and King, D. C. (1997). *Why People Don't Trust Government.* Cambridge, MA: Harvard University Press.

Obenour, W. L., and Cooper, N. (2010). Tourism planning and power within metropolitan community development. *Community Development*, 41:3, 323–339.

O'Neill, O. (2001) *Autonomy and Trust in Bioethics.* Cambridge, UK: University of Cambridge Press.

O'Neill, O. (2002) *A Question of Trust.* Cambridge, UK: University of Cambridge Press.

Oxford Dictionary (2003) *Compact Oxford English Dictionary*, Second Edition. Oxford: Oxford University Press.

Park, H., and Blenkinsopp, J. (2011). The roles of transparency and trust in the relationship between corruption and citizen satisfaction. *International Review of Administrative Sciences*, 77:2, 254–274.

Pastras, P., and Bramwell, B. (2013). A strategic-relational approach to tourism policy. *Annals of Tourism Research*, 43, 390–414.

Reed, M. (1997) Power relations and community-based tourism planning. *Annals of Tourism Research*, 24:3, 566–591.

Rousseau, D., Sitkin, S., Burt, R. and Camerer, C. (1998) Introduction to special topic forum: Not so different after all: A cross-discipline view of trust. *Academy of Management Review*, 23, 393–404.

Schlicher, D. (2007) Growth versus equity: The continuum of pro-poor tourism and neoliberal governance. *Current Issues in Tourism*, 10:2–3, 166–193.

Shone, M. C., and Ali Memon, P. (2008). Tourism, public policy and regional development: A turn from neo-liberalism to the new regionalism. *Local Economy*, 23:4, 290–304.

Simmons, D. (1994) Community participation in tourism planning. *Tourism Management*, 15, 98–108.

Stein, S., and Harper, T. (2003) Power, trust, and planning. *Journal of Planning Education and Research*, 23, 125–139.

Swain, C., and Tait, M. (2007) The crisis of trust and planning. *Planning Theory & Practice*, 8, 229–247.

Uslaner, E. (2002) *The Moral Foundations of Trust*. Cambridge, UK: Cambridge University Press.

Uslaner, E. (2004) Trust and social bonds: Faith in others and policy outcomes reconsidered. *Political Research Quarterly,* 57, 501–507.

Uslaner, E., and Brown, M. (2005) Inequality, trust, and civic engagement. *American Politics Research,* 33, 868–894.

Uslaner, E., and Conley, R. S. (2003) Civic engagement and particularized trust: The ties that bind people to their ethnic communities. *American Politics Research,* 31, 331–360.

Webster, C., Ivanov, S. and Illum, S. F. (2011). The paradigms of political economy and tourism policy. In J. Mosedale (Ed.), *Political Economy of Tourism: A Critical Perspective* (pp. 55–73). London: Routledge.

Yeoman, I., Munro, C. and McMahon-Beattie, U. (2006) Tomorrow's: World, consumer and tourist. *Journal of Vacation Marketing*, 12:2, 174–190.

Yüksel, F., Bramwell, B. and Yüksel, A. (2005) Centralized and decentralized tourism governance in Turkey. *Annals of Tourism Research,* 32:4, 859–886.

3 Trust, governance and sustainable tourism

Bill Bramwell

Introduction

Researchers examining sustainable tourism have often focused on policies and on how policies might be strengthened. Several academic studies, for example, investigate individual policies or policy instruments intended to encourage sustainable tourism, such as assessments of interpretation policies, codes of conduct, land use regulations, carrying capacity limits, and sustainability indicators (Ayuso 2007; Miller and Twining-Ward 2005; Mycoo 2006). However, researchers have generally shown far less interest in the political circumstances that make the adoption of such policies less or more likely (Bramwell 1998). But behind policies there is always politics, and getting the politics right appears to be a prerequisite to securing sustainable tourism (Meadowcroft 2011). More research is needed on the practical politics and governance processes in specific circumstances that favor, obstruct or contradict sustainable tourism principles.

Governance processes involve the steering of social development and the coordination of social action. In the most straightforward sense, governance for sustainable tourism refers to tourism's socio-political steering and coordination in order to orient it toward sustainable development. It encompasses public debate, political decision making, policy formation and implementation, and interactions among government agencies, private-sector businesses and civil society associated with steering societal development along more sustainable lines (Bramwell and Lane 2011; Meadowcroft 2007). Tourism research would benefit if greater attention was paid to these governance processes for sustainable tourism and to the underlying politics. More particularly, this research would be assisted by having an improved understanding of the interests, capacities, rules, values and attitudes affecting these issues.

Some attention in tourism research in this field has been directed specifically to how power and conflict affect politics and governance behind the adoption of, and resistance to, sustainable tourism policies (Bianchi 2004; Bramwell 2006 and 2011; Lovelock 2002). By contrast, there has been a relative neglect of how trust affects these relationships. It has been claimed that "viewing the politics of tourism only in terms of power relations may be insufficient. Other ingredients such as trust are equally important for a democratic and sustainable form of tourism development" (Nunkoo *et al.* 2012: 1540). As with the case of conflict, trust can help, hinder or even contradict the adoption and application of sustainable tourism policies. Indeed, it may often do these simultaneously.

Social theorists have claimed that trust is necessary for the smooth functioning of a democratic society, including when negotiating policy objectives. At its simplest, trust involves interdependence between an actor who trusts and an actor or entity that is trusted (Vangen and Huxham 2003). Although *trust* is a contested term, some agreement exists that trust is relational because it involves expectations about the aims and behavior of actors and institutions, it is accorded to other parties and entities with respect to particular issues or activities and it is a judgment that can be measured dichotomously or in a more graded form (Baral 2012: 43). These features of trust can all be important for actors for the adoption or rejection of sustainable tourism policies. While trust is relatively neglected in research on tourism politics and governance, this also applies in other policy fields. In planning studies, for instance, Laurian (2009: 370) notes that "Despite the importance of trust, theory on the subject has not been fully developed in the planning literature."

Complex and often contradictory relationships exist among trust, governance and the adoption of sustainable tourism policies. There is often considered to be a need for cooperation between actors, such as between government, businesses and civil society, in order to agree and implement sustainable tourism policies, and that can depend on developing and maintaining trust between the actors. Yet such trust can result in tourism proposals being adopted despite them having clearly damaging implications for society and the environment.

Relationships between trust, governance and sustainable tourism are complex, in part because trust is multidimensional. It has varied features, it is entangled with many other relationships and it differs according to the specific circumstances of each case. The context or object of trust related to sustainable tourism governance also varies – it might be an individual, an institution, a political ideology, a policy domain, an activity or even society in general. In each context and its particular circumstances, there are also often varying degrees of trust and distrust, and they co-exist and interact with each other.

Relations between trust and sustainable tourism are also complex because people's trust in individuals, groups and institutions can encourage either support or opposition to sustainability aims. Thus, government agencies advocating sustainable tourism initiatives can be ascribed with either high or low trust by the public, and that ascription tends to affect how positively the initiatives are received and hence their likely success. And, similarly, government organizations promoting environmentally damaging tourism proposals may be ascribed with either a high or low degree of trust, and that ascription, too, has implications for whether the public accepts or opposes the proposals.

The analysis that follows, first, explains why governance is of fundamental importance for sustainable tourism. Second, the specific character of trust is considered within tourism governance, including its relations with political legitimacy. Third, an assessment is conducted of how trust and distrust can be important for the governance of sustainable tourism, and thus why they require study. This is followed, fourth, by evaluation of selected features of trust in two governance contexts that are often significant for sustainable tourism: for national governments and for collaborative partnerships. Fifth, the complexity and varying potential consequences or outcomes associated with the relations between trust, governance and sustainable tourism are considered. And, finally, an associated typology is developed for the potential relations between the degree of trust among actors involved in tourist destination governance and whether the resulting tourism policies are likely to promote or damage destination sustainability.

The importance of governance for sustainable tourism

The term *sustainable tourism* became popular in the years after the release in 1987 of the World Commission on Environment and Development (or Brundtland) Report, which presented highly influential ideas about the sustainable development concept. Most basically, sustainable tourism may be regarded as the application of sustainable development ideas to the tourism sector (Bramwell and Lane 2011). The close association between these two sets of ideas has led to sustainable tourism often being depicted in terms closely integrated with those of sustainable development, notably as tourism that meets the needs of present generations without compromising the ability of future generations to meet their own needs. It is regularly linked with the promotion of human welfare, the preservation of ecosystems, inter- and intragenerational equity and public participation in development decision making. The Brundtland Report's concept of sustainable development was not intended primarily to be part of the vocabulary of academic social science, or as a set of practical rules allowing policies automatically to be decided based on the situational inputs. Instead, it was designed more as a normative point of reference for policy making for environment and development (Jacobs 1999; Meadowcroft 1999). As with such political terms as *justice* and *democracy*, *sustainable development* is subject to much debate and re-interpretation, but it also provides an essential foundation – a frame and focus – for contemporary political and policy debate about development (Meadowcroft 1999). The same applies to the more specific concept of sustainable tourism. Thus, it is to be expected that there are many different interpretations of what sustainable tourism entails and of the scale of reforms required to give it force.

The governance of sustainable tourism can be depicted as efforts to shape the structures and processes of tourism governance so that they promote more sustainable development trajectories (Bramwell and Lane 2011; Meadowcroft 2007). Governance involves "systems of governing" – that is, the ways that societies are governed, ruled or "steered" (Bulkeley 2005; Stoker 1998). It encompasses the processes for regulating and mobilizing social action and for producing social order. According to Atkinson (2003: 103), governance entails processes "whereby some degree of societal order is achieved, goals decided on, policies elaborated and services delivered." The concept of governance is seen as broader than that of government, in recognition that often it is not just the formal agencies of government that are involved in governance tasks (Goodwin and Painter 1996).

Non-state actors that can be involved in governance include actors in the business, community and voluntary sectors.

There are several reasons why governance is an essential and integral requirement of sustainable tourism (Meadowcroft 2013). First, sustainable tourism involves a normative orientation to re-direct long-term societal development toward the normative goals of sustainable development, and it is suggested that this requires the societal steering involved in governance. Second, increasingly it is suggested that the operation of society's institutions is unlikely spontaneously to result in a sustainable development path focused on long-term socio-economic change (Bramwell and Lane 2011; Meadowcroft 2007). As a consequence, sustainable tourism is becoming understood as requiring conscious and collective – that is, political – actions through the institutions and processes of governance. The political project to encourage sustainability may require, for example, changes to law to modify the regulatory frameworks within which economic actors conduct their affairs (for example, by introducing planning regulations or a carbon tax) as well as direct government expenditure (for example, to support the setting up of community tourism initiatives, to interpret a destination's history and culture and to deploy energy-saving technologies in transport and tourist accommodation). Political processes that are legitimized and enforced through the institutions of the state are needed to achieve such changes.

Third, it is widely considered that sustainable tourism requires the transformation of existing governance processes, notably to incorporate broad processes of societal mobilization. This societal mobilization is often depicted as requiring increased use of collaborative or partnership arrangements among diverse societal actors, so that businesses, civil society organizations and citizens are actively engaged in policy making and policy implementation. This widens the democratic basis of tourism development, draws on different knowledge and viewpoints and encourages more locally sensitive and innovative responses. Fourth, it is often suggested that all levels of government, such as local and national government, should be active in promoting sustainable tourism, partly because they have the financial, organizational and legal resources substantially to advance sustainable tourism's ambitious objectives. And, fifth, sustainable tourism involves fundamental choices about basic values and the sort of society that we want, and thus it is a political project that requires democratic involvement. This is another justification often given for the need for government involvement and for broad civil society engagement in policy decisions.

The objectives of sustainable tourism, sixth, will threaten some interests, and this involves a requirement for political engagement in governance, such as to build coalitions of actors to bring about the necessary changes. These political struggles are likely to involve both established political groups, such as tourism industry associations and political parties, as well as emerging groups and social movements. Moving toward sustainable tourism is inevitably a long-term agenda, and this means that, seventh, it is necessary to develop an understanding of how governance processes can be used most effectively in the long term. It is important that lessons learned along the way are incorporated into the governance of sustainable tourism.

Trust within tourism governance

As with other important social relations, trust is an elusive and complex concept (Gambetta 1988; Lachapelle and McCool 2012). Many accept, however, that trust involves particular types of relations between actors and between actors and other entities, such as institutions, that are embedded in networks of social relations and norms. According to Laurian (2009), trust is relational, so that actor A trusts actor or entity B with regard to a specific activity or issue. In an interpersonal context, trust is A's subjective assessment of the probability that B will act as agreed when B's actions affect A. These relations between actors are affected by A's and B's socio-cultural values, commitment to goals, and perceptions of the value of trustworthiness. Trust is an expectation of future appropriate behavior, and it is often based on people's accumulated experience of past cycles of exchanges and whether they were considered reliable and fulfilled expectations (Lachapelle and McCool 2012; Vangen and Huxham 2003). Hall (2008: 220) suggests that trust of others in tourism-related governance emerges when "Ongoing interactions and flows of information over time have built up a bond of confidence that anticipated outcomes can be relied upon to be achieved." The resulting interdependence is characterized by a reliance on others to act in good faith, resulting in mutually beneficial interactions.

The role of trust in local-level tourism governance is explored by Saxena (2006) for the case of three local tourism business associations in an English national park. Social bonds, trust and commitment among the participating tourism businesses are shown to be important for their involvement in joint marketing and lobbying activities. These businesses engaged in market intelligence exchanges and other social exchanges to steer the local tourism industry's rebranding and repositioning to attract targeted visitor segments. This steering was underpinned by "trust acquired as a result of [a] previous history of working together" (p. 271), which was evident in their honesty, accessibility to each others' time and skills and open communication. While there were significant social bonds among the associations' participants based on trust, Saxena notes that there also could be conflicts, with the relationships varying on a spectrum from collaboration to confrontation, and also evolving as their interactions unfolded over time.

Trust is clearly important in the specific governance context of sustainable tourism, although the relationships are often complex. Trust between actors, for instance, is needed for them to cooperate in democratic processes and for them to agree and implement sustainable tourism policies. But it can also be the case that such trusting relations result in the acceptance of tourism initiatives proposed by influential actors despite them being environmentally or socially damaging.

Three broad research perspectives, among others, can be applied to trust and governance for sustainable tourism (Baral 2012; Laurian 2009). These are trust as an individual-level process that leads an actor to decide to trust another actor or entity, such as a tourism organization; trust as a broad social construct within human relations that is formed by, and simultaneously shapes, our social contexts, including through the relations around sustainable tourism development; and trust as the legitimacy accorded to an entity, such as a national ministry of tourism, that its actions are proper and appropriate, and through that legitimacy the entity is conferred with authority (Curry and Fisher 2012; Edelenbos and Eshuis 2012).

The first perspective, of trust as an individual-level process, concerns trust between one actor and another or between an actor and another entity, such as a tourism-related government agency. Rational choice theory is often used in research on individual-level trust. In this theory individuals analyze the benefits and costs of trusting, or being trustworthy, in specific situations. With this interpersonal trust, A's decision to trust B is based on A's comparison of the expected benefits and costs of cooperating and transferring some power to B with the expected benefits and costs of a failure of trust due to B's incompetence or betrayal (Laurian 2009). From this theoretical position, actors make rational assessments of the benefits and costs of developing and maintaining relations of trust, aware in so doing that trusting relationships, for example, can reduce people's power and expose them to risks (Baral 2012). Trust in tourism governance is likely to develop in a situation when individuals perceive that trusting another person accords with their personal self-interest, such as when trustors perceive an action performed by the trustee as beneficial (Welch *et al.* 2005).

Such rational assessments of trust might operate not only at the individual level but also between individuals and organizations, such as between a citizen and an environmental agency or between a business owner and a tourism business association. Thus, an individual's trust in an organization may depend on his evaluation of whether the organization can meet his needs (Kehoe and Ponting 2003; McDermott 2012). Trust in an institution may involve faith that the entity is benevolent and has integrity, such as belief that an organization has a fair record of protecting the environment or encouraging local community initiatives (Edelenbos and Eshuis 2012). Individuals may weigh the benefits and costs associated with, for example, joining a sustainable tourism partnership. It could be expected, for instance, that participants in a partnership will have higher levels of trust if they perceive that the benefits of participating will outweigh the costs. Having joined a tourism partnership, an individual may have higher levels of trust in the partnership's administering agencies if she feels that the partnership depends on those agencies to function properly. It should be noted, however, that people are not always rational or instrumental in their societal interactions and assessments, and that, for example, trust can be based on a leap of faith.

In the second perspective, trust is considered more generally as a social construct within human relations that is affected by social mores, institutional structures and social practices. Trust is more likely in society, for example, if there is recourse to the institutional protections of the law or to an arbitrator (Bannister and Connolly 2011). Regulations for reduction of waste and pollution by tourism businesses, for example, are more likely to be successful if business owners know that effective legal procedures and sanctions enforce compliance. This recognition encourages trust in the agencies establishing the regulations and in the likely compliance by other businesses so that all bear the costs (Bramwell 1998 and 2004). From this perspective, trust is necessary because social life is not predictable, and this uncertainty may encourage people to recognize their interdependence and their need to trust each other. Trust is necessary for the stability of society, including the protection of social order and continuity in the institutions, rules of exchange and claims to rights and justice. Societal-level trust also is needed to maintain "the legitimacy of systems that allocate power, prestige and wealth, define the public good and regulate the distribution of public goods" (Laurian 2009: 372).

The third perspective to be considered is that of trust as the legitimacy which is accorded to an actor or other entity. This perspective is often invoked in contexts where there is conflict, and it is generally viewed as a response to distrust as well as to desires for control. Legitimacy is seen as a collective belief that the position and actions of an actor or entity are desirable, proper or appropriate, with this conferring authority on that actor or entity (McDermott 2012). Legitimacy is "the acceptance and justification of shared rule by a community . . . the question of legitimacy concerns who is entitled to make rules" (Bernstein 2005: 142–143; Lockwood 2010). Legitimacy justifies authority among the governed, it empowers the authorities, and it increases the likelihood that the authorities' wishes and requirements will be followed (Bernstein 2011). It is a key issue, therefore, in the acceptability of governance arrangements and of the associated policies. In liberal democratic systems, governments typically gain legitimacy through elections, and their decisions are given weight by legislation and other forms of regulation and policy that they can put into place because of their democratic authority (Lockwood 2010). Bramwell (2011) suggests that a degree of legitimacy is usually required by governments, or other institutions, when they lead tourism policy processes, and through leading these processes they may seek to consolidate their political authority and hegemony. A politically relatively stable relationship among the state, its institutions and its citizens is important for the state to maintain effective authority (Nunkoo *et al.* 2012; Purcell and Nevins 2005). Legitimacy can mean that actors and entities involved in tourism governance secure the institutionalized power that enables them to control distrusted actors. Actors also may argue on behalf of a broader social collective that a particular governing approach holds legitimacy, and this may be debated and contested among different actors.

All three perspectives on trust suggest that, while trust involves mutual acceptance, confidence and support, it is also affected by, and affects, control and power. Where there is trust and thus voluntary cooperation between two parties, for example, both parties can gain power to pursue their long-term interests, although there also may be imbalances in control and power between these actors. Trust also implies that trustors are vulnerable to trustees, and this further indicates how power relationships are embedded in trust (Laurian 2009). By contrast, where trust is lacking, then both sides may be more inclined to vie for control and power. In all such situations, the consequences can include conflicts between the parties, and varying degrees of trust and conflict between actors can co-exist (Murnighan *et al.* 2004).

Trust within governance for sustainable tourism

The potential importance of trust for sustainable tourism governance is illustrated here through the governance arrangements for protected areas, which often attract many tourists. This example illustrates the value of studying trust to gain a deeper understanding of sustainable tourism governance.

The regulation and management of protected areas, including promoting more sustainable forms of tourism within them, is often undertaken by one or more public agencies or authorities. These often have responsibilities for steering a protected area's tourism management system, including its legislative framework, system of management planning and range of management goals, policies and actions (Dredge and Jenkins 2007). These agencies are often appointed and significantly funded by government, and they are commonly presented as operating in the "common good," although what that entails is regularly contested. Some shift has occurred away from government-led agencies, with more partnership arrangements and privatizations, and some distrust of government exists in many societies. Yet public sector–led protected area agencies often secure a degree of public support and trust because of respect for the democratic electoral processes behind government, their presumed focus on the common good and the possibility of legal recourse if proper management procedures and processes are not applied (Laurian 2009). Trust in protected area authorities is important because, in effect, citizens voluntarily delegate powers to these often relatively unknown organizations. Trust in these agencies as legitimate authorities in turn promotes citizens' voluntary compliance and deference to decisions made in the name of the common good. This voluntary compliance is necessary as more coercive power is likely to be less welcome and possibly less effective in practice.

Trust in protected area public agencies will depend on their perceived legitimacy, which is often affected by their conferred or earned powers and by their objectives for the protected area (Lockwood 2010). The agencies' mandate and powers – which help to delineate their scope of legitimate action – may be specified in legislation, a constitution, a charter or customary law. Failure by these agencies to act in ways consistent with their mandate can undermine people's trust and the agencies' overall legitimacy. This trust also depends on agency activities being consistent with such principles as transparency, accountability, inclusion, respect for cultural differences and fairness (Bramwell 1998). According to Brockington *et al.* (2008: 93), an erosion of trust has occurred among local communities connected with some African protected areas, partly because "of their experiences over many decades of being marginalized, impoverished or disempowered by conservation policies." Trust can break down when local populations affected by protected areas feel that the authorities overlook their traditions, rights and aspirations. In many situations a considerable portion of people's trust probably hinges on whether they believe the trustee adequately considers their interests (Höppner 2009).

The form taken by governance arrangements may affect public trust in protected area agencies. A study of actors' views about park governance in two Canadian provinces found that there were more favorable perceptions of a parastatal governance model, where the park agency directly provided most services, compared to a private sector governance model, where profit-making companies provided the park services (Eagles *et al.* 2013). Thus, governments potentially could see a loss of legitimacy for their park policies if they shift protected area funding from public subsidies to tourism fees and charges.

Contexts for trust within sustainable tourism governance

The context or object of trust within sustainable tourism governance can vary from an individual to an institution and from a specific policy instrument to a policy domain. Some of the features of trust are examined next for two governance contexts that are often significant for sustainable tourism: national governments and collaborative partnerships.

Governments potentially represent important contexts for building trust for sustainable tourism governance. Although many other actors are involved in steering sustainable tourism, in practice much of the responsibility for ensuring that progress is made rests with government. It is government which often has a general mandate to promote the public good, and in democratic political systems it may have clear lines of public accountability (Meadowcroft 1999). Yet there are often doubts about the genuine political commitment of politicians and governments to sustainable tourism, including at a national level (Dinica 2009). A study by Yüksel *et al.* (2012) of statements made by recent tourism ministers in Turkey observes that their stated objectives were strongly economically driven and growth oriented. "The ministers are in support of environmental protection, while also calling for new investments. This may signify that the ministers hold economic aspirations with respect to sustainably developed tourism, without being too much concerned about likely environmental issues" (p. 527).

Although national government policies can be important for sustainable tourism, there has been a trend in many countries away from steering by government toward more complex, co-management arrangements among several parties, including greater use of public–private sector partnerships. Some suggest this trend may have been influenced by a decline in the general level of trust in government within society (Bramwell 2010; Swain and Tait 2007). This potential loss in confidence in government may reflect judgments about the general commitment and competence of elected politicians and government officials to do something right or to seek to do the right thing (Bannister and Connolly 2011). Further, in specific contexts where the government can be corrupt or bypassed in decisions affecting tourism development and environmental protection, then the legitimacy of regulations can be weaker and the tourism industry and developers may not voluntarily comply with the regulations (Yüksel and Yüksel 2008). There is much debate about whether confidence is declining in various nations' governments. Many nonacademic commentators and some academics contend that trust in government is in long-term decline in the United States and in several European countries, but this is rejected by other scholars (Bannister and Connolly

2011). It should be noted, too, that the factors determining trust in government are not necessarily the same for every country or political culture, and they may differ over time (Bouckaert and van de Walle 2003).

Horizontal co-management arrangements or partnerships are increasingly important in modern society, and they are a second potential governance context where sustainable tourism might be pursued. It can be argued that trust has gained increased significance as a coordination mechanism because uncertainties can no longer be managed through hierarchical power or direct surveillance, and instead there is more use of partnerships and other diffuse governance arrangements (Edelenbos and Eshuis 2012). It is often suggested that trust among members of a group is essential for the effectiveness of co-governance arrangements, such as collaborative partnerships (Kumar and Paddison 2000). Collaboration and trust seem to be reciprocal processes, with each depending on and fostering the other. Yet only a limited amount of attention has been directed to the associated importance of trust within the proliferating research on tourism partnerships. Many dimensions of trust exist in such arrangements, including trust in a partnership as an institution, among actors not directly involved in a partnership but affected by its actions and interpersonal relations of trust among a partnership's participants.

The limited amount of research that does consider trust within tourism partnerships tends to focus on the general character of the interpersonal relations among the partnerships' participants. The factors contributing to member satisfaction with tourism collaborations in northern Thailand are examined by Yodsuwan and Butcher (2012). From a literature analysis and feedback from members of one partnership, five factors were considered most likely to contribute to partnership member satisfaction: the perceived gains for individuals, trust, the quality of communication in the partnership, the quality of participation and interdependency. According to the surveyed tourism partnership members, all the suggested factors could positively affect their satisfaction. The strongest overall predictor of satisfaction, however, was mutual trust among participants, followed by the perceived gains for individuals and then by the quality of communications.

A study by Laing *et al.* (2008) similarly examined factors mentioned by partnership participants as accounting for the success of two partnerships for urban fringe parks in Australia that involved park managers, other government agencies, the tourism industry and community groups. But they found that only a few participants mentioned trust between partners as a success factor. On some occasions, however, they did mention how trust underpinned other features, such as open communication, commitment and addressing problems as they occur. The importance attached to shared accountability in one of the partnerships also may have rested on concerns with trust. The authors consider that the limited discussion of trust was "an unexpected finding, given the centrality of trust in social capital and related discussions and praxis about collaborative enterprises" (p. 116). They suggest that it probably reflected the difficulties of assessing and describing trust, given its intangibility and dynamism (Schuett *et al.* 2001), and thus they call for more research on the issue of trust due to its likely underlying importance for such partnerships.

Trust may be such a basic, fundamental and overarching requirement that it could be overlooked by respondents when asked about specific factors contributing to successful tourism partnership working. Research on the features of successful tourism partnership operations seems to have been most concerned with the elements that are more immediately tangible and easily measured (Waayers *et al.* 2012). This conclusion is reached by Roberts and Simpson (1999) from an evaluation of tourism-related partnerships in two rural regions of Bulgaria and Romania. They found evidence of the significance of six features of successful partnership previously identified by Jamal and Getz (1995). These features were the working of aims and objectives, the inclusion of key stakeholders, the appointment of a legitimate convenor, recognition of a high degree of interdependence, recognition of benefits from collaboration and perceptions that decisions arrived at will be implemented. Roberts and Simpson see these as relatively easily measured criteria, however, and they suggest that this is why they often feature in assessments of tourism partnership success. In that context, they assert that "This may have led to the lack of recognition of underlying, less tangible elements of collaboration, which the authors believe are the factors critical to success in partnership working" (p. 325). The case study partnerships are seen by these authors as illustrating the importance of two intangible and less easily measured, but more fundamental, influences: trust and sincerity, and the balance of power between stakeholders. They regard these as key layers to be placed over the six more specific dimensions of partnership working identified by Jamal and Getz.

While tourism partnerships may often depend on a reasonable level of trust, it also may be the case that they only occasionally promote sustainable outcomes. More participants, with diverse viewpoints, can be involved in decision making through partnerships, and this is often praised by advocates of sustainable tourism. But it is probably rare that every participant in a partnership is fully engaged and that in-depth consideration is given to the views of actors with limited resources and influence (Vangen and Huxham 2003). Further, tourism partnerships often have fairly narrow business development agendas, and they may fail to concentrate on sustainability objectives and outcomes. Thus, research on tourism governance is misleading if it simply assumes that institutional arrangements encouraging networked interactions and cooperation (and, by implication, greater trust among participants) are inherently good and desirable (Hall 2011).

Complexity of trust in governance and sustainable tourism

The discussion next considers the complex connections among trust, governance and sustainable tourism. Too often there can be implicit assumptions of a simple relationship, with trust seen as a necessary ingredient for sustainable tourism because it encourages cooperation between actors representing sustainability's varied economic, social and environmental concerns. Such cooperative decision making is also often considered valuable for sustainable development because it promotes wider political access and democracy. Yet a presumption that there is a necessary positive relationship among trust, governance and sustainable tourism is oversimplified and misleading.

For example, while many propose a positive relationship between trust and democracy, other researchers argue that the opposite can apply. Bouckaert and van de Walle (2003) note that in Anglo-Saxon research low trust is often considered to reflect a healthy democratic attitude, because high levels of trust may encourage repressive governments. It must also be remembered that authoritarian rulers often enjoy an apparently high level of public trust and that clientelistic relations can promote trust. In addition, it should not be assumed that a society that generally trusts government and its agencies will necessarily promote sustainable tourism policies. This is a dangerous assumption, because trusted government organizations may advocate environmentally harmful policies. Rather, there should be recognition of various potential relationships between trust in institutions and the promotion of sustainable tourism. For example, government agencies may positively promote sustainable tourism initiatives, but the degree of trust in these agencies can vary from high to low, and this ascription is likely to affect the degree of success of the initiatives. By contrast, government agencies may promote tourism proposals that are environmentally damaging, and again the degree of trust in these agencies – whether high or low – is likely to affect whether the proposals are welcomed or opposed by the public.

These varying potential relationships mean that trust in governance institutions should not be considered as intrinsically beneficial or detrimental for sustainable tourism. It is necessary to recognize that these relationships are context dependent, varying by the institutions involved and by whether they promote sustainable tourism. Research that considers an actor's trust in an institution only in a generalized way, and does not explore what this institution is trusted to be and do, is unlikely to be illuminating (Aitken 2012). It is more revealing if research on trust in tourism governance reflects upon which institution is being trusted and what it is trusted to do.

These varying relationships indicate that distrust can be helpful for the governance of sustainable tourism. People's distrust can help them resist the efforts of agencies to promote tourism schemes that are environmentally damaging and socially unacceptable, especially if distrust is combined with a belief in positive political action (Laurian 2009). In such cases, people can act as watchdog activists to resist unsustainable tourism activities. Lovelock (2002: 5), for example, suggests that it is necessary to recognize "the potential advantages of stakeholders adopting non-cooperative approaches in the policy processes surrounding the quest for sustainable tourism." Actors and interest groups that are concerned about community issues and environmental protection, but are also distrustful of collaborative and consultative governance processes, may be more successful in achieving their political ends if they ignore such governance processes and instead lobby, protest and use the media to further their interests (Bramwell 2010). Some commentators have depicted the expansion of collaborative and consultative governance as an "anti-political strategy" that marginalizes the importance of political contestation in socio-economic development. They suggest that a consensus strategy is often a way to avoid turning questions of interests, representation, justice or power into political questions and community controversies (Brand and Gaffikin 2007; Hickey and Mohan 2005; Jayasuriya and Hewison 2004). In these circumstances, distrustful relations as well as conflict and struggle among actors and organizations can be important for progress toward sustainable tourism.

Typology of trust, governance and sustainable tourism

A typology is presented here of potential relations between the degree of trust among actors involved in tourist destination governance and whether the associated tourism policies are likely to promote or damage destination sustainability. The typology contains four potential relations. First, there is a situation in which agencies positively promote sustainable tourism and there is a high level of trust among relevant actors or entities, which increases the chances for its successful adoption. Second, there is a position where again the agencies positively promote sustainable tourism, but in this case there is low trust among the pertinent actors or entities, which reduces the likelihood of positive results. Third, there is the very different case in which agencies advocate tourism proposals that are damaging to sustainability, and low trust among some relevant actors results in opposition to the proposals. Finally, a situation can occur in which again the agencies push for tourism proposals that are unsustainable, but in this case a high level of trust allows them to be put into practice. Of course, this typology represents a set of ideal types, and one should not expect to find these ideal types in practice in their pure form. The typology is a considerable simplification of the complex and often contradictory relations often found in real cases. In addition, these relations are dynamic and they evolve over time. The discussion that follows uses examples from the tourism literature to illustrate the potential relevance of these scenarios, although space constraints mean only the first three are examined.

Sustainable tourism policies and relatively high trust

The first situation is where agencies positively promote sustainable tourism and there is a high level of trust among relevant actors or entities, with that trust increasing the chances that it is adopted successfully. This has relevance for some of the tourism development processes identified by Iorio and Corsale (2013) in a study of the remote and poor rural village of Viscri in Romania. According to their study, tourism in Viscri is relatively sustainable because it is people-centred and it focuses on local community assets and skills and other local resources. Tourists are drawn to the village by the preservation of its colourful farmhouses, which were originally occupied by Transylvanian Saxons, and by the original settlement pattern of the houses along village streets. The village's model of relatively sustainable tourism has been promoted by an influential local leader and a few external agencies, which have worked with local residents in several community initiatives. Their cooperation in promoting this form of tourism has been successful because of the relatively strong bonds of trust within the community and between the community and the local leader.

The influential local leader had run a guesthouse, established a village museum and undertaken house restoration, all within the village, and she took the important step of seeking and working with international supporters to attract funding for village projects (Iorio and Corsale 2014). This person was

> generally respected and trusted by the community and knows how to build social capital. Such local leadership can make vital contributions to the building of a network of internal and external stakeholders, and they can work as a mediator preventing the community from feeling ruled by outsiders. As locals, they understand local systems and know how to work within them but they also have the ability to reach out and establish vital connections outside of the community.
>
> (p. 252)

This leader, for example, worked with an external British and Romanian non-profit foundation to secure funding for projects to develop cultural and rural tourism in the village. These networks also have reinforced relations inside the community that depend on mutual help and trust. This was evident, for example, when local guesthouse owners exchanged guests among accommodation providers according to their vacancies, and also when they employed local people to help with cooking and cleaning.

Sustainable tourism policies but relatively low trust

The second scenario is again where agencies positively promote sustainable tourism, but in this instance low trust among the pertinent parties reduces the likelihood of positive results. Similar, although more complex, circumstances are described by Ioannides (1995: 583) in an account of the economically disadvantaged and relatively pristine rural area of the Akamas Peninsula, situated on the coast of Cyprus, where the government sought to introduce "alternative tourism as a sustainable development tool." The government advocated small-scale, village-based tourism in the area, which would involve locally-owned enterprises and use of the existing building stock. It was suggested that these proposals meant that environmental protection objectives could be matched with the economic development wishes of the villagers. Ioannides (p. 590) argues, however, that a

> stumbling block to implementing truly sustainable tourism in the Akamas region is the climate of distrust between the government and local communities. Villagers maintain they were never approached about their opinions on community development and have been excluded from all stages of the plan-making process.

The locals appear to have resented external government officials and consultants telling them how to use their land without them being consulted or involved in the decision making.

The potential relevance of the second scenario is also illustrated by Holland's (2000) study of tourism in two rural communities in southern Albania. She explains that European Union–funded projects to encourage local residents to participate in policy making for sustainable rural tourism faced major difficulties because of the extent of distrust within the communities and distrust within the communities of outside agencies. The development projects sought to use tourism to encourage sustainable economic regeneration, social integration and participatory community development. But Holland (2000: 517) argues that "it became transparent that the villagers did not trust the process. Despite painstaking preparation, ensuring widespread community access to the process, the very notion of collective action was anathema to the villagers." Distrust had undermined the social capital of mutual cooperation and reciprocity as well as abilities to take risks and think long-term – characteristics needed for communities to work together for tourism development.

Holland identifies several long-established influences behind the lack of trust and the associated reluctance to cooperate that had hindered attempts by outside agencies to develop sustainable tourism activities. These included Albania's history of foreign occupation and domination, totalitarian suppression of human rights and hierarchical political and economic organization. The history of foreign domination, for example, had encouraged a continuing disbelief in the power of the state to protect and defend Albanians' political and economic rights. The communist regime's rigid command economy after the Second World War had also meant that there was no experience of the social relations necessary to underpin a market economy. Collective action was associated with collectivization under communism, and this hindered the collective action required for community participation in sustainable tourism initiatives. The historic lack of institutions to combat distrust had thus meant that civic engagement and voluntary cooperation in the public sphere remained stifled. The many years of hardship caused by economic and political repression had hindered any notion of the community acting together for the benefit of the whole. The reaction to a transition to market capitalism was expressed in the need to accumulate resources as rapidly as possible and by whatever means, illegal if necessary.

Unsustainable tourism policies and low trust

The third scenario involves the government, private-sector commercial interests or other agencies proposing environmentally or socially damaging tourism developments, but in this case low trust among some relevant actors or entities may encourage opposition and possibly conflict that can block the proposals. Distrust can lead to negative public opinion, hostility, resistance and conflicts, and they can be important influences that might halt development proposals that appear unsustainable.

Relationships associated with a lack of trust and with oppositional politics are examined by Warren (1998) in a study of resort development in the 1990s on the Indonesian island of Bali. She examines emerging disagreements among Bali's residents with government policies for tourism and the environment and with proposals for resort complexes put forward by commercial interests, some led by developers based elsewhere in Indonesia, following a property investment boom in the late 1980s and early 1990s. "In the wake of this investment boom, popular reaction to the effects of the increasingly visible Jakarta conglomerates began to shake the sacred cow status of the tourist industry and government development policy itself" (pp. 230–231). The rapid growth of tourism led to a range of environmental problems, including unregulated mining of limestone and coral for hotel construction and an airport extension, the incursion of high-class hotels into remote parts of the island, pollution from sewage and plastic, the diversion of water to hotels and golf courses and the conversion of productive land to tourist facilities. Emerging local criticisms of such developments in Bali in part reflected increasing unease about the power of interests based outside the island in Jakarta to shape their local environment, culture and ways of life and about the sway of national government in Jakarta over provincial government as well as concerns about corruption and social inequalities. Warren (1998: 240) contends that the result was "a significant shift in attitude among Balinese towards the large-scale tourism development that was entering a new phase in the 1990s."

Despite a public debate about these issues, organized and active resistance to Bali's resort complex schemes was rare, in part reflecting a fairly repressive political climate. This changed, however, with proposals for a mega-resort near the religious site of Tannah Lot, which has major cultural-religious symbolism for the Balinese. The public outcry, including displaced farmers presenting a petition in opposition to the project, and the formation of a political coalition among students and intellectuals, "culminated in the first major political demonstrations on the island, and swelling opposition brought about an unprecedented eight-month suspension of construction on the project" (p. 245). Yet the eventual "compromise" saw only the number of hotel and residential units in the mega-resort being reduced to an earlier approved number.

Conclusion

The discussion here has been a response to the important and timely observation made by Nunkoo *et al.* (2012: 1540) that "research on political trust in the context of tourism development has remained virtually silent in the literature." The analysis has drawn together the few scattered ideas in the literature and extended those ideas concerning the roles of trust in the practical politics and governance processes of sustainable tourism. When trust in tourism governance has been touched on previously, it appears sometimes to be assumed that trust is inevitably positive both for democracy and for sustainable tourism. It has been argued here that such assumptions are oversimplified and misleading. Instead, the discussion explored aspects of the complexity of the relationships in practice among trust, governance and sustainable tourism. Notably, it considered how trust and distrust can tend to favor, obstruct or contradict sustainable tourism principles in different specific circumstances.

The analysis developed and explained a typology of different potential ideal-type scenarios of the relationships among trust, governance and sustainable tourism. The typology was used to begin to disentangle some of the complexities and contradictions, but it should not be expected that the ideal types will be found in practice in their pure form. In reality, there are often complex combinations of these relationships as well as interactions between them, and the relationships will vary between different policies and proposals, governance arrangements, past legacies and specific contemporary contexts. It is hoped that researchers will begin to explore these issues in a range of contexts, and this should add to our understanding of how trust interacts with governance and has important consequences for sustainable tourism.

References

Aitken, D. (2012) 'Trust and participation in urban regeneration', *People, Place and Policy*, 6(3): 133–147.

Atkinson, R. (2003) 'Addressing urban social exclusion through community involvement in urban regeneration', in R. Imrie and M. Raco (eds.) *Urban Renaissance? New Labour, Community and Urban Policy*, pp. 101–119, Bristol: Policy Press.

Ayuso, S. (2007) 'Comparing voluntary policy instruments for sustainable tourism: the experience of the Spanish hotel sector', *Journal of Sustainable Tourism*, 15(2): 144–159.

Bannister, F. and Connolly, R. (2011) 'Trust and transformational government: a proposed framework for research', *Government Information Quarterly*, 28: 137–147.

Baral, N. (2012) 'Empirical analysis of factors explaining local governing bodies' trust for administering agencies in community-based conservation', *Journal of Environmental Management*, 103: 41–50.

Bernstein, S. (2005) 'Legitimacy in global environmental governance', *Journal of International Law and International Relations*, 1(1/2): 139–166.

Bernstein, S. (2011) 'Legitimacy in intergovernmental and nonstate global governance', *Review of International Political Economy*, 18(1): 17–51.

Bianchi, R. (2004) 'Tourism restructuring and the politics of sustainability: a critical view from the European periphery (the Canary Islands)', *Journal of Sustainable Tourism*, 12: 495–529.

Bouckaert, G. and van de Walle, S. (2003) 'Comparing measures of citizen trust and user satisfaction as indicators of "good governance": difficulties in linking trust and satisfaction indicators', *International Review of Administrative Sciences*, 69: 329.

Bramwell, B. (1998) 'Selecting policy instruments for sustainable tourism', in W. Theobald (ed.) *Global Tourism*, 2nd ed., pp. 361–379, Oxford: Butterworth-Heinemann.

Bramwell, B. (2004) 'The policy context for tourism and sustainability in Southern Europe's coastal regions', in B. Bramwell (ed.) *Coastal Mass Tourism. Diversification and Sustainable Development in Southern Europe*, pp. 32–47, Clevedon: Channel View.

Bramwell, B. (2006) 'Actors, power, and discourses of growth limits', *Annals of Tourism Research*, 33(4): 957–978.

Bramwell, B. (2010) 'Participative planning and governance for sustainable tourism', *Tourism Recreation Research*, 35(3): 239–249.

Bramwell, B. (2011) 'Governance, the state and sustainable tourism: a political economy approach', *Journal of Sustainable Tourism*, 19(4/5): 459–477.

Bramwell, B. and Lane, B. (2011) 'Critical research on the governance of tourism and sustainability', *Journal of Sustainable Tourism*, 19(4/5): 411–421.

Brand, R. and Gaffikin, F. (2007) 'Collaborative planning in an uncollaborative world', *Planning Theory*, 6(3): 282–313.

Brockington, D., Duffy, R. and Igoe, J. (2008) *Nature Unbound. Conservation, Capitalism and the Future of Protected Areas*. London: Earthscan.

Bulkeley, H. (2005) 'Reconfiguring environmental governance: towards a politics of scales and networks', *Political Geography*, 24(8): 875–902.

Curry, N. and Fisher, R. (2012) 'The role of trust in the development of connectivities amongst rural elders in England and Wales', *Journal of Rural Studies*, 28: 358–370.

Dinica, V. (2009) 'Governance for sustainable tourism: a comparison of international and Dutch visions', *Journal of Sustainable Tourism*, 17(5): 583–603.

Dredge, D. and Jenkins, J. (2007) *Tourism Planning and Policy*. Milton: Wiley.

Eagles, P., Romagosa, F., Buteau-Duitschaever, C., Havitz, M., Glover, T. and McCutcheon, B. (2013) 'Good governance in protected areas: an evaluation of stakeholders' perceptions in British Columbia and Ontario provincial parks', *Journal of Sustainable Tourism*, 21(1): 60–79.

Edelenbos, J. and Eshuis, J. (2012) 'The interplay between trust and control in governance processes: a conceptual and empirical investigation', *Administration and Society*, 44(6): 647–674.

Gambetta, D. (1988) 'Can we trust trust?' in D. Gambetta (ed.) *Trust: Making and Breaking Cooperative Relations*, pp. 213–237, Oxford: Blackwell.

Goodwin, M. and Painter, J. (1996) 'Local governance, the crisis of Fordism and the changing geographies of regulation', *Transactions of the Institute of British Geographers*, 21: 635–648.

Hall, M. (2008) *Tourism Planning. Policies, Processes and Relationships*. Harlow: Pearson.

Hall, M. (2011) 'Policy learning and policy failure in sustainable tourism governance: from first- and second-order to third-order change?' *Journal of Sustainable Tourism*, 19 (4/5): 649–671.

Hickey, S. and Mohan, G. (2005) 'Relocating participation within a radical politics of development', *Development and Change*, 36(2): 237–262.

Holland, J. (2000) 'Consensus and conflict: the socioeconomic challenge facing sustainable tourism development in southern Albania', *Journal of Sustainable Tourism*, 8(6): 510–524.

Höppner, C. (2009) 'Trust – A monolithic panacea in land use planning?', *Land Use Policy*, 26: 1046–1054.

Ioannides, D. (1995) 'A flawed implementation of sustainable tourism: the experience of Akamas, Cyprus', *Tourism Management*, 16(8): 583–592.

Iorio, M. and Corsale, A. (2014) 'Community-based tourism and networking: Viscri, Romania', *Journal of Sustainable Tourism*, 22(2), 234–255.

Jacobs, M. (1999) 'Sustainable development as a contested concept', in A. Dobson (ed.) *Fairness and Futurity: Essays on Environmental Sustainability and Social Justice*, pp. 21–45. Oxford: Oxford University Press.

Jamal, T. and Getz, D. (1995) 'Collaboration theory and community tourism planning', *Annals of Tourism Research*, 22(1): 186–204.

Jayasuriya, K. and Hewison, K. (2004) 'The antipolitics of good governance: from global social policy to a global populism?' *Critical Asian Studies*, 36(4): 571–590.

Kehoe, S. and Ponting, R. (2003) 'Value importance and value congruence as determinants of trust in health policy actors', *Social Science and Medicine*, 57(6): 1065–1075.

Kumar, A. and Paddison, R. (2000) 'Trust and collaborative planning theory: the case of the Scottish planning system', *International Planning Studies*, 5(2): 205–223.

Lachapelle, P. and McCool, S. (2012) 'The role of trust in community wildland fire protection planning', *Society and Natural Resources*, 25(4): 321–335.

Laing, J., Moore, S. A., Wegner, A. and Weiler, B. (2008) 'Identifying success factors behind partnerships for managing recreation and tourism in urban fringe parks', *Annals of Leisure Research*, 11(1–2): 101–122.

Laurian, L. (2009) 'Trust in planning: theoretical and practical considerations for participatory and deliberative planning', *Planning Theory and Practice*, 10(3): 369–391.

Lockwood, M. (2010) 'Good governance for terrestrial protected areas: a framework, principles and performance outcomes', *Journal of Environmental Management*, 91: 754–766.

Lovelock, B. (2002) 'Why it's good to be bad: the role of conflict in contributing towards sustainable tourism in protected areas', *Journal of Sustainable Tourism*, 10(1): 5–30.

McDermott, C. (2012) 'Trust, legitimacy and power in forest certification: a case study of the FSC in British Columbia', *Geoforum*, 43: 634–644.

Meadowcroft, J. (1999) 'The politics of sustainable development: emergent arenas and challenges for political science', *International Political Science Review*, 20(2): 219–237.

Meadowcroft, J. (2007) 'Who is in charge here? Governance for sustainable development in a complex world', *Journal of Environmental Policy and Planning*, 9(3/4): 299–314.

Meadowcroft, J. (2011) 'Engaging with the politics of sustainability transitions', *Environmental Innovation and Societal Transitions*, 1: 70–75.

Meadowcroft, J. (2013) 'Sustainable development', in M. Bevir (ed.) *The Sage Handbook of Governance*, pp. 535–551, London: Sage.

Miller, G. and Twining-Ward, L. (2005) *Monitoring for a Sustainable Tourism Transition: The Challenge of Developing and Using Indicators*. Wallingford: CABI.

Murnighan, J., Malhotra, D. and Weber, J. (2004) 'Paradoxes of trust: empirical and theoretical departures from a traditional model', in R. Kramer and K. Cook (eds.) *Trust and Distrust in Organizational Dilemmas and Approaches*, pp. 293–326. New York: Russell Sage.

Mycoo, M. (2006) 'Sustainable tourism using regulations, market mechanisms and green certification: a case study of Barbados', *Journal of Sustainable Tourism*, 14(5): 489–511.

Nunkoo, R., Ramkissoon, H. and Gursoy, D. (2012) 'Public trust in tourism institutions', *Annals of Tourism Research*, 39(3): 1538–1564.

Purcell, M. and Nevins, J. (2005) 'Pushing the boundary: state restructuring, state theory, and the case of US–Mexico border enforcement in the 1990s', *Political Geography*, 24(2): 211–235.

Roberts, L. and Simpson, F. (1999) 'Developing partnership approaches to tourism in Central and Eastern Europe', *Journal of Sustainable Tourism*, 7(3/4): 314–330.

Saxena, G. (2006) 'Beyond mistrust and competition – the role of social and personal bonding processes in sustaining livelihoods of rural tourism businesses: a case of the Peak District National Park', *International Journal of Tourism Research*, 6: 263–277.

Schuett, M., Selin, S. and Carr, D. (2001) 'Making it work: keys to successful collaboration in natural resource management'. *Environmental Management*, 27(4): 587–593.

Stoker, G. (1998) 'Governance as theory: five propositions', *International Social Science Journal*, 50(155): 17–28.

Swain, C. and Tait, M. (2007) 'The crisis of trust and planning', *Planning Theory and Practice*, 8(2), 229–247.

Vangen, S. and Huxham, C. (2003) 'Nurturing collaborative relations: building trust in interorganizational collaboration', *Journal of Applied Behavioral Science*, 39: 5–30.

Waayers, D., Lee, D. and Newsome, D. (2012) 'Exploring the nature of stakeholder collaboration: a case study of marine turtle tourism in the Ningaloo region, Western Australia', *Current Issues in Tourism*, 15(7): 673–692.

Warren, C. (1998) 'Tanah Lot. The cultural and environmental politics of resort development in Bali', in P. Hirsch and C. Warren (eds.) *The Politics of the Environment in Southeast Asia. Resources and Resistance*, pp. 229–261, London: Routledge.

Welch, M., Rivera, R., Conway, B., Yonkoski, J., Lupton, P. and Giancola, R. (2005) 'Determinants and consequences of trust', *Sociological Enquiry*, 75(4), 453–473.

Yodsuwan, C. and Butcher, K. (2012) 'Determinants of tourism collaboration member satisfaction in Thailand', *Asia Pacific Journal of Tourism Research*, 17(1): 63–80.

Yüksel, F. and Yüksel, A. (2008) 'Perceived clientelism: effects on residents' evaluation of municipal services and their intentions for participation in tourism development projects', *Journal of Hospitality and Tourism Research*, 32(2): 187–208.

Yüksel, A., Yüksel, F. and Culha, O. (2012) 'Ministers' statements: a policy implementation instrument for sustainable tourism?', *Journal of Sustainable Tourism*, 20(4): 513–532.

4 Trust and participatory tourism planning

Heather L. Mair

It is nearly an unchallenged truth that the long-term success of tourism development depends first and foremost on the support of the host community. Indeed, for many concerned with the sustainability of the places where tourism activities take place, as well as the tourism sector itself, one of the most central and complex issues is the role of members of the host community in tourism development. Concerns about this role extend beyond seeing community members as key allies in terms of crafting, shaping and supporting the tourism experience to assessing their part in the process of planning the tourism development in the first instance. These, of course, are complex issues, and critiques of tourism planning processes abound. Researchers have begun to challenge us to ask tough questions about unthinking and uncritical endorsements of tourism planning that 'engages' the community. For instance, Blackstock (2005) asked: What or who is 'the community' in community-based tourism? Reed (1997; see also Mair and Reid 2007) asked: How are these planning processes developed, and who has the real power to make decisions and affect change? Deeper considerations tackle questions related not just to the degrees or types of involvement, but even more fundamentally in terms of the broader context that shapes the capacity of community members to participate in the planning process and how that might change over time. For example, Wray (2011) wonders about the impact of the socio-political context within which all tourism planning endeavours must be located.

As someone trained in the techniques of tourism planning, I draw on personal experience as well as insights from relevant scholarly literature to consider critically the notion of participation in the tourism planning context. I argue that to contribute to the discussion of participatory tourism planning, one must first come to terms with the issue of meaningful and engaged participation in the tourism planning process. What must we consider when we talk about tourism planning that is participatory or collaborative? I argue a key concern is whether the goals of development are limited to the tourism enterprise or if they speak to broader community development objectives. Moreover, the rather confounding matter of trust must be brought to bear on this topic, because trust is arguably the key element for successful participatory tourism planning processes and yet it is often a missing or overlooked ingredient. Certainly, trust is essential to the success of all public planning endeavours, and so should be for essential for all tourism planning activities.

However, and as I plan to argue, participatory planning endeavours that start from a community development perspective stand a better chance of success because the processes by which they work can help to build trust and confidence in planning decisions over the long term.

The chapter has five sections. The first part presents a critical look at the context of the planner and planning and sets the stage for the rest of the discussion by considering the extent to which planning goals and processes are fully understood and how challenges to the nature of planning (and who has the right to plan) are ultimately issues of trust in the process. Next, the discussion turns more directly to tourism planning and provides a brief overview of the variety of approaches that can be considered to have a participatory flavour in that the need to bring in the views of community members is made clear. Third, a look at the critiques of these various participatory approaches to tourism planning is briefly presented and matched with a discussion of community development as a potential process and goal for tourism planning. Fourth, a discussion of a handful of tourism planning endeavours, which seem to align most closely with a community development perspective, is presented, and the notion of trust – particularly as it can be developed through planning processes – is engaged directly. The chapter concludes with a provocation to consider whether sustainable tourism is ultimately about sustaining community or sustaining the industry; I argue trust will emerge from the former but not the latter.

I should also make clear that I am writing from a Western (and specifically Canadian) viewpoint and so am unable to speak with confidence about tourism development processes beyond that particular context. As Bramwell argues, 'the "Western" or contemporary models of partnerships may be both unwanted by local communities and also inappropriate in relation to encouraging greater sustainability' (2004: 545).

Context: planning – by whom and to what end?

Central to any discussion of tourism planning processes and trust is a brief consideration of planning and the role of the planner. In his landmark book, *Planning in the Public Domain*, Friedmann (1987) traced the evolution of the role of the professional, public planner in society. He argued the power of the planner's role was rooted in epistemological assumptions; based in questions about *what knowledge* was relevant to making development decisions and, perhaps most importantly, *who* had that knowledge. In the post–World War II era, economic crises and rising concerns about growing poverty, environmental issues and social inequality led citizens to question the goals and implications of growth and development, to challenge the dominant view of planner-as-expert and to seek alternatives:

> Citizens around the world have begun to search for an 'alternative' development that is less tied to the dynamics of industrial capitalism. Emancipatory movements have emerged to push for a more positive vision of the

future . . . and in serious pursuit of a balanced natural environment, gender equality, the abolition of racism and the eradication of grinding poverty.

(Friedmann 1987: 10)

While the tone of agency and empowerment underscored in this quotation is valid, others have traced the ideological impact of neoliberalism for opening up space for more community-driven (and corporate) involvement in planning. Briefly, neoliberalism is a political-economic viewpoint that encourages a reduction in government involvement in business activity and industrial development with a view to unhampering economic growth. While not an overly popular investigative theme in tourism studies, many authors are coming to realise the significance of this broad ideological context, which serves to shape all public policy decisions, not just tourism. Hall and Wilson (2011; see also Mair 2006; Mair and Reid 2007), for example, noted the transformation of the local state under neoliberalism, where government is either unwilling or unable to manage issues of social provision, which are then left in the hands of private and corporate interests. Dredge and Jenkins pointed out the implications of the growing immersion of private and corporate interests in the public planning and policy-making process:

Industry bodies and corporate interests have become integrated into policy making processes so seamlessly in some cases that industry interests have been responsible for substantially writing and informing policy . . . At a practical level, it reduces political tensions and improves the chances of policy being supported by industry and criticised less. Issues of public interest, social justice, equity, transparency and accountability, while certainly drawing increased critical interest in academic circles, remain outside the focus (or interest) of planning and policy practice in many cases.

(Dredge and Jenkins 2011: 4–5)

Thus, in an era of increased desire for broad democratic engagement in public policy processes, which are underscored by a withdrawal of government influence, the stage becomes set for developing participatory processes for (tourism) planning. Further, linked to these intertwined forces are concerns about power, knowledge and ultimately trust as these developments challenge traditional assumptions regarding who can be trusted to have the expertise or the knowledge and the skills to meet the challenges of our times. Indeed, how can these insights be brought more deeply into the planning process? As Friedmann put it:

Thus, there is renewed urgency in the question posed by the philosophers of the Enlightenment: Are reason and democracy compatible? Can ordinary people be trusted to use their heads in the conduct of their own affairs, or is superior wisdom needed? Can people free themselves from tutelage by state and corporate power and become autonomous again as active citizens in households, local communities and regions?

(Friedmann 1987: 10)

Alongside the questioning of expert knowledge in planning comes a broader recognition or perhaps a growing awareness that planners are hardly objective experts with access to unchanging truths. They are instead value-driven agents who are active in shaping the way the planning process works. Forester is particularly insightful about the power of the planner:

> The planner does not just present and collect information, reach agreements, set meeting times, and call for further work to be done – all these the production of instrumental results. The planner also establishes, refines, and recreates, and thus reproduces, social relations of trust or distrust, cooperation or competition, amiability or hostility, encouragement of discouragement, and so on. Every organizational interaction or practical communication (including the nonverbal) not only produces a result, it also reproduces, strengthening or weakening, the specific social working relations of those who interact.
>
> (Forester 1989: 71)

Thus, planners and indeed everyone involved in planning activities must be seen as subjective beings, deeply embedded in the processes by which information is both provided to the community and to one another. Further, their actions can expand or limit the avenues by which planning participants can act on that information (see, for example, Forester 1989; Healey 1997). Healey made the point forcefully:

> Planning practice is thus not an innocent, value-neutral activity. It is deeply political. It carries value and expresses power. The power lies in the formal allocation of rights and responsibilities, in the politics of influence, the practices through which 'bias' is mobilised, and in the taken-for-granted assumptions embedded in cultural practices.
>
> (Healey 1997: 84)

As Healey and Forester argued, seeing planners as powerful shapers of the planning process, and viewing them not just as objective facilitators but as active agents, opens up opportunities to consider how the role of the tourism planner might be equally powerful. Lew (2007) reflected on the role of planners in the context of sustainable tourism and considered their perhaps rather under-appreciated role as agents of change:

> The one area of tourism where tourism planners are recognized as a participant in social change is sustainable tourism planning. Unlike more traditional business-oriented tourism planning, sustainable tourism is supposed to have a goal of supporting and sustaining environmental and local community values. This potentially activist role is, however, not recognized as such in tourism planning textbooks, most of which now claim to be sustainable development oriented, but continue to view the tourism planner simply as a person who attempts to bring rationality to the economic development process.
>
> (Lew 2007: 386)

If we accept that the context of (tourism) planning has changed under the ideological rules of neoliberalism as well as the epistemological challenge to planner-as-all-powerful-expert, and we agree we need to move to investigate opportunities to empower and engage ordinary citizens while remaining cognizant of how complex and difficult this is, perhaps we can begin to assess the different ways of engagement and to consider the role of trust therein. Stein and Harper also reflect on trust and its role in planning and are powerfully clear on its role in society more broadly:

> So, we believe that trust is at least as basic as power to understanding human relationships and institutions and to reforming them. Trust is also a necessary condition for any kind of communication, understanding, knowledge, or learning. If there were literally no trust, then nothing any other party says could be accepted; everything would have to be verified, guaranteed, enforced.
>
> (Stein and Harper 2003: 136)

Laurian (2009; see also Swain and Tait 2007) argued that the shift away from seeing planners as all-knowing experts, while embedded in broader challenges to (and mistrust of) authority and government, as well as a greater sense of insecurity, have fostered a general sense of distrust with regard to the planning profession. She argued further that this trust may be restored only through participatory and deliberative planning practices (2009: 370). Further, Laurian reflected on the so-called collaborative turn in planning (see also Healey 1997), whereby efforts to address public distrust have included a more open approach to planning. Collaborative, or what might be called participatory, approaches to planning were developed, and, as Laurian made clear, the role of trust in the success of these plans is vital, because it can create a 'positive feedback loop' over time (2009: 379).

However, we must be careful not to imbue ordinary citizens with some sort of unbiased access to a particular truth or solution to a problem, because they, too, are subjective beings with values, assumptions, goals and expectations. Moreover, these ordinary citizens may not have the motivation, skills or even the interest to be deeply engaged in planning despite efforts to involve them. As Forester (1989) pointed out, citizens may distrust planners, but seeing themselves as capable of doing the job themselves may be another matter:

> (1) uncertain and uninformed about policy opportunities and consequences, yet believing that others 'know better'; (2) cynical about the promise of their own participation and deferential to those with expert, official or investor status, consenting through deference, not participation; (3) doubting their own social and community capacities for cooperation, and trusting instead in the good faith of professionals or the hidden hand of market advocates; and (4) confused about and distracted from planning and policy options that could address social needs in more than a 'trickle down' fashion.
>
> (Forester 1989: 80)

Thus, this is a remarkably interesting time. As is discussed in more depth in the next section, many students and practitioners of tourism planning have come to advocate approaches that either mitigate or challenge the all-powerful role of the expert planner by placing trust in the knowledge, ability and power of ordinary citizens (i.e., community members) to plan for tourism development on their own behalf.

Tourism planning: bringing in the community

It is beyond the scope of this chapter, and it is rather well-trod ground, to review the extent of information now available in terms of measuring the social, economic, political and environmental impacts of tourism development. Alongside the multitude of indicators extolling the economic virtues of tourism growth worldwide one now can nearly always expect to see a companion discussion of its enormously damaging effects. This was and is, ultimately, an issue of planning. As Costa (2001) pointed out, a 1980 report published by the World Tourism Organization was something of a watershed, as it concluded, based on a review of 1,619 tourism plans, that tourism planning was a dismal failure; overtly pursuing an economic rationale and systematically ignoring social and physical factors. Costa (2001: 431) argued this led to a search for more alternative, efficient and effective tourism planning approaches.

Nonetheless, the most pervasive objective of tourism plans was (and remains) the pursuit of business and economic development goals. Instead of dismissing the obvious opportunities of tourism development, then, most researchers, planners and policy makers look instead for processes whereby negative impacts could be mitigated and the benefits enhanced. Wray (2011; see also Okazaki 2008 and Grybovych *et al.* 2011) traced the growing interest in participatory and collaborative approaches to tourism planning. This interest is not just a means for enhancing broad engagement but a way of addressing the impacts of tourism while capturing and expanding upon its primarily economic benefits.

What all this discussion has led to is a proliferation of terminology, myriad approaches and not much certainty. For instance, students of tourism development may assess methods and models, including participatory tourism planning, collaborative tourism planning and community-based tourism planning. Grybovych *et al.* (2011) provided a thoughtful list of these various models. Table 4.1, while hardly exhaustive, lists some of them and encourages us to reflect on the language and the broad scope of scholarly attention devoted to this issue.

Although sometimes used interchangeably, these various terms have different elements and yet they all adhere to a fundamental commitment to fostering deep and meaningful engagement with members of the host community in the tourism planning process. Indeed, while most of the tourism literature makes a rather fleeting case for the necessity of involving the community in planning endeavours, and some authors have developed innovative models and approaches for bringing community members or stakeholders into the planning process for tourism, a few others have put at the forefront a concern for not only community engagement but a direct consideration of the role of tourism development in community

Table 4.1 Types of tourism planning

Tourism planning model	Author
Integrated and integrative tourism planning	Hung *et al.* (2011); Inskeep (1988); Ioannides (1995); Marcouiller (1997); Pearce and Moscardo (1999)
Responsible and responsive tourism planning	Haywood (1988); Reid (2003); Ritchie (1993)
Comprehensive and balanced tourism planning	Madrigal (1995); Murphy (1985)
Collaborative tourism planning	Bramwell (2004); Bramwell and Lane (2004); Bramwell and Sharman (1999); Hall (2000); Jamal and Getz (1995); Reed (1997, 1999); Sautter and Leisen (1999); Vernon *et al.* (2005)
Participatory tourism planning	Mair and Reid (2007); Reid *et al.* (2004); Timothy (1999); Tosun (2000, 2006)
Inclusive tourism planning	Costa (2001); Madrigal (1995); Prentice (1993)
Dialogic tourism planning	Jamal *et al.* (2002)
Community-based planning	Blackstock (2005); Okazaki (2008)
Transactive tourism planning	Wray (2011)

Source: adapted from Grybovych *et al.* (2011: 84).

development more generally. Blackstock (2005), for instance, pointed out that the dependence of the tourism sector on residents' goodwill has led to interest in broader issues of community development and participatory planning philosophies. She builds on Gilchrist's definition of community development as 'building active and sustainable communities based on social justice and mutual respect' (Gilchrist 2003: 22; as cited in Blackstock 2005: 40) and then adds, 'thus community development explicitly seeks to dismantle structural barriers to participation and develop emancipatory collective responses to local issues' (Blackstock 2005: 40).

However, critiques of these tourism planning processes over the past twenty years have alerted us to the potential for tourism planning processes aiming to engage the community to fall apart or simply to reinforce the power structures already in place. For instance, Koutsouris (2009) reflected on the challenge of using a community-based or participatory approach to tourism development, explaining that if genuine networks for interaction and learning are not established, interventions may generate uncertainties, alienation and potentially social disintegration, and will not lead to sustainable tourism development (as cited in Wray, 2011: 622).

Bramwell's work has been deeply influential in the realm of participatory or collaborative tourism planning. Indeed, it was an article by Bramwell and Sharman (1999) that first sparked my personal interest in these kinds of approaches to tourism planning. Bramwell listed three strategies that could be used to address what he called 'the problems that limit stakeholder participation in multi-party working' (2004: 542). First is the need for increased inclusion, 'thereby widening involvement in this participatory democratic form'. Importantly, the argument here is that there must first be an underlying foundation of democracy; meaningful engagement in planning processes can only work if participants have had experience in being part of the decision-making processes that affect them. Second, and related to the first, Bramwell argues there is a need to ensure that those who are not involved in the process be able to 'build their own institutional capacities and self-confidence' to participate. Bramwell also noted the importance of appreciating different ways of knowing about the world, because power is situated in knowledge, and if equity is a goal, then these different worldviews will have to be brought together and validated in the process:

> Some people are familiar with the language of consequences, grounded in economic reasoning or scientific evidence. Others are more accustomed to the language of belief or the political assertion of rights. Others again may be more comfortable with the expression of fears and dangers. If the hegemony of the powerful is to be reduced, all these forms of reasoning need to be learned about and shown respect in the collaborative process.
>
> (Bramwell 2004: 546)

Last, an effort must be made to consult with those who are not involved in the process, for whatever reason. However, Bramwell issues a caution and an inherent resistance to merely assuming that consultation will ultimately lead to change in power structures. He follows Mowforth and Munt:

> Looked at critically, partnerships and other approaches to widening participant in tourism policy-making could be seen largely as providing improved means for economic and political elites to incorporate dissenting groups and to manage potential conflicts more broadly within their own agendas.
>
> (Mowforth and Munt 1998; as cited in Bramwell 2004: 550–551)

Blackstock (2005: 40) made the essential critique that community-based tourism diverges from what she calls the 'ethos of community development' and, as a result, risks becoming a mere 'community development imposter' for three reasons. First, its focus on sustaining tourism development over meeting community needs leads to a lack of transformative potential; second, communities are treated as 'homogeneous blocks' instead of groups of people with differing power and values. Last, it ignores the extent to which local decisions are situated within broader ideological contexts, which limit their power to affect change.

And yet, more than a decade of experience in participatory tourism planning research and practice leaves me optimistic with regard to the potential of participatory approaches to tourism planning. As Reid argued:

> Those championing the corporate globalization project know exactly what kind of world we are moving towards. It is one where the wealthy have

become wealthier, and the poor poorer; it is a world where the disenfranchised are left to serve the wealthy, without processes under their control which can assist them out of their condition. The tourism industry is not only a participant in that process, but perhaps a major contributor to it. This need not be the case, however. Tourism development can be a bottom-up activity, one that allows for control at the grass-roots level, and provides an improved standard of living to those engaged in it, particularly those at the community level.

(Reid 2003: 21)

Thus, given the critiques and concerns outlined above, one is left wondering how to address these challenges. Indeed, is it too much to ask of tourism planning to address issues of power, equity and access? As Lew (2007) speculated, perhaps because tourism planning issues are not considered as all-pervasive as some other planning concerns, they tend to deal more directly with recreation and hospitality sectors in a community and could leave out broader public, community concerns. Of course, given what we know to be the economic, social, political, environmental and cultural impacts of tourism, which are ultimately felt at the community level, perhaps it is not too much to ask that tourism planning tackles bigger issues and questions.

Community development scholar Jnanabrata Bhattacharyya (2004) reviewed the many definitions of community and presented his own. He crafted a theory of community development, arguing it had two components: 'community' was essentially solidarity (comprised of a shared identity and shared values and norms), and the goal of 'development' was essentially agency or autonomy, which, building on de Certeau (1986) and Giddens (1984), he defined in the following way:

the capacity of people to order their world, the capacity to create, reproduce, change, and live according to their own meaning systems, to have the powers to define themselves as opposed to being defined by others.

(Bhattacharyya 2004: 12)

Bhattacharyya further outlined three principles of community development, which he argued are central to any process. First, community developers must recognize people are productive by nature and must have opportunities to be producers of their own life chances (what he called self-help). Second, people have needs and demands about which only they should be allowed to speak (what he called felt needs). Third, he developed the notion of participation, calling it the 'most recognized principle of community development' (2004: 23), and argued that it must be encouraged at every opportunity.

Although the influence of this theory has yet to be felt in the literature on participatory tourism planning, it provides a provocative platform upon which to build the rest of this discussion, especially when we start to delve more deeply into the issue of trust. The next section provides a brief review of recent efforts to utilise these approaches in tourism planning with a view to reinforcing both the potential and the need for an even more radical, community development approach.

Participatory tourism planning: the community development question

As should be clear by now, the issue of participation in planning processes, tourism and otherwise, has received much attention, evaluation and debate. Indeed, as tourism becomes an ever-present component of urban and rural development strategies, all such plans are increasingly subject to scrutiny in terms of how (and how much) broad participation there was during the plan's development. There may be, however, an emergent shift in the discourse of participatory (tourism) planning; a growing expectation that it takes on broader goals of community development. These expectations are beginning to shape scholarly assessments of participatory planning approaches. For instance, Mahjabeen *et al.* (2009) evaluated the process by which the Sydney Metropolitan Strategy was developed in Australia, paying particular attention to the participation of traditionally marginalised groups (so-called voiceless groups). The authors found that despite many 'participation platforms' instituted during the consultation and planning process, the voices of Aboriginal and non-English speaking Australians were virtually nonexistent. For those concerned with the connection between community development and planning (including tourism planning), this is a serious limitation. As they noted:

> There are, however, increasing concerns among community groups and scholars that the current plan-making process, particularly in developed countries such as Australia, is dominated by powerful politicians, senior bureaucrats and professional planners who are principally concerned with pre-determined standards, targets, time-frames and economic imperatives.
>
> (Mahjabeen *et al.* 2009: 46)

In a similar vein, Duffy *et al.* (2012) pointed out that, despite efforts to bring community-based approaches to tourism planning to the forefront, there remains a lack of inclusive techniques to bring out the views and voices of marginalised community members. Their own work, for example, highlights the role of gendered ideology in shaping the process of participation during community-based tourism planning in Ecuador. Wray (2011) evaluated two tourism planning approaches that arguably pursued a collaborative or participatory approach (what she calls transactive). She concluded:

> More importantly, transactive planning requires planners to understand diverse stakeholder values and learning processes. The contrast between [the two case studies] has demonstrated that despite efforts to foster learning and dialogue, if principal destination stakeholders are not committed to this approach at the outset, or if governance and sociopolitical agendas dominate, the transactive process may be ineffectual.
>
> (Wray, 2011: 624)

And yet, like me, these authors held out hope for an improved process. As Mahjabeen *et al.* argued: 'When community groups are actively engaged in planning and implementation processes, plans are likely to be more closely matched with stakeholders' needs, interests and expectations, motivating them to achieve social and ecological benefits' (2009: 46). Moreover, these authors see community participation, much like Bhattacharyya (2004), as part of a 'global movement promoting democracy, justice and sustainability' (Mahjabeen *et al.* 2009: 46) and, as such, were deeply concerned about a process that merely reinforced existing power structures and met the needs of elites. Okazaki (2008) puts issues of power and self-development right at the centre of thinking about participation in tourism planning and follows Connell, who argues that participation is

> not only about achieving the more efficient and more equitable distribution of material resources: it is also about the sharing of knowledge and the transformation of the process of learning itself in the service of people's self-development.
>
> (Connell 1997: 250; as cited in Okazaki 2008: 511)

Grybovych *et al.* (2011) reinforce and expand these ideas in their development of the often taken-for-granted notion of democracy, and they consider the role it could play in participatory tourism planning. They follow Weeks (2000 in Grybovych *et al.* 2011: 85) and provide the following definition of deliberative democracy: 'informed participation by citizens in the deliberative process of community decision making'. Once again, we hear elements of community development theory. Interestingly, Grybovych *et al.* concluded their rather favorable assessment of a community engagement process for tourism planning in Ucluelet, British Columbia, this way:

> Creating avenues for broad and informed public participation and fostering partnerships and collaboration among various stakeholders opened up a broad range of opportunities for Ucluelet and helped secure some of the widely praised benefits of participatory and collaborative tourism planning initiatives. Among them – increased accountability to the public, an opportunity to make balanced and better-informed decisions and properly address community concerns, initiating a process of social learning, securing legitimacy of decisions made, increasing chances to overcome power imbalances through collaboration and initiating a process of community building and development.
>
> (Grybovych *et al.* 2011: 98)

Writing about their experiences with participatory tourism planning in rural Ontario, Canada, Mair and Reid (2007) called for an approach to tourism planning that put at the forefront a concern with power and end goals. They advocated moving toward what Friedmann (1987) delineates as models of social learning or radical planning as a way to counter unequal power relations in communities and to see tourism as merely a means for meeting collectively defined community development goals, not an end in itself. Mair and Reid attempted to extend the discussion about participatory tourism planning to foster a broader consideration of community development and to decentre the tourism development imperative. They argued the potential of a radical, participatory approach to community planning and development that may or may not make tourism part of the development strategy:

> The focus of a radical planning approach to community development, whether or not tourism is a part, is to create spaces where community members can gather together and discuss the future of their communities on an equitable footing and in an atmosphere of open dialogue and trust.
>
> (Mair and Reid 2007: 420)

The next section explores the potential of a participatory tourism planning process that has community development at its core focus in an effort both to inject the tourism discourse with these broad principles and to draw a more direct connection with the topic of trust.

Participatory tourism planning: building trust through process

In the handful of evaluations and assessments of participatory tourism planning endeavours that are favorable, the notion of trust seems to play a key role. While not well enough understood, trust is clearly an essential component in making participatory tourism plans work, particular those with broader community development goals. More specifically, the essential component may be trust in the *process* of decision making. Nunkoo and Ramkissoon (2011) builds on Lovell (2001) to argue that 'institutional trust is a basic preconditioned [*sic*] for cooperation between two parties and is important to liberal democracy and civil society as it lays the foundation for people's confidence in government decisions'. However, what needs to be laid bare is the extent to which the processes of government decision making are trustworthy. Laurian argued that the connection between trust and successful planning is becoming ever more important as most individuals trust based on a careful evaluation of their experience with the processes of governance and decision making:

> Modern society is reflexive. Individuals' decisions to trust institutions are not based on tradition, but on their experience with, and rational analysis of, institutions. Information sharing, deliberation and democratic governance are thus increasingly important to support the emergence and sustenance of trust, and planners play an integral role in this process.
>
> (Laurian, 2009: 375)

Further, because participatory planning or collaborative planning approaches have at their core a commitment to engaging outside voices, the flattening of power relationships and equity, their potential to enhance trust is clear. Laurian (2009: 376) reflected on the mutually reinforcing relationship between trust and collaborative planning and argued these approaches both facilitate and rely on trust through 'undistorted communication, collaboration within and outside organizations and the decentralization of decision making'.

Bramwell touches on the potential of participatory action research because the core elements of this methodology are very much like participatory planning approaches:

> Here the subjects being studied are encouraged to take part in shaping the research, such as by defining their own criteria and identifying their own ways of representing and interpreting the issues being examined. Action research is particularly reliant on establishing mutual trust between the researchers and the people being studied.
>
> (Bramwell 2004: 549)

In their report on the use of a collaborative approach to tourism planning in Quebec, Canada, which had elements of action research and planning, Blangy *et al.* (2008) highlighted the following process-based outcomes: it created a sense of ownership of the project; gave people a chance to share knowledge, build bridges, develop links between communities and operators and work together at the regional level; put at the forefront the needs of the community in question, including the desire to build small-scale, culturally and land-based experiences rather than lodges and community hotels; and gave the local tourism development officers a set of tools they can use in other ways.

Mair *et al.* (2005) candidly described the somewhat bumpy road they took to developing what they felt was a context-sensitive and clearly written process for participatory tourism development that had a community development agenda. They realised that building interest, engagement and trust in the process of planning tourism in small communities were things they needed to take more seriously. Their manual, *Visiting Your Future: A Community Guide to Planning Rural Tourism* (Reid *et al.* 2000) was based upon extensive experience in tourism planning and consultation with several rural communities in Ontario, Canada. The development of the planning manual borrowed heavily from a community-development technique called a 'community search conference' (Emery and Purser 1996), which involved bringing citizens together over an extended period of time (i.e., ideally a weekend) to address collectively issues of concern in their community.

In 2005, Mair *et al.* reported on the application of this process in one particular community and noted that many of the outcomes and strategies of that session were bigger than tourism: fostering partnership and community support, identification of community resources and image, coordination of community and economic activity, coordination of marketing and communication activity and long- and short-term infrastructure planning (pp. 174–175). While the search conference methodology is not without critics (Schafft and Greenwood 2003), as Mair *et al.* argued, it provided an invaluable platform for launching a broad-based discussion about tourism, for building trust and capacity in the communities and for taking on community development concerns that may or may not be tourism related.

Other research on the potential of a search conference approach for non–tourism-related issues also reinforces its potential. Schusler *et al.* (2003), for instance, utilised and then assessed the search conference model to develop a collaborative process for natural resource management. Perhaps unsurprisingly, trust figured largely in their findings:

> Collaborative relationships require trust. Twenty-four interviewees (83%) reported that through the search conference they gained trust in others to a moderate or great extent. They emphasized mutual respect, listening, and open-mindedness as essential to developing collaborative working relationships and enhancing trust. A few participants responded that they had established trusting relationships with others prior to this experience.
>
> (Schusler *et al.* 2003: 317)

Nevertheless, these authors also concluded that the issue of trust, while a common factor in the success of the search conference and the relationships that came from that conference, remained relatively unexplored.

Clearly, it is not enough to state simply that trust is a prerequisite for tourism planning generally and participatory approaches to tourism planning specifically. One must give thought to how trust can be built into the tourism planning process, and this requires thinking about knowledge and power. For members of communities where tourism is merely a last-ditch effort to sustain community life, trust in the tourism planning process risks being sacrificed for the sake of meeting the sector's needs. However, where tourism is treated as one component in the mix of economic, social and cultural development options for a community, time can be taken to situate the consideration of tourism, and its planning, in ways that build trust relationships.

Planners, as outlined above, need to be cognizant of both the influence of their values and their need to take into account the views and values of others in the community. In their book on rural tourism development, George *et al.* (2009) outline five questions that planners and those involved in planning for tourism must ask and be prepared to answer as the planning process unfolds. Moreover, and as the discussion above made clear, in order for trust to be built and sustained, as many people as possible must be involved in the crafting of these answers over time. Following Bhattacharyya (2004), they need to be at the forefront of deciding what is important to them, building a shared understanding of what the community needs and working on their own behalf as agents of change.

1   What is an appropriate product for our community?
2   What is our motivation for doing this?
3   Who is in control of what we are doing?
4   What is the right development process for us?
5   What form of knowledge will we rely on as we build this product?

(George *et al.* 2009: 246)

Of course, this is no easy task and requires a long-term view. Planners committed to participatory processes need to build the trust in the communities *before* a discussion of tourism planning even takes place. Moreover, they need to be self-reflexive, humble and able to challenge the neoliberal worldview within which all tourism development considerations are situated. And, as Macbeth puts it:

> One needs to be prepared to argue for no tourism! More precisely, treat this industry like any other development option and assess its viability to contribute to the wider sustainable development of the region, the state, the country and the 'living earth', but without ignoring the political economic of the North–South divide in the early 21st century.
>
> (Macbeth 2005: 980; as cited in Mair 2012: 51)

Conclusion

In 1997, House asked us to evaluate what was meant by sustainable tourism development and to consider critically whether the emphasis was on tourism development or on sustainability. Indeed, when we talk about sustainable tourism, what is it that we are sustaining? If we imagine that tourism can and should play a role in and among various strategies for community development, our view can open to consider a long-term, community-supported approach to tourism development that both relies on and builds trust. Community members can trust the tourism endeavour if and when they trust the planning process. They can trust that tourism is employed in service of the community. If, however, we imagine that the community is to be employed in service of the tourism industry, then the process will be dominated by elite interests and short-term economic development, and community members will rightly suspect that few are benefiting while the majority bear the brunt of the pressure from the development. They will not trust tourism development, and their mistrust may come to impact the tourism experience itself.

This chapter has sought to provoke discussion and debate about the kind of tourism development processes we need in the future and to put on the table the idea that following a community development perspective and process may help build trust in tourism planning and may also lead to developments that are sustainable in the broadest environmental, social and economic sense. There is much work to do as we continue to explore the opportunities and to rework and refine participatory approaches to tourism, and perhaps we can agree that this needs to be a major focus of our attention in the future.

Bibliography

Bhattacharyya, J. (2004) 'Theorising community development', *Community Development Journal*, 34(2): 5–34.

Blackstock, K. (2005) 'A critical look at community based tourism', *Community Development Journal*, 40(1): 39–49.

Blangy, S., McGinley, R., and Chevalier, J. (2008) 'Aboriginal tourism in northern Canada: How collaborative research can improve community engagement in tourism projects', in Chevalier, J. (ed.) *Proceedings of Celebrating Dialogue: An International SAS2 Forum*, Ottawa, Canada: Carleton University. Online: www.sas2.net (accessed on June 18, 2013).

Bramwell, B. (2004) 'Partnerships, participation, and social science research in tourism planning', in Lew, A. L., Hall, C. M., and Williams, A. M. (eds), *A Companion to Tourism*, Oxford, England: Blackwell, 541–554.

Bramwell, B., and Sharman, A. (1999) 'Collaboration in local tourism policymaking', *Annals of Tourism Research*, 26: 392–415.

Connell, D. (1997) 'Participatory development: An approach sensitive to class and gender', *Development in Practice*, 7(3): 248–259.

Costa, C. (2001) 'An emerging tourism planning paradigm? A comparative analysis between town and tourism planning', *International Journal of Tourism Research*, 3: 425–441.

De Certeau, M. (1986) *Heterologies: Discourse on the Other*, B. Massoumi (trans.). Minneapolis, Minnesota: University of Minnesota Press.

Dredge, D., and Jenkins, J. (2011) 'New spaces in tourism planning and policy', in Dredge, D. and Jenkins, J. (eds), *Stories of Practice: Tourism Policy and Planning*, Surrey, England: Ashgate: 1–12.

Duffy, L. D., Mowatt, R. A., Chancellor, H. C., and Cardenas, D. A. (2012) 'Machismo–marianismo and the involvement of women in a community-based tourism project in Ecuador, South America', *Tourism Analysis*, 17: 791–803.

Emery, M., & Purser, R. E. (1996) *The Search Conference: A Powerful Method for Planning Organizational Change and Community Action*, San Francisco: Jossey-Bass Publishers.

Forester, J. (1989) *Planning in the Face of Power*, Berkeley, California: University of California Press.

Friedmann, J. (1987) *Planning in the Public Domain: From Knowledge to Action*, Princeton, New Jersey: Princeton University Press.

George, E. W., Mair, H., and Reid, D. G. (2009) *Rural Tourism Development*, Bristol, England: Channel View Publications.

Giddens, A. (1984) *The Constitution of Society*, Glasgow, Scotland: Bell and Bain.

Gilchrist, A. (2003) 'Community development in the UK—possibilities and paradoxes', *Community Development Journal*, 38(1): 16–25.

Grybovych, O., Hafermann, D., and Mazzoni, F. (2011) 'Tourism planning, community engagement and policy innovation in Ucluelet, British Columbia', in Dredge, D. and Jenkins, J. (eds), *Stories of Practice: Tourism Policy and Planning*, Surrey, England: Ashgate: 79–104.

Hall, C. M. (2000) *Tourism Planning: Policies, Processes and Relationships*. Harlow, England: Prentice Hall.

Hall, C. M., and Wilson, S. (2011) 'Neoliberal urban entrepreneurial agendas, Dunedin stadium and the Rugby World Cup: Or 'if you don't have a stadium, you don't have a future', in Dredge, D. and Jenkins, J. (eds), *Stories of Practice: Tourism Policy and Planning*, Surrey, England: Ashgate: 133–152.

Haywood, K. M. (1988) 'Responsible and responsive tourism planning in the community', *Tourism Management*, 9(2): 105–118.

Healey, P. (1997) *Collaborative Planning: Shaping Places in Fragmented Societies*, Vancouver, British Columbia: University of British Columbia Press.

House, J. (1997) 'Redefining sustainability: A structural approach to sustainable tourism', in Stabler, M. J. (ed.), *Tourism and Sustainability: Principles to Practice*, Oxfordshire: United Kingdom: CAB International, 89–104.

Hung, K., Sirakaya-Turk, E., and Ingram, L. J. (2011) 'Testing the efficacy of an integrative model for community participation', *Journal of Travel Research*, 50(3): 276–288.

Inskeep, E. (1988) 'Tourism planning: An emerging specialization', *Journal of the American Planning Association*, 54(3): 360–372.

Ioannides, D. (1995) 'Planning for international tourism in less developed countries: Toward sustainability?' *Journal of Planning Literature*, 9(3): 235–254.

Jamal, T. B., and Getz, D. (1995) 'Collaboration theory and community tourism planning', *Annals of Tourism Research*, 22(1): 186–204.

Jamal, T. B., Stein, S. M., and Harper, T. L. (2002) 'Beyond labels: Pragmatic planning in multistakeholder tourism-environmental conflicts', *Journal of Planning Education and Research*, 22: 164–177.

Koutsouris, A. (2009) 'Social learning and sustainable tourism development; local quality conventions in tourism: A Greek study', *Journal of Sustainable Tourism*, 17(5): 567–581.

Laurian, L. (2009) 'Trust in planning: Theoretical and practical considerations for participatory and deliberative planning', *Planning Theory and Practice*, 10(3): 369–391.

Lew, A. (2007) 'Invited commentary: Tourism planning and traditional urban planning theory – The planner as an agent of social change', *Leisure/Loisir*, 31(2): 383–391.

Lovell, D. W. (2001) 'Trust and the politics of post-communism', *Communist and Post-Communist Studies*, 34: 27–38.

Macbeth, J. (2005) 'Towards an ethics platform for tourism', *Annals of Tourism Research*, 32(4): 962–984.

Madrigal, R. (1995) 'Residents' perceptions and the role of government', *Annals of Tourism Research*, 22(1): 86–102.

Mahjabeen, Z., Shresha, K. K., and Dee, J. A. (2009) 'Rethinking community participation in urban planning: The role of disadvantaged groups in Sydney metropolitan strategy', *Australiasian Journal of Regional Studies*, 15(1): 45–63.

Mair, H. (2006) 'Global restructuring and local responses: Investigating rural tourism policy in two Canadian communities', *Current Issues in Tourism*, 9(1): 1–45.

Mair, H. (2012) 'The challenge of critical approaches to rural tourism studies and practice', in Ateljevic, I., Morgan, N., and Pritchard, A. (eds), *The Critical Turn in Tourism Studies*. London, England: Routledge, 42–54.

Mair, H., and Reid, D. G. (2007) 'Tourism and community development vs. tourism for community development: Conceptualising planning as power, knowledge and control', *Leisure/Loisir*, 31(2): 403–426.

Mair, H., Reid, D. G., and George, E. W. (2005) 'Globalisation, rural tourism and community power', in Hall, D., Kirkpatrick, I., and Mitchell, I. (eds), *Rural Tourism and Sustainable Business*, Clevedon, England: Channel View Publications: 165–179.

Marcouiller, D. W. (1997) 'Toward integrative tourism planning in Rural America', *Journal of Planning Literature*, 11(3): 337–357.

Mowforth, M., and Munt, I. (1998) *Tourism and Sustainability: Development and New Tourism in the Third World*, London: Routledge.

Murphy, P. E. (1985) *Tourism: A Community Approach*, New York, New York: Methuen.

Nunkoo, R., and Ramkissoon, H. (2011) 'Developing a community support model for tourism', *Annals of Tourism Research*, 38(3): 964–988.

Okazaki, E. (2008) 'A community-based tourism model: Its conception and use', *Journal of Sustainable Tourism*, 16(5): 511–529.

Pearce, D. G., and Moscardo, G. (1999) 'Tourism community analysis: Asking the right questions', in Pearce, D. G. and Butler, R. W. (eds), *Contemporary Issues in Tourism Development*, London, England: Routledge, 31–51.

Prentice, R. (1993) 'Community-driven tourism planning and residents' preferences', *Tourism Management*, 14(3): 218–226.

Reed, M. G. (1997) 'Power relations and community-based tourism planning', *Annals of Tourism Research*, 24(3): 566–591.

Reed, M. G. (1999) 'Collaborative tourism planning as adaptive experiments in emergent tourism settings', *Journal of Sustainable Tourism*, 7(3–4): 331–355.

Reid, D. G. (2003) *Tourism, Globalization and Development: Responsible Tourism Planning*, London, England: Pluto Press.

Reid, D. G., Mair, H., and George, E. W. (2004) 'Community tourism planning: A self-assessment instrument', *Annals of Tourism Research*, 31(3): 623–639.

Reid, D. G., Mair, H., George, E. W., and Taylor, J. (2000) *Visiting Your Future: A Community Guide to Planning Rural Tourism*, Guelph, Ontario: Ontario Agriculture Training Institute.

Ritchie, J.R.B. (1993) 'Crafting a destination vision: Putting the concept of resident-responsive tourism into practice', *Tourism Management*, 14: 379–89.

Sautter, E. T., and Leisen, B. (1999). 'Managing stakeholders: A tourism planning model', *Annals of Tourism Research*, 26(2): 312–328.

Schafft, K. A., and Greenwood, D. J. (2003) 'Promises and dilemmas of participation: Action research, search conference methodology, and community development', *Community Development Society Journal*, 34(1): 18–35.

Schusler, T. M., Decker, D. J., and Pfeffer, M. J. (2003) 'Social learning for collaborative natural resource management', *Society & Natural Resources: An International Journal*, 16: 309–326.

Stein, S. M., and T. L. Harper. (2003) 'Power, trust and planning', *Journal of Planning Education and Research*, 23(2): 125–139.

Swain, C., and Tait, M. (2007) 'The crisis of trust and planning', *Planning Theory and Practice*, 8(2): 227–245.

Timothy, D. J. (1999) 'Participatory planning: A view of tourism in Indonesia', *Annals of Tourism Research*, 26(2): 371–391.

Tosun, C. (2000) 'Limits to community participation in the tourism development process in developing countries', *Tourism Management*, 21: 613–633.

Tosun, C. (2006) 'Expected nature of community participation in tourism development', *Tourism Management*, 27(3): 493–504.

Vernon, J., Essex, S., Pinder, D., and Curry, K. (2005) 'Collaborative policy-making: Local sustainable projects', *Annals of Tourism Research*, 32(2): 325–345.

Wray, M. (2011) 'Adopting and implementing a transactive approach to sustainable tourism planning: Translating theory into practice', *Journal of Sustainable Tourism*, 19(4–5): 605–627.

5 Social capital, trust and tourism development

Gianna Moscardo

Introduction

As governments, businesses and communities around the world begin to seriously address a wide range of sustainability issues, tourism has come under increasing criticism. This criticism of tourism highlights its contributions to negative environmental impacts such as climate change (Verbeek and Mommaas, 2008), its continued exploitation of global North–South economic and political inequalities (Klein-Vielhauer, 2009) and its foundation in what is increasingly seen as unnecessary consumption (Lansing and de Vries, 2007). This growing pressure on tourism to justify its existence and to better manage its impacts, both positive and negative, creates a challenge for tourism researchers to better understand the nature of tourism development and its impacts on destinations (Mason, 2008).

Despite a long history of literature on tourism impacts, the subject still remains largely descriptive and atheoretical, especially in the social domain (Moscardo *et al.*, 2013; Wall and Mathiesen, 2006). Research in this area continues to focus primarily on resident perceptions of impacts with little detailed analysis of the links among these perceptions and actual features of tourism and its development (Andereck and Nyuapane, 2010). There is a growing consensus that better conceptual models are needed to describe and explain in detail the mechanisms that link tourism processes and characteristics to effects on destination regions, especially effects on the people who live and work in these places (Deery *et al.*, 2012; Moscardo *et al.*, 2013). Such models are necessary to improve the practice of tourism development.

Two themes in the tourism literature offer some promise for developing better explanations of tourism impacts. The first is the use of the wider literature on community well-being and quality of life to examine tourism impacts (Macbeth *et al.*, 2004: McGehee *et al.*, 2010; Moscardo, 2012). This work has adopted the concepts of different forms of capital to analyze the nature of tourism impacts in detail (Andereck and Nyuapane, 2010; McGehee *et al.*, 2010; Moscardo, 2009). The second theme is that of more critical and detailed analyzes of tourism planning, community participation, political processes and governance (Bramwell, 2011; Moscardo, 2011a; Nunkoo and Ramkissoon, 2012). The concept of trust links these two themes, with trust recognized as an important concept in both understanding the nature of tourism impacts on social capital (Moscardo, 2012) and analyzing the political dimensions of tourism development (Nunkoo and Smith, 2013).

This chapter will focus on the relationships among tourism development, social capital in destinations and the concept of trust. To understand the relationships between tourism development and trust, it is critical to have a clear understanding of both the nature of trust and the social capital construct. Thus, the chapter begins with an overview of what has been called the capitals approach to sustainability, including a brief review of the use of this approach to understanding tourism development and impacts. It then examines in more detail the complex nature of the social capital construct providing a framework for the creation and operation of social capital. The concept of trust is briefly analyzed to provide a sound foundation for the main focus of the chapter, which is on how tourism development impacts on the different forms and levels of trust in a destination region. The primary goal of this analysis is to suggest ways in which tourism development can maximise its positive impacts and minimise its negative impacts by contributing to the development of trust among the stakeholders connected to a tourist destination. This analysis will then consider the cultural challenges associated with understanding and managing the tourism–trust relationship, before concluding with a set of recommendations for improving tourism development practice.

A capitals approach to sustainability and tourism development

The rise of public and government concern about sustainability reflects a shift in attitudes toward the concept of a "good life." Diener and Suh (1997) describe three interrelated approaches to deciding what makes a good life: (1) the individual freedom of choice or economic approach, (2) the subjective quality of life approach and (3) the "good society" approach. In the first approach, a good life arises where individuals have the freedom to pursue personal preferences. This is usually associated with higher incomes, a wider range of employment opportunities, and financial wealth (Diener and Suh, 1997). In the second approach, a good life is one where individuals believe themselves to be happy or satisfied (Diener and Suh, 1997). The third approach argues that a good life can be had only in a good society, and a good society is one that offers its members safety, rule of law, health and educational support, opportunities to participate in governance and freedom of personal and cultural expression (Diener and Suh, 1997). Taking a sustainability approach to the idea of good life suggests a move away from focussing solely on the economic approach and expanding the good society approach to include social justice, corporate responsibility and environmental quality (Moscardo, 2013). In this sustainable good life perspective, it is proposed that individual and collective well-being or quality of life depends on a wide range of factors beyond financial wealth and that the pursuit of economic growth often comes at the cost of other dimensions that are at least as important as economic freedom of choice (Moscardo, 2013).

Consistent with this argument is the capitals approach to sustainability described by Lehtonen (2004) and Vermuri and Costanza (2006). This approach argues that there are many forms of capital beyond those usually considered in economic and financial analyzes. It further argues that we need to recognize that personal, business and government actions can affect all these forms of capital and that we must acknowledge and assess these impacts to have, what Costanza and colleagues (2010) have called, a full-world economic model. This full-world model identifies a range of different capitals and proposes that the process of production of goods and services can both deplete and enhance stocks of these capitals. According to Lehtonen (2004), a sustainable approach to decisions is one that considers the full range of capitals and results in "the maintenance and increase of the total stock of different types of capital" (pp. 200–201), recognizing that one form of capital, natural capital, is particularly important because it is not easy to replace or substitute.

This raises the question of what these additional forms of capital are. A review of the types of capital usually listed as essential for community well-being (Moscardo, 2008) and reviews of the various factors that have been proposed as important for individual quality of life (Sirgy, 2002; Moscardo, 2009, 2012) reveal considerable consensus about the things that are necessary for well-being or a good quality of life. Matching the two sets of literature results in a range of different types of capital that might be considered when analyzing the sustainability of different actions, decisions or policies. These are summarised in Table 5.1.

Table 5.1 Summary of main types of capital

Types of capital	Summary description
Financial	Income and accumulated wealth in the forms of savings, stocks, precious metals and/or land that can be used to invest in other activities
Built	Buildings of all types and infrastructure such as transport, resources and energy distribution systems that can be used to support the production of other capitals, goods and services
Manufactured	Goods created through manufacturing activity that can in turn be used to generate other forms of capital
Natural	The services, assets, resources and support for life provided by the ecosystems and processes that exist and operate within the natural environment
Human	The sum of the skills, capacity to provide labour, knowledge, health and abilities of individuals that they can use in exchange for other forms of capital
Political	The opportunities that are available for individuals to access and influence the decisions and governance relevant to their lives
Cultural	The features of culture and cultural expression, such as arts, crafts, knowledge, rituals, performances, events and heritage resources, that can be used to maintain and affirm cultural identity
Social	The number, type and capacity of social relationships and networks that can be used to access and convert different forms of capital

Sources: Costanza *et al.* (2010); Emery and Flora (2006); McGehee *et al.* (2010); Moscardo (2008, 2012, 2013).

It is important to recognize that there is opposition to expanding the use of the concept of capital beyond the financial and economic realm. A detailed discussion of these critiques is provided by Macbeth *et al.* (2004), Lehtonen (2004) and Adler and Kwon (2002). These critiques focus on two main concerns. The first is a more philosophical issue with opponents challenging the dominance of the economic exchange paradigm in thinking about sustainability and arguing that expanding the use of the concept of capital does not address the core drivers of unsustainable action (Macbeth *et al.*, 2004). The second concern is a more theoretical one with critics suggesting that these newer forms of capital are not well defined, and researchers using them often confuse what the capital is with how it is generated, stored and/or used in production or exchange (Adler and Kwon, 2002). It is important to remember that the general concept of capital implies that it is something of value, an asset or resource, that can be either used to produce desirable goods and services or offered in exchange for goods and services or other capitals (Bourdieu, 1986). Despite these concerns, there continues to be expansion of the concept of capital to include multiple forms and a growing use of the idea of multiple capitals in the analysis and consideration of sustainability (Lehtonen, 2004).

Consistent with this increasing use in the broader sustainability literature there has been an emergence in recent years of the use of a capitals approach to understand tourism development and impacts (Macbeth *et al.*, 2004). Several works have used the idea that well-being depends on multiple forms of capital as a starting point for analyzing changes resulting from tourism in the destination and its associated communities (Andereck and Nyuapane, 2010; McGehee *et al.*, 2010; Moscardo, 2012; Moscardo *et al.*, 2013; Zahra and McGehee, 2013). To date, most attention has been paid to natural, cultural and social capital in the tourism literature.

Social capital: definitions, source and effects

The concept of social capital was one of the first forms of capital to be added to the traditional financial, built and manufactured capitals, being described by Bourdieu in 1986. Despite both this lengthy history in sociology and economics and the widespread use of this particular form of capital, there continues to be considerable confusion around its definition (Adler and Kwon, 2002; Moscardo, 2012). Major definitions of social capital include:

- "the aggregate of the actual or potential resources which are linked to the possession of a durable network of more or less institutionalized relationships of mutual acquaintance and recognition" (Bourdieu, 1986, p. 51).
- "friends, colleagues, and more general contacts through whom you receive opportunities to use your financial and human capital" (Burt, 1992, p. 9).
- "features of social organization such as networks, norms and social trust that facilitate coordination and cooperation or mutual benefits" (Putnam, 1995, p. 67).
- "the information, trust and norms or reciprocity inhering in one's social networks" (Woolcock, 1998, p. 153).

- "goodwill available to individuals or groups. Its sources lie in the structure and content of the actor's social relations. Its effects flow from the information, influence and solidarity it makes available to the actor" (Adler and Kwon, 2002, p. 19).
- "resources embedded in one's social networks . . . that can be accessed or mobilized through ties in the network" (Lin, 2008, p. 51).

Pawar (2006) conducted a simple content analysis of social capital definitions and reported that the most common words and phrases included relationships, networks, trust, collective action, norms, cooperation and social interaction. While this review confirms the importance of social interactions through relationships and networks to descriptions of social capital, it further highlights the confusion about which of these listed concepts are the social capital and which are the processes that allow social capital to be generated or used (Abbott and Freeth, 2008; Lin, 2008; Moscardo, 2012).

To clarify this confusion, Figure 5.1 provides a simple framework for social capital that draws upon more recent analyzes that explicitly distinguish social capital from its antecedents, uses and effects. Following on from Woolcock (1998), Adler and Kwon (2002) and Lin (2008), social capital is defined as goodwill, access to resources and/or other capitals and potential assistance that an individual or group can use to achieve goals and solve problems. Social capital is generated through or from social relationships and networks, but is distinct from these structures (Lin, 2008). In this framework, having social relationships and being connected to networks is a necessary but not sufficient condition for social capital to exist (Moscardo, 2012).

The existence of the social capital depends upon the quality of the relationships and the nature of an individual's or group's social networks (Abbott and Freeth, 2008; Fisher, 2013; Lin, 2008). Individuals and groups can have any number of relationships, but these do not offer social capital unless they are characterised by reciprocity and/or obligations and responsibilities (Abbott and Freeth, 2008). Where relationships do offer the possibility of social capital, the nature and extent of the social capital depends upon a number of features of the relationship, including who the relationship is with, the frequency and familiarity of contact and the norms and rules that apply to the relationships, which are in turn based on culture (Fisher, 2013). Similarly, social capital can be generated only from networks when the networks have relevant resources (Lin, 2008). Simply being a member of a network does not provide social capital if the other members of the network do not have, or have access to, other forms of capital (Stephens, 2008). Social capital also depends upon the nature of networks, their density, extent, the presence of any hierarchies within them and the dynamics of different types of ties or linkages between different nodes (Fisher, 2013; Lin, 2008). Three main types of ties can be identified: (1) bonding ties that connect members within groups or collectives, (2) bridging ties that connect groups to other groups or organizations and (3) linking ties that connect individuals and/or groups to those in the higher levels of hierarchical organizations or institutions

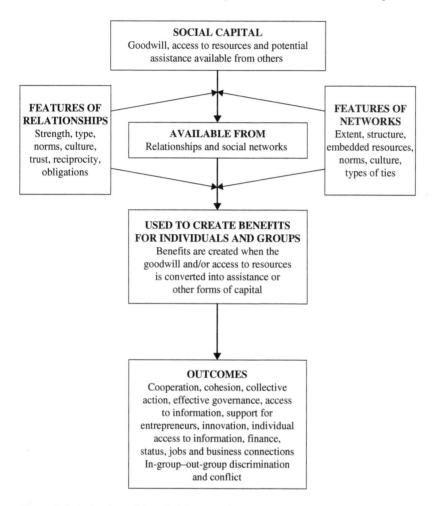

Figure 5.1 A simple social capital framework

(Fisher, 2013; Leahy and Anderson, 2013; Lin, 2008; Woolcock, 1998). These different types of ties offer different pathways for using social capital to achieve different goals. Bonding ties, for example, are more likely to support what Lin (2008) calls "expressive goals" such as social cohesion and identity. Bridging ties, on the other hand, seem more effective for "instrumental goals" such as financial support, recommendations for employment and access to information (Lin, 2008).

Understanding the balance among the different types of ties is important, because not all the outcomes of having and using social capital are positive. While many positive effects and uses are listed in the literature (Bachman and Inkpen, 2011; Kwon and Arenius, 2010) and are included in Figure 5.1, social capital can also be used to protect the interests of group members and deny nonmembers access to resources and opportunities and can create tension and conflict between groups (Fisher, 2013; Leahy and Anderson, 2013; Lin, 2008; Rothstein and Stolle, 2008).

This brief review of social capital highlights the need to be more careful in defining what social capital is, how it is generated, how it is used and what it is used for. Within this more critical and complex approach to social capital, the concept of trust has been recognized as an important factor in the development and operation of social capital but is increasingly defined as distinct from social capital (Abbott and Freeth, 2008; Fisher, 2013; Lin, 2008; Rothstein and Stole, 2008). This distinction is an important one, and this importance will be clarified in the following discussion of trust.

The nature of trust

Given the discussion of the concept of trust elsewhere in this volume, this section will only briefly define and describe trust to set the context for an analysis of tourism development, social capital and trust. This chapter will use Rousseau and colleagues' (1998) definition, which describes trust as "a psychological state comprising the intention to accept vulnerability, based upon positive expectations of the intentions or behavior of another" (p. 395). This definition contains the three most common elements of trust definitions:

- The willingness to accept vulnerability;
- beliefs and expectations about the trustworthiness of others; and
- the intention to act under these conditions (Sharp *et al.*, 2012).

This definition also recognizes that trust involves both an attitude and a behavior or action (Abbott and Freeth, 2008; Bachmann and Inkpen, 2011), and it highlights that trust becomes important only under conditions of risk and uncertainty and where at least one actor in a relationship is dependent upon another (Davenport *et al.*, 2007; Lin, 2008). Several different types of trust have been identified based on the nature of the relationship between the trustor and trustee and the type of trustee (Bachmann and Inkpen, 2011; Lin, 2008; White-Cooper *et al.*, 2009). These types include:

- Individualised trust, which refers to trust between two individuals. This type of trust can be further categorised by whether the individuals are familiar to each other and have regular and/or frequent contact, referred to as personal or particularised trust (Kwon and Arenius, 2010), or whether the individuals are strangers, referred to as generalised trust (Abbott and Freeth, 2008; Kwon and Arenius, 2010).
- Institutionalised trust, where the target of trust is an organization or institution (Bachmann and Inkpen, 2011).
- Political trust, which is a specific form of institutional trust defined as "the belief that the political system or some part of it will produce preferred outcomes even in the absence of constant scrutiny" (Nunkoo *et al.*, 2012).

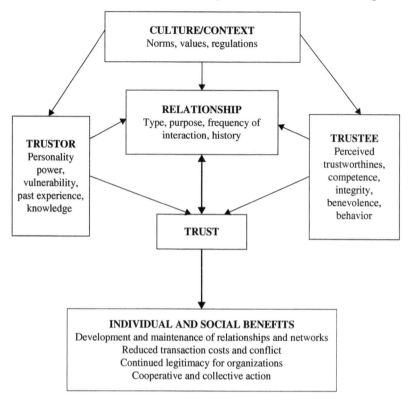

Figure 5.2 A simple trust framework

Figure 5.2 provides a simple framework for understanding the trust construct. Trust exists as a characteristic of the relationship between the trustee and the trustor and is influenced by the nature of that relationship and characteristics of the trustee and trustor. All these elements are in turn influenced by culture and context. The relationship between trustee and trustor varies according to the type, frequency and purpose of the contact and the nature of the norms and regulations relevant to the relationship (Lin, 2008; White-Cooper *et al.*, 2009). Important features of trustors include their personal disposition to be trusting, their cultural background, their power in the relationship, their vulnerability to risk and their experiences (Kwon and Arenius, 2010; Rothstein and Stolle, 2008; Sharp *et al.*, 2012). The most important feature of the trustee is her/his perceived trustworthiness (Sharp *et al.*, 2012). Perceived trustworthiness depends upon the trustor's knowledge of the trustee, the history of relationship and the perceived competence, integrity and benevolence of the trustee (Fisher, 2013; Sharp *et al.*, 2012). Sharp and colleagues (2012) provide a detailed review of the factors (summarised in Table 5.2) that are connected to the three core elements of perceived trustworthiness: competence, integrity and benevolence.

Table 5.2 Summary of dimensions of trustworthiness

Competence/ability	Benevolence/care	Integrity
• Knowledge and skills relevant to the goal • Expertise • Flexibility • Consistency of effort and response	• Belief that the trustee will act in the best interests of the trustor • Empathetic • Willing to listen • Respectful of others' needs, values and knowledge	• Open/transparent • Honest • Credible • Inclusive • Commitment • Acts according to expectations and/or shared values and norms

Note: Based on Davenport *et al.* (2007); Leahey and Anderson (2013); Sharp *et al.* (2012).

Benefits claimed from the development and maintenance of trust in relationships and networks include:

- Development, extension or maintenance of relationships and networks;
- reduced transaction costs and perceived risks in relationships;
- reduced conflict and social anxiety;
- continued legitimacy for institutions and support for their actions and policies; and
- cooperation and collective action (Abbott and Freeth, 2008; Leahy and Anderson, 2013; Sharp *et al.*, 2012; White-Cooper *et al.*, 2009).

The features included in Figure 5.2 and Table 5.2 provide insights into the variables that can encourage trust in relationships. The conditions that encourage trust include:

- Frequent positive interactions between trustor and trustee that support extensive knowledge of each other.
- regular and reliable meeting of obligations and maintaining of reciprocity;
- demonstrations of competence on the part of the trustee;
- shared values and goals;
- consistency, effort and predictability on the part of the trustee;
- mutual interdependence between trustor and trustee; and
- a trustee that is willing to listen to the trustor and to respect the trustor's needs and values (Abbott and Freeth, 2008; Bachmann and Inkpen, 2011; Davenport *et al.*, 2007; Fisher, 2013; Leahy and Anderson, 2013; Sharpe *et al.*, 2012; White-Cooper *et al.*, 2009).

These conditions are applicable to both individualised and institutionalised trust. Additional factors are applicable to situations where the trustee is an institution such as a business or government agency. Several researchers have noted that when the trustee is an institution, two levels of trust are to be considered: trust in the institution and trust in the individuals who represent the institutions (Bachman and Inkpen, 2011; Davenport *et al.*, 2007; Leahy and

Anderson, 2013; White-Cooper *et al.*, 2009). Institutional representatives are important links between individual trustors and institutions, and, in addition to the conditions already listed, institutional representatives need to be seen as hardworking and supported by the institution (Davenport *et al.*, 2007; White-Cooper *et al.*, 2009). At the macro level, institutions are more likely to be seen as trustworthy if they:

- Have effective communication strategies;
- value local/trustor knowledge;
- focus on procedural fairness, which consists of transparent, predictable, equitable decision making that includes opportunities for trustor involvement.
- flexibility, openness and willingness to respond to trustor concerns; and
- adherence to regulations and codes of conduct (Bachmann and Inkpen, 2011; Davenport *et al.*, 2007; Leahy and Anderson, 2013; White-Cooper *et al.*, 2009).

Nunkoo and colleagues (Nunkoo and Ramkissoon, 2011, 2012, Nunkoo and Smith, 2013; Nunkoo *et al.*, 2012) have focussed on trust, in particular political trust, and its connection to effective tourism development, providing the impetus for the present edited volume. These studies confirm many of the conclusions reported in this section. More specifically, Nunkoo and colleagues argue that trust is an essential element for effective tourism governance and sustainable tourism development, a finding consistently reported in case studies of tourism development experiences (cf. Alipour *et al.* 2011; Bertella, 2011; Hwang *et al.* 2012; Mbaiwa and Stronza, 2010; Onyx and Lenard, 2010). They also report consistent relationships between political trust, specifically destination resident trust in local government, and perceived competence in managing tourism impacts, perceived political performance, which includes transparency and justice in decision making and incorruptibility, perceived economic performance and perceived power in tourism, defined as the ability to participate in and influence tourism decisions. Like many other authors in the area of trust, Nunkoo and colleagues conceptualise trust as closely connected to social capital.

Connecting trust and social capital

Although trust is often considered part of social capital, this chapter concurs with more recent discussions in which trust is linked to, but not a component of, social capital. Figure 5.3 summarises the relationships proposed in this chapter between trust and social capital. In the simple model presented in Figure 5.3, trust is the critical catalyst that allows the use of social relationships and networks to access resources and to support effective collective action (Fisher, 2013; Leahy and Anderson, 2013; Lin, 2008; Woolcock, 1998). In other words, the ability to use relationships to create and access social capital is dependent on trust being a core characteristic of those relationships. Within the model are two feedback loops. In the first, trust supports the expansion of social relationships and networks, as trusted

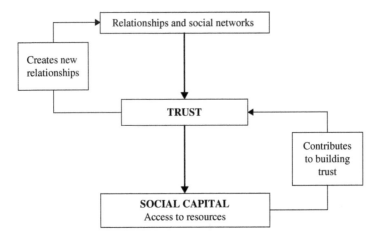

Figure 5.3 Connecting trust to social capital

individuals/organizations are more likely to be introduced and recommended to others (Davenport *et al.*, 2007; Lin, 2008). In the second feedback loop, the successful use of social relationships to access and generate social capital can in turn enhance trust as the actors involved demonstrate that they can meet social obligations and offer expected reciprocal exchanges (Kwon and Arenius, 2010; Lin, 2008).

Tourism development, social capital and trust

Using this preliminary model of the nature of the relationships between trust and social capital and an understanding of the factors that support trust in general, it is possible to systematically review the emerging literature on tourism impacts on social capital to identify the ways in which tourism development processes impact all types of trust within the destination. This review will first examine the negative impacts of tourism on social capital, highlighting the role of trust, and then describe major themes from research reporting positive impacts from tourism development for both social capital and trust.

Three main pathways linking tourism to negative impacts on destination social capital can be identified: (1) conflict within a destination over a proposed tourism development, (2) competition within a destination over opportunities to access and benefit from tourism business and (3) the failure of tourism to realise promised outcomes. Many authors have described the negative outcomes of contested tourism proposals (Blackstock, 2005; Dredge, 2010; Lee *et al.* 2010; Shepherd, 2002). Analysis of these and similar cases has identified a consistent pattern in which a tourism venture is put forward by an external actor or from within a local elite; this is followed by opposition to the proposal, usually based on concerns over its size and appropriateness for the local context; and this conflict alters social relationships between destination residents, heightening awareness of differences in values and goals within the community and eroding interpersonal trust (Moscardo, 2012). In some cases, the external actors establish close connections to local government agencies that can lead to actual and perceived corruption and nepotism generating political distrust between residents and their governments (Yamamoto and Yamamoto, 2013).

The second theme is also about community conflict over tourism, but in this case the research emphasises the negative effects of intradestination competition for tourism business opportunities and benefits (Jones, 2005). Reviews of a number of community-based tourism programs in Africa, for example, found that many destination communities experienced conflict over how to distribute the funds generated by the tourism activities with a breakdown in relationships and trust between individuals (Ashley *et al.* 2001). In a similar fashion, Holladay and Powell (2013) describe the breakdown of trust in tourism networks that results from destination residents being unable to participate in tourism business and employment opportunities.

The third theme refers to situations in which a proposed tourism development begins with widespread destination resident and stakeholder support but then fails to deliver the promised benefits (Park *et al.*, 2012). This can reflect either a specific tourism enterprise failure or a failure of the tourism overall to generate the level and type of benefits initially predicted (Stone and Stone, 2011). This discourages participants and so has a direct negative impact on community identity. It also brings into question the competence of those most closely associated with the tourism plans and activities and, through that, erodes trust in those actors.

These three themes are consistently associated with limited or nonexistent tourism planning processes, ineffective tourism governance, a dominance of external actors, a lack of knowledge among local destination stakeholders about tourism systems, processes and impacts, poor communication, limited public participation and engagement in tourism planning and business activities and failures to effectively market the available tourism opportunities and connect to wider tourism distribution systems (Aref, 2010; Moscardo, 2011a, 2011b). These findings confirm Nunkoo *et al.*'s (2012) argument that improvements to tourism governance on all dimensions are necessary to achieve better outcomes for destination social capital and trust.

While conflict about, and opposition to, tourism proposals is usually associated with negative impacts on social capital for destination stakeholders, there are examples where a controversial tourism development has had positive impacts on the social capital. In these instances, destination residents found common ground in their opposition, engaged in cooperative and collaborative behavior and developed new networks and social organizations (Hwang, *et al.* 2012; Lee, *et al.* 2010; Moscardo, 2011a; Yamamoto and Yamamoto, 2013). Two aspects of these cases are of particular interest to the present discussion of trust: the importance of shared values and the role of tourism leaders. Yamamoto and Yamamoto (2013) described a coalition among different sectors of a Japanese community opposed to a proposed resort, which included both long-term residents and more recent migrants. The protest offered opportunities for these different types of residents to have direct interactions with each other and to appreciate the extent to which they shared values. Ruiz-Ballesteros (2011) argues that these types of interactions with diverse groups encourages greater generalised trust as residents learn that they can work with, and rely upon, previously unknown people. Hwang *et al.* (2012) further propose that this increase in generalised trust can help with other collective activities.

Yamamoto and Yamamoto (2013) also discussed the importance of strong leadership in the opposition organizations. The importance of effective tourism leadership for building and using destination social capital has been recognized in many case studies. (cf. Mahony and Van Zyl, 2002; Nel and Binns, 2002). Moscardo (2014) analyzed detailed case studies of the actions of 55 tourism leaders or entrepreneurs focussing on how these individuals used and either contributed to or depleted different forms of capital in the 47 destinations in which they acted. This critical examination concluded that the most effective tourism leaders in terms of both the financial success of the tourism ventures and net benefits across the different types of capital in the destination community were those that:

- had strong existing relationships within the destination and used these to expand social networks and enhance bridging ties both within the destination and between groups in the destination and outside the location.
- shared and promoted destination community values and sought forms of tourism that were consistent with these values.
- were motivated by a desire to improve community well-being beyond tourism, often acting as a social entrepreneur.
- built trust at multiple levels by behaving in an ethical fashion (Moscardo, 2014).

Coalitions organised to oppose a tourism development are one form of tourism-focussed organizations. Three other types of tourism-focussed organizations also can enhance social capital: (1) groups formed to plan tourism development, (2) partnerships focussed on coordinating and offering tourism experiences and products and (3) networks formed as part of cooperative tourism marketing efforts. Tourism planning groups that explicitly seek to maximise destination stakeholder engagement and empowerment have been described as powerful tools for improving social capital in destinations (Beritelli, 2011; Macbeth *et al.*, 2004; McGehee *et al.*, 2010). Such groups often are generated by local governments and driven by a desire to support more community-based tourism. The evidence in this area is that mutual trust between governments and residents is particularly important, with government agencies needing to be responsive, flexible and prepared to relinquish control over tourism to these community-driven processes and groups (Johnson *et al.* 2009).

The third type of tourism-focussed group refers to partnerships among locally owned businesses, other destination residents and tourism coordination and marketing organizations focussed on providing services and experiences for tourists. Evidence that these types of groups can make positive contributions to destination social capital has been described for the development of regional tours (Bertella,

2011; Halme and Fadeeva, 2000), themed touring routes (Briedenhann and Wickens, 2004), the restoration and presentation of heritage sites for tourists (Hamilton and Alexander, 2013) and various forms of community-based tourism ventures (Hospers, 2003; Matarrita-Cascante *et al.* 2010; Ruiz-Ballesteros, 2011). Similar results have been reported for a final type of tourism-focussed group: networks engaged in the cooperative activities required for marketing and promoting a destination or tourism experience (Saxena, 2005; von Friedrichs Grangsjo and Gummesson, 2006; Wang and Xiang, 2007). These examples reveal a set of common characteristics of all these types of groups:

- compatibility of actors, especially with regard to shared values and goals;
- recognition of interdependence;
- effective communication and exchange of knowledge;
- conflict resolution mechanisms; and
- opportunities for positive interpersonal interaction.

Finally, there are situations in which the nature of the tourism product within a destination encourages positive interaction between tourists and destination residents. Moscardo and colleagues (2013), for example, reported on a study of tourism impacts of community well-being in three rural Australian regions in which destination residents talked positively about the interpersonal interactions they had with tourists in shared public spaces and tourist places. In this case, the interactions resulted in new social connections or bridging ties, supported greater tolerance of a diversity of people and resulted in expanded interpersonal trust. This kind of outcome was likely associated with what might be called forms of "slow tourism," where the tourists stayed for longer periods of time, made direct contributions to the community through volunteer work, supported local cultural activities and casual and seasonal labour and maintained regular contact. Although the positive interactions in this study were associated with particular forms of tourism, such interactions can happen in any location where tourists and residents come into contact (Upchurch and Teivane, 2000).

This building of bridging ties with tourists has also been reported in other examples of volunteer tourism (Novo-Corti *et al.* 2010; Zahra and McGehee, 2013). In these studies, the volunteer tourism program had a number of positive effects on a range of different aspects of the destination, but it was especially significant in creating positive self-identity and community pride and encouraging further collective action. Novo-Corti *et al.* (2010) conclude that these outcomes were possible because the residents saw the volunteers as competent and knowledgeable, and the resulting trust in the actions and opinions of the volunteers carried great weight among destination residents.

Cultural cautions and challenges

Cultural context was presented as a foundation factor in the model of trust presented in Figure 5.2, and its importance has been raised in many discussions of trust, social capital and tourism development (Beritelli, 2011; Kwon and Arenius,

2010; Nunkoo and Smith, 2013; Xu *et al*. 2010). There exist three cultural dimensions of trust that can be considered: (1) differences among cultures in the way they define, extend and develop trust and trustworthiness, (2) issues of trust in cross-cultural interactions and (3) challenges to Western models of trust and governance. Most of the available research into culture and trust has examined the first of these dimensions, cultural differences in various aspects of trust, primarily in the context of national cultures. This research has identified cultural differences in features of trust, including:

- Overall levels of generalised trust (Delhey *et al*. 2011; Kwon and Arenius, 2010).
- The radius of trust or the extent of the circle of unknown people that would be trusted (Delhey *et al*., 2011; Reeskens and Hooghe, 2008).
- Willingness to perceive others as benevolent (Balliet and van Lange, 2013; Joy and Kolb, 2009).
- Conditions under which people are willing to trust others (Niu and Xin, 2012; Yuki *et al*., 2005).
- The emphasis given to action and competence versus cooperation and benevolence in judgments of relationships (Schoorman *et al*., 2007).
- Assessment of risk and thus willingness to trust others (Park *et al*., 2010; Schoorman *et al*., 2007).
- Expectations about, and norms for, the regulation and transparency of business interactions (Hofstede *et al*., 2010).

Differences in trust also exist in organizational cultures (Bachman and Inkpen, 2011; Davenport *et al*., 2007).

The second dimension of culture and trust – that of issues of trust in cross-cultural interactions – has received less research attention, but arguably is more relevant to understanding tourism development and trust, because tourism often involves cross-cultural communication and transactions. Cultural differences can be a barrier to both meaningful interactions and mutual trust (Chua and Morris, 2009; Matarrita-Cascante and Stocks, 2013). In general, it is harder to build trust in a relationship if there is a greater cultural distance between the actors involved (Giannetti and Yafeh, 2012), if the actors involved have limited experience and skill at intercultural interaction (Ochieng and Price, 2010) and if there has been only limited contact between the cultural groups involved (Boehnke and Rippl, 2012).

Finally, there is the issue of the cultural context of the prevailing models of social capital and governance and the assumptions made about the value of trust and cooperation. Xu *et al*. (2010) and Yamamoto and Yamamoto (2013) all note that current models of social capital and its importance in supporting democratic, cooperative governance processes are embedded in Western traditions of individualism and, as such, may not be applicable in other cultures. Similar issues have been raised in other areas of governance, particularly those associated with governance and sustainability (Aras and Crowther, 2009). This presents a particular challenge for tourism researchers working in complex, cross-cultural situations.

Conclusions, recommendations and future directions

Although the evidence available on trust and tourism development is limited, the existing conclusions are consistent with the wider literature on trust. Within these conclusions there is, however, convergence on some themes that suggest particular aspects of trust that may be especially important in the tourism context and that tourism may have specific features that make it especially useful for building certain types of trust in communities. This final concluding section will present a preliminary framework for using tourism to build trust in destination communities that can be used to generate principles for improving tourism impacts and as a guide for further research.

A preliminary framework for using tourism to build trust in destination communities

Using the results reported in the tourism literature and remembering the basic processes outlined in Figures 5.2 and 5.3, it is possible to begin building a more complex framework linking tourism to trust and social capital. A preliminary version of this framework is presented in Figure 5.4. At the centre of this framework are shared values and compatible goals. Trust in tourism situations depends on the different stakeholders sharing an understanding of the important values associated with the destination and having compatible goals in terms of why tourism is being proposed and what each party believes tourism can offer the destination. This understanding and recognition of shared values and compatible goals is enhanced by positive interpersonal interactions with tourists and with other stakeholders in tourism-focussed groups. These positive interactions are, in turn, supported by appropriate forms of tourism development and effective tourism-focussed groups. Appropriate forms of tourism are those that are compatible with the values of the destination community, directly and specifically aligned to the goals of that community, and offer opportunities for meaningful engagement between tourists and residents. Effective tourism-focussed groups require tourism leaders with a social entrepreneurship style that seeks to use tourism as a means to achieve other social and cultural outcomes for the destination and the support of responsible institutions such as local governments. Both the tourism-focussed groups and responsible institutions need to practice good governance characterised by all the features listed for integrity in Table 5.2. These conditions support enhanced trust at the individualised, generalised and institutional levels. This trust acts to support access to and use of social capital. Finally, successful tourism ventures build institutional trust and enhance social capital support of collective action beyond tourism. In summary, perceived trustworthiness of tourism leaders appears to rely mostly on benevolence; perceived trustworthiness of responsible institutions

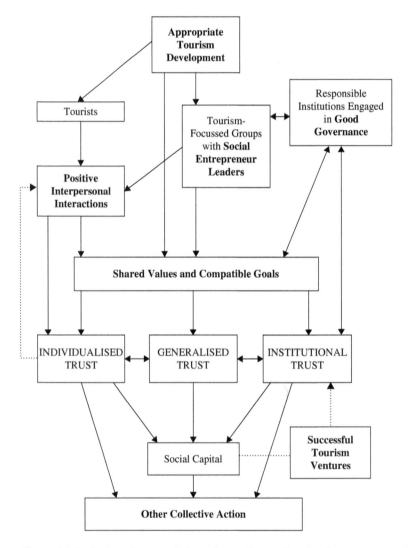

Figure 5.4 Preliminary framework for understanding tourism development, trust and social capital

relies mostly on integrity; and perceived trustworthiness of tourism itself as a development tool relies mostly on the competence of all the actors involved in its planning and management. These perceptions of the trustworthiness of the various tourism actors are enhanced by the building of interpersonal trust through positive interactions.

The preliminary framework presented in Figure 5.4 proposes five key principles that direct tourism governance and development processes in directions likely to build trust, especially trust in the institutions and organizations responsible for tourism. First, it is vital that the forms and styles of tourism development proposed for a destination are compatible with the core values of the destination community and its needs, goals and aspirations. This means that more time and effort need to be focussed on determining what these values, goals and needs might be before beginning tourism development proposals, and this needs to happen before analyzes of the available tourism resources and potential tourism markets are conducted. Of particular importance is a consideration of the types of tourism that are most likely to provide opportunities for positive interpersonal interactions between tourists and residents. Second, the organizations and institutions responsible for tourism planning and management need to engage in good governance. Although some challenges to Western models of governance have been made, the available evidence from across a range of situations still supports the value of integrity, justice, transparency, clear communication, stakeholder empowerment and recognition of mutual knowledge and interdependence. Third, more attention needs to be paid to development and support of effective tourism leaders and social entrepreneurs. Fourth, greater education is required for all stakeholders in the commercial and marketing realities of tourism to improve tourism venture success.

Finally, tourism has several characteristics that, taken together, distinguish it from other commercial and development activities, especially in its potential to contribute to enhanced trust in destination communities. Tourism requires the building of bridging ties because of the need to connect to global distribution systems and distant markets. Unlike other activities, tourism markets actually come to the destination, and this brings opportunities for personal interactions among a diverse range of people and to build both interpersonal and generalised trust. Tourism also comes in many forms and so can be shaped and influenced to focus on and support destination community values. To use these opportunities for maximum benefit, tourism researchers and practitioners will need to more explicitly pursue tourism development as a means to achieving community goals beyond the success of the tourism itself. The overall aim of tourism development should be to build all forms of capital, but especially trust and social capital, to support other effective collective action.

References

Abbott, S. and Freeth, D. (2008) 'Social capital and health: Starting to make sense of the role of generalized trust and reciprocity', *Journal of Health Psychology*, 13: 874–883.
Adler, P. S. and Kwon, S-W. (2002) 'Social capital: Prospects for a new concept', *Academy of Management Review*, 27(1): 17–40.
Alipour, H., Vaziri, R. K. and Ligay, E. (2011) 'Governance as catalyst for sustainable tourism development: Evidence from North Cyprus', *Journal of Sustainable Development*, 4(5): 32–49.
Andereck, K. and Nyuapane, G. (2010) 'Exploring the nature of tourism and quality of life perceptions among residents', *Journal of Travel Research*, 50(3): 248–260.
Aras, G. and Crowther, D. (2009) 'Corporate governance and corporate social responsibility in context', in G. Aras and D. Crowther (eds) *Global Perspectives on Corporate Governance and CSR*, Farnham: Gower Publishing (pp. 1–42).

Aref, F. (2010) 'Barriers to community capacity building for tourism development in Shiraz, Iran', *Journal of Sustainable Tourism,* 19(3): 347–359.

Ashley, C., Roe, D. and Goodwin, H. (2001) *Pro-poor Tourism Strategies: Making Tourism Work for the Poor.* Nottingham: Overseas Development Institute.

Bachman, R. and Inkpen, A. C. (2011) 'Understanding institutional-based trust building processes in inter-organizational relationships', *Organization Studies,* 32(2): 281–301.

Balliet, D. and Van Lange, P. A. (2013) 'Trust, punishment, and cooperation across 18 societies: A meta-analysis', *Perspectives on Psychological Science,* 8(4): 363–379.

Beritelli, P. (2011) 'Cooperation among prominent actors in a tourist destination', *Annals of Tourism Research,* 38(2): 607–629.

Bertella, G. (2011) 'Communities of practice in tourism: Working and learning together', *Tourism Planning and Development,* 8(4): 381–397.

Blackstock, K. (2005) 'A critical look at community based tourism', *Community Development Journal,* 40(1): 39–49.

Boehnke, K. and Rippl, S. (2012) 'General and "neighbourly" trust in border regions', *Czech Sociological Review,* 6: 1075–1092.

Bourdieu, P. (1986) 'The forms of capital', in J. E. Richardson (ed.) *Handbook of Theory of Research for the Sociology of Education,* New York: Greenwood Press (pp. 241–258).

Bramwell, B. (2011) 'Governance, the state and sustainable tourism: A political economy approach', *Journal of Sustainable Tourism,* 19(4/5): 459–477.

Briedenhann, J. and Wickens, E. (2004) 'Tourism routes as a tool for the economic development of rural areas – vibrant hope or impossible dream?' *Tourism Management,* 25: 71–79.

Burt, R. S. (1992) *Structural Holes: The Social Structure of Competition,* Cambridge, MA: Harvard University Press.

Chua, R. Y. and Morris, M. (2009) 'Innovation communication in multicultural networks: Deficits in inter-cultural capability and affect-based trust as barriers to new idea sharing in inter-cultural relationships", *Harvard Business School Organizational Behavior Unit Working Paper,* 09–130.

Costanza, R., Cumberland, J. C., Daly, H. E., Goodland, R. and Norgaard, R. (2010) *Introduction to Ecological Economics,* Boca Raton: St Lucie Press.

Davenport, M. A., Leahy, J. E., Anderson, D. H., and Jakes, P. J. (2007) 'Building trust in natural resource management within local communities: A case study of the Midewin National Tallgrass Prairie', *Environmental Management,* 39: 353–368.

Delhey, J., Newton, K. and Welzel, C. (2011) 'How general is trust in "most people"? Solving the radius of trust problem', *American Sociological Review,* 76(5): 786–807.

Deery, M., Jago, L. and Fredline, L. (2012) 'Rethinking social impacts of tourism research: A new research agenda', *Tourism Management,* 33(1): 64–73.

Diener, E. and Suh, E. (1997) 'Measuring quality of life: Economic, social and subjective indicators', *Social Indicators Research,* 40(1–2): 189–216.

Dredge, D. (2010) 'Place change and tourism development conflict: Evaluating public interest', *Tourism Management,* 31, 104–112.

Emery, M. and Flora, C. B. (2006) 'Spiraling-up: Mapping community transformation with community capitals framework', *Community Development,* 37: 19–35.

Fisher, R. (2013) '"A gentleman's handshake": The role of social capital and trust in transforming information into usable knowledge', *Journal of Rural Studies,* 31, 13–22.

Giannetti, M. and Yafeh, Y. (2012) 'Do cultural differences between contracting parties matter? Evidence from syndicated bank loans', *Management Science,* 58(2): 365–383.

Halme, M. and Fadeeva, Z. (2000) 'Small and medium-sized tourism enterprises in sustainable development networks', *Greener Management International,* 30: 97–118.

Hamilton, K. and Alexander, M. (2013) 'Organic community tourism: A cocreated approach', *Annals of Tourism Research,* 42: 169–190.

Hofstede, G. J., Fritz, M., Canavari, M. and Oosterkamp, E. (2010) 'Towards a crosscultural typology of trust in B2B food trade', *British Food Journal,* 112(7): 671–687.

Holladay, P. J. and Powell, R. B. (2013) 'Resident perceptions of social-ecological resilience and the sustainability of community-based tourism development in the Commonwealth of Dominica', *Journal of Sustainable Tourism*. Available online at http://dx.doi.org/10.1080/09669582.2013.776059.

Hospers, G. (2003) 'Localization in Europe's periphery: Tourism development in Sardinia', *European Planning Studies*, 11(6): 629–645.

Hwang, D., Stewart, W. P. and Ko, D. W. (2012) 'Community behavior and sustainable rural tourism development', *Journal of Travel Research*, 51(3): 328–341.

Johnson, A. J., Glover, T. D. and Yuen, F. C. (2009) 'Supporting effective community representation: Lessons from the Festival of Neighbourhoods', *Managing Leisure*, 14(1): 1–16.

Jones, S. (2005) 'Community-based ecotourism: The significance of social capital', *Annals of Tourism Research*, 32(2): 303–324.

Joy, S. and Kolb, D. A. (2009) 'Are there cultural differences in learning style?' *International Journal of Intercultural Relations*, 33(1): 69–85.

Klein-Vielhauer, S. (2009) 'Framework model to assess leisure and tourism sustainability', *Journal of Cleaner Production*, 17: 447–454.

Kwon, S-W. and Arenius, P. (2010) 'Nations of entrepreneurs: A social capital perspective', *Journal of Business Venturing*, 25: 315–330.

Lansing, P. and De Vries, P. (2007) 'Sustainable tourism: Ethical alternative or marketing ploy?' *Journal of Business Ethics*, 72: 77–85.

Leahy, J. E. and Anderson, D. H. (2013) ' "Cooperation gets it done": Social capital in natural resources management along the Kaskaskia River', *Society and Natural Resources*, 23: 224–239.

Lee, T. J., Riley, M. and Hampton, M. P. (2010) 'Conflict and progress: Tourism development in Korea', *Annals of Tourism Research*, 37(2): 355–376.

Lehtonen, M. (2004) 'The environmental-social interface of sustainable development: Capabilities, social capital, institutions', *Ecological Economics*, 49: 199–214.

Lin, N. (2008) 'A network theory of social capital', in D. Castiglione, J. van Deth and G. Wolleb (eds) *A Handbook of Social Capital*, Oxford: Oxford University Press (pp. 50–69).

Macbeth, J., Carson, D., and Northcote, J. (2004) 'Social capital, tourism and regional development: SPCC as a basis for innovation and sustainability', *Current Issues in Tourism*, 7(6): 502–522.

Mahony, K. and Van Zyl, J. (2002) 'The impacts of tourism investment on rural communities: Three case studies in South Africa', *Development Southern Africa*, 19(1): 83–103.

Mason, P. (2008) *Tourism Impacts, Planning and Management*, 2nd edition, Amsterdam: Butterworth-Heinnemann.

Matarrita-Cascante, D., Brennan, M. A. and Luloff, A. E. (2010) 'Community agency and sustainable tourism development: The case of La Fortuna, Costa Rica', *Journal of Sustainable Tourism*, 18(6): 735–756.

Matarrita-Cascante, D. and Stocks, G. (2013) 'Amenity migration to the global south: Implications for community development', *Geoforum*, 49: 91–102.

Mbaiwa, J. E. and Stronza, A. L (2010) 'The effects of tourism development on rural livelihoods in the Okavango Delta, Botswana', *Journal of Sustainable Tourism*, 18(5): 635–656.

McGehee, N. G., Lee, S., O'Bannon, T. L. and Perdue, R. R. (2010) 'Tourism-related social capital and its relationship with other forms of capital', *Journal of Travel Research*, 49(4): 486–500.

Moscardo, G. (2008) 'Community capacity building: An emerging challenge for tourism development', in G. Moscardo (ed.) *Building Community Capacity for Tourism Development,* Wallingford: CABI (pp. 1–15).

Moscardo, G. (2009) 'Tourism and quality of life: Towards a more critical approach', *Tourism and Hospitality Research*, 9(2): 159–170.

Moscardo, G. (2011a) 'Exploring social representations of tourism planning: Issues for governance', *Journal of Sustainable Tourism*, 19(4): 423–436.

Moscardo, G. (2011b) 'The role of knowledge in good governance for tourism', in E. Laws, N. Scott and H. Richins (eds) *Tourist Governance: Practice, Theory and Issues*, Wallingford: CABI (pp. 67–80).

Moscardo, G. (2012) 'Building social capital to enhance the quality of life of destination residents', in M. Uysal, R. Perdue and M. J. Sirgy (eds) *Handbook of Tourism and Quality of Life Research*, New York: Springer (pp. 403–422).

Moscardo, G. (2013) 'Sustainability, economy and society', in G. Moscardo, G. Lamberton, G. Wells, W. Fallon, P. Lawn, A. Rowe, J. Humphrey, R. Wiesner, B. Pettitt, D. Clifton, M. Renouf and W. Kershaw (eds) *Sustainability in Australian Business: Principles and Practice*, Milton: Wiley-Blackwell (pp. 1–34).

Moscardo, G. (2014) 'Tourism and community leadership in rural regions: Linking mobility, entrepreneurship, tourism development and community well-being', *Journal of Tourism Planning and Development*, 11(3): 354–370.

Moscardo, G., Konovalov, E., Murphy, L. and McGehee, N. (2013) 'Mobilities, community well-being and sustainable tourism', *Journal of Sustainable Tourism*, 21(4): 532–556.

Nel, E. and Binns, T. (2002) 'Place marketing, tourism promotion, and community based local economic development in post-apartheid South Africa: The case of Still Bay—the "Bay of Sleeping Beauty"', *Urban Affairs Review*, 38(2): 184–208.

Niu, J. and Xin, Z. (2012). 'Trust discrimination tendency of trust circles in the positive and negative information-sharing/disclosing domains and cultural differences between Canada and China', *Journal of Social, Evolutionary, and Cultural Psychology*, 6(2): 233–252.

Novo-Corti, I. N., Marola, P. N. and Castro, M. B. (2010) 'Social inclusion and local development through European voluntourism: A case study of the project realized in a neighbourhood of Morocco', *American Journal of Economics and Business Administration*, 2(3): 221–231.

Nunkoo, R. and Ramkissoon, H. (2011) 'Developing a community support model for tourism', *Annals of Tourism Research*, 38(3): 964–988.

Nunkoo, R. and Ramkissoon, H. (2012) 'Power, trust, social exchange and community support', *Annals of Tourism Research*, 39(3): 997–1023.

Nunkoo, R., Ramkissoon, H. and Gursoy, D. (2012) 'Public trust in tourism institutions', *Annals of Tourism Research*, 29(3): 1538–1564.

Nunkoo, R. and Smith, S.L.J. (2013) 'Political economy of tourism: Trust in government actors, political support, and their determinants', *Tourism Management*, 36: 120–132.

Ochieng, E. G. and Price, A.D.F. (2010) 'Managing cross-cultural communication in multicultural construction project teams: The case of Kenya and UK', *International Journal of Project Management*, 28(5): 449–460.

Onyx, J. and Leonard, R. (2010) 'The conversion of social capital into community development: An intervention in Australia's outback', *International Journal of Urban and Regional Research*, 34(2), 381–397.

Park, D. B., Lee, K. W., Choi, H. S. and Yoon, Y. (2012) 'Factors influencing social capital in rural tourism communities in South Korea', *Tourism Management*, 33(6): 1511–1520.

Park, J., Gunn, F. and Han, S. L. (2012) 'Multidimensional trust building in e-retailing: Cross-cultural differences in trust formation and implications for perceived risk', *Journal of Retailing and Consumer Services*, 19(3): 304–312.

Pawar, M. (2006) ' "Social" "capital"?' *Social Science Journal*, 43(2): 211–226.

Putnam, R. D. (1995) 'Bowling alone: America's declining social capital', *Journal of Democracy*, 6(1): 65–78.

Reeskens, T. and Hooghe, M. (2008) 'Cross-cultural measurement equivalence of generalized trust: Evidence from the European social survey (2002 and 2004)', *Social Indicators Research*, 85(3): 515–532.

Rothstein, B. and Stolle, D. (2008) 'The state and social capital: An institutional theory of generalized trust', *Comparative Politics*, 40(4): 441–459.

Rousseau, D. M., Sitkin, S. B., Burt, R. and Camerer, C. (1998) 'Not so different after all: A cross-discipline view of trust', *Academy of Management Review*, 23(3): 393–404.

Ruiz-Ballesteros, E. (2011) 'Social-ecological resilience and community-based tourism: An approach from Agua Blanca, Ecuador', *Tourism Management*, 32(3): 655–666.

Saxena, G. (2005) 'Relationships, networks and the learning regions: Case evidence from the Peak District National Park', *Tourism Management*, 26(2): 277–289.

Schoorman, F. D., Mayer, R. C. and Davis, J. H. (2007) 'An integrative model of organizational trust: Past, present, and future', *Academy of Management Review*, 32(2): 344–354.

Sharp, E. A., Thwaites, R., Curtis, A. and Millar, J. (2012) 'Trust and trustworthiness: Conceptual distinctions and their implications for natural resources management', *Journal of Environmental Planning and Management*. Available online at www.tandfonline.com/doi/full/10.1080/09640568.2012.717052#.UetA5rp-_Mw.

Shepherd, N. (2002) 'How ecotourism can go wrong: The cases of Seacanoe and Siam Safari, Thailand', *Current Issues in Tourism*, 5(3–4): 309–318.

Sirgy, M. J. (2002) *The Psychology of Quality of Life*. New York: Springer.

Stephens, C. (2008) 'Social capital in its place: Using social theory to understand social capital and inequalities in health', *Social Science and Medicine*, 66(5): 1174–1184.

Stone, L. S. and Stone, T. M. (2011) 'Community-based tourism enterprises: Challenges and prospects for community participation; Khama Rhino Sanctuary Trust, Botswana', *Journal of Sustainable Tourism*, 19(1): 97–114.

Upchurch, R. S. and Teivane, U. (2000) 'Resident perceptions of tourism development in Riga, Latvia', *Tourism Management*, 21(5): 499–507.

Verbeek, D. and Mommaas, H. (2008) 'Transitions to sustainable tourism mobility: The social practices approach', *Journal of Sustainable Tourism*, 16(6): 629–644.

Vermuri, A. W. and Costanza, R. (2006) 'The role of human, social, built and natural capital in explaining life satisfaction at the country level: Toward a national well-being index', *Ecological Economics*, 58: 119–133.

Von Friedrichs Grangsjo, Y. and Gummesson, E. (2006) 'Hotel networks and social capital in destination marketing', *International Journal of Service Industry Management*, 17(1): 58–75.

Wall, G. and Mathieson, A. (2006) *Tourism: Change, Impacts and Opportunities*, Harlow: Pearson Education.

Wang, Y. and Xiang, Z. (2007) 'Toward a theoretical framework of collaborative destination marketing', *Journal of Travel Research*, 46, 75–85.

White-Cooper, S., Dawkins, N. U., Kamin, S. L. and Anderson, L. A. (2009) 'Community–institutional partnerships: Understanding trust among partners', *Health Education and Behavior*, 36(2): 334–347.

Woolcock, M. (1998) 'Social capital and economic development: Toward a theoretical synthesis and policy framework', *Theory and Society*, 27: 151–208.

Xu, Q., Perkins, D. D. and Chow, J. C. (2010) 'Sense of community, neighboring, and social capital as predictors of local political participation in China', *American Journal of Community Psychology*, 45(3–4): 259–271.

Yamamoto, D. and Yamamoto, Y. (2013) 'Community resilience to a developmental shock: A case study of a rural village in Nagano, Japan', *Resilience: International Policies, Practices and Discourses*, 1(2): 99–115.

Yuki, M., Maddux, W. W., Brewer, M. B. and Takemura, K. (2005) 'Cross-cultural differences in relationship-and group-based trust', *Personality and Social Psychology Bulletin*, 31(1): 48–62.

Zahra, A. and McGehee, N. G. (2013) 'Volunteer tourism: A host community capital perspective', *Annals of Tourism Research*, 42: 22–45.

6 Tourism planning and human security

Knowledge and intervention construction and trust in "solving" environmental change

C. Michael Hall

Introduction

In tourism, there has been increasing interest in issues of security in recent years. This has arguably stemmed primarily from industry and consumer concerns with respect to the effects of terrorism, wars and criminal activity on perceptions of personal safety and the likelihood of destination avoidance. However, the notion of security potentially provides a useful framework within which to consider issues of trust in tourism planning, because it highlights not only the ways in which individuals are affected by other events and individuals but also that individuals are embedded in communities and other collectivities that are themselves affected by broader system change. All of which influence both the need to trust and the capacity to trust.

"Human security is not a concern with weapons – it is a concern with human life and dignity" (United Nations Development Program 1994: 22–23). In a general sense, security is "the condition of being protected from or not exposed to danger" (Barnett 2001b: 1). Environmental, social and economic issues are now recognized as underlying contemporary understandings of security. Concepts of common and collective security, although not universally accepted and even actively opposed by some jurisdictions, have been integral in making significant tourism planning issues such as environmental change, including climate change, and sustainable development security issues (Page and Redclift 2002; Hall *et al.* 2003; O'Brien *et al.* 2010a; Intergovernmental Panel on Climate Change [IPCC] 2012). These concerns also reflect a growing awareness that feelings of security are a function of not only individual and collective trust in human institutions and relationships but the physical environment (Schmidt and Gifford 1989; Greenberg and Williams 1999; Parker *et al.* 2007), especially at a time when the impact, magnitude and frequency of natural disasters are increasing. For example, the IPCC (2012: 293) concluded with "high agreement" that "[t]he impacts of climate extremes and weather events may threaten human security at the local level." Indeed, O'Brien *et al.* (2010b: 4) argue that climate change is "a problem that can only be resolved by focusing on climate change as an issue of human security, which includes a thorough investigation of what it means for humans to be 'secure'." However, the potential of such a discourse has not yet been captured in tourism research on the implications of climate change, where the focus has been set more on the economic behavioral conditions of industry, destinations and consumers to respond than their social practices.

The relationship among climate change, security and sustainable development also frames a significant emerging post- or transdisciplinary research agenda that seeks to move between and integrate physical and social science perspectives, and the potential development of a broad range of answers to the questions of "security from what and secure to do what?" (Hall *et al.* 2003: 8–9). Environmental change, and climate change in particular, is used as the starting point for a discussion on security and trust, because it is arguably the most important tourism planning issue of all given its tourism system-wide effects. And, although often appreciated by many, including the tourism sector, with respect to its local effects, the system-wide implications of global change mean that it requires a response at multiple scales at different parts of the system. Nevertheless, local capacity to act and adapt clearly remains important and is usually the main focus of most tourism planning initiatives. Indeed, in the case of the less developed countries, Barnett (2001a) argues that environmental insecurity is the double vulnerability of people that arises when underdevelopment and impoverishment are compounded by anthropogenic environmental change. However, also important to note is that this chapter has as a basic assumption that the role of tourism planning is not to seek to achieve what is in the greatest interest of the tourism sector but instead to use tourism to further the interests of destination communities. As Hall (2008) suggests, this will mean that the best form of tourism planning in some circumstances will likely be minimal tourism or no tourism at all. If other assumptions were used, the resultant chapter and series of arguments would look very different. For example, in the case of tourism planning in the less developed countries, it becomes important to assess the value of international tourism for not only the short-term income it may bring to a destination community but the longer-term impacts on the environment and human vulnerability as a result of continued growth in emissions (Hall *et al.* 2013).

This chapter therefore explores some of the tourism planning issues relating to the emerging human security and environmental change agenda at the community and individual scale. It argues that the challenge is as much conceptual with respect to paradigms of behavior and governance as it is to the impacts of environmental change on tourism and tourism's contribution to environmental change. Indeed, the intellectual capacity to consider other ways of doing and decision making are potentially the most important of all. However, this requires a much more fundamental understanding of how problems are defined and planning and policy interventions selected, especially with respect to the "rules of the game."

The chapter is divided into three main sections. The first discusses the ways in which issues of security and environmental change response are framed. Such a discussion is regarded as fundamental to considering capacities of planning interventions to adapt to change. The chapter then examines the way that communities and individuals are embedded within broader social and economic structures that are intrinsically political in nature. The critical role of trust and values in communities is noted, but it is stressed that communities should not be romanticized as appears to be the case in some discussions of the role of the community in tourism planning. Similarly, individuals may lack capacity or willingness to respond to environmental change, even if this may appear to be a rational response. The challenges that this provides for planning communication is highlighted. Finally, the chapter returns to the vital role of different political paradigms of behavior and governance and the implications that this has for the nature of behavioral interventions given the potential of the "lock in" of communities and individuals within certain socio-technical systems (Hall 2013b).

Framing human security and tourism

The short- and long-term economic, environmental, health and welfare risks that environmental changes, such as biodiversity loss and climate change, pose to human well-being are acknowledged in both scientific and policy circles. However, like environmental change itself, the impacts of which are not evenly distributed in space and time, so policy, planning and institutional responses are also uneven. Yet this makes local approaches even more important with vulnerability at the local level attributable "to social, political, and economic conditions and drivers including localized environmental degradation and climate change" (IPCC 2012: 293).

Following Alkire (2003), Barnett and Adger defined human security as "the condition where people and communities have the capacity to manage stresses to their needs, rights, and values" (2007: 640). This approach also reflects the relationship of human security discourse to that of vulnerability, which is itself an emerging discourse with respect to the potential adverse effects of environmental, economic and political change on ecosystems, infrastructure, economic sectors, social groups, communities and regions (Füssel and Klein 2006; Füssel 2007; O'Brien *et al.* 2007; IPCC 2012), including with respect to tourism (Calgaro and Lloyd 2008; Scheyvens and Momsen 2008; Dawson *et al.* 2009).

As with notions of vulnerability, the assessment of human security requires considering levels of risk, susceptibility to loss, and capacity to recover (Barnett and Adger 2007). However, also like ideas of vulnerability and risk, human security tends to be "more socially constructed than objectively determined" (Barnett 2001b: 2). Yet recognition that notions of security, vulnerability and risk are socially constructed has clear planning and research implications for risks and framing tourism development and environmental problems.

Figure 6.1 proposes a model of the way in which tourism planning problems are defined and interventions selected via the interaction of political and scientific approaches and community responses. In some cases, the way in which the problem is defined to make it "solvable" and the selection of appropriate planning interventions will be the same between the political and scientific approaches. In other cases, it will not. For example, Hall (2010) suggests that one of the reasons

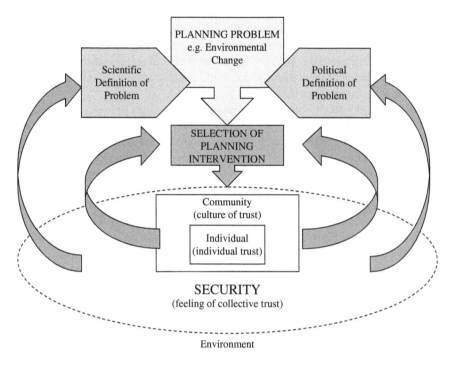

Figure 6.1 Selection of planning interventions and relationship to security

why tourism research has had little practical effect on making tourism more sustainable in real terms may lie in the notion of "epistemic community," a concept used in international relations to explain how policy makers are influenced by the providers of knowledge. An epistemic community refers to a network of knowledge-based experts or professionals with a recognized authoritative claim to knowledge and skill in a particular issue area and the domain of their expertise (Hass 1992; Sebenius 1992; Antoniades 2003).

Hall (2010) suggests that academics active in sustainable tourism research have not become a publicly recognized group with an unchallenged claim to understand the nature of the sustainable tourism issue arena and therefore able to interpret the area and influence political decisions, actions and interventions. Such epistemic communities, where successful, can introduce new policy alternatives and encourage their implementation. In environmental policy, the cases of concern over the protection of the stratospheric ozone layer and Mediterranean pollution control via the Mediterranean Action Plan (Med Plan) provide examples of when new research actors were consulted on policy formulation because of uncertainties about environmental problems (Hass 1989). However, in the case of sustainable tourism, as with climate change, the influence of researchers may be vitiated by the countering interests of business and other interest groups, thereby diminishing not only access to decision makers but also claims as to authoritative knowledge.

Although another explanation may lie in that members of the sustainable tourism epistemic community do not hold a sufficiently common set of causal beliefs and shared notions of validity to be effective (Haas 1989, 1992). This is a practical as well as an academic issue, because the development of an agreed conceptualization and definition of what a problem actually is are fundamental to its solution in policy and planning terms (Majone 1989).

As Meijerink (2005) notes, identifying the intersections between policy advocacy coalitions that are often grounded in shared political values and epistemic communities is important in understanding policy and governance continuity and change, and why some interventions are selected out of a range of possible intervention choices. To which we can also add, as Figure 6.1 suggests, the acceptability and trust in the success of such interventions by communities and individuals. The extent to which communities accept particular interventions is important for not only their implementation but their political acceptability. Indeed, in some cases, policy coalitions will engage in political marketing campaigns to make planning interventions more acceptable (Hall 2014). Examining the relationship of human security to tourism planning and the potential of planning interventions to succeed means engaging in the broader issues of identifying the relationships between values and interests as well as the political capacities to intervene and implement policies and the potential integration of social and biophysical research perspectives (Füssel and Klein 2006) along with accompanying ontological shifts (Turnpenny *et al.* 2010). However, this also requires that particular attention be given to the ways in which security threats and responses are framed and how different assumptions about individual and community behavior are interrelated to different modes of governance (Hall 2013b).

The power to frame tourism development issues

Knowledge is produced locally and globally in different forms, including with respect to the social dimensions of the communities that study environmental and climate change and the roles of social science in change models and projections (Demeritt 2001a, 2001b, 2006; Yearley 2009; Wainwright 2010). Demeritt's (2001a, 2001b) examination of the construction of climate change science and the politics of science is particularly informative (see also the response of Schneider 2001). Demeritt focused on the way in which climate change science is constructed and how this leads into political issues as to how environmental issues are framed with respect to both problem and solution. "For the most part, climate change model projections have been driven by highly simplistic business-as-usual scenarios of human population growth, resource consumption, and GHG emissions at highly aggregated geographic scales" (Demeritt 2001a: 312). A no less valid and relevant alternative approach would be to frame the problem in terms of the structural imperatives of the capitalist economy that drives emissions; the north–south gap in terms of emissions; or regionalized, community or individual conceptions that focus on issues of poverty and deprivation. As Demeritt (2001a: 316) notes, "by treating the objective physical properties of [greenhouse gases] in isolation from the surrounding social relations serves to conceal, normalize, and thereby reproduce those unequal social relations." In the case of tourism, for example, this could be understood with respect to the issue that tourism emissions are disproportionately caused by the wealthier more mobile elements of society (Scott *et al.* 2012).

The appeals of formal quantitative evaluation methods are social and political as much as technical and scientific, particularly as it also makes them more credible from a public perspective of natural science (Hall 2013c):

> insofar as adherence to rigidly uniform and impersonal and in that sense 'procedurally objective' . . . rules limits the scope for individual bias or discretion and thereby guarantees the vigorous (self-)denial of personal perspective necessary to make knowledge seem universal, trustworthy and true.
>
> (Demeritt 2001a: 324)

However, such rules are socially and politically constructed. The "rules of the game" are a set of predominant values, beliefs, rituals and instructional procedures that operate systematically and consistently to the benefit of some groups at the expense of others (Bachrach and Baratz 1962).

Power is not evenly distributed within a community, whether it is a destination or an academic community, and some groups and individuals have the ability to exert greater influence over the policy and planning process than others through access to financial resources, expertise, public relations, media, knowledge and time to put into contested situations (Church and Coles 2007). Importantly, the use of such power occurs throughout the entire planning process from problem definition and policy setting through to choice of intervention and its implementation (Hall 2007). The actions of interests to influence policy making does not stop when a plan is written but continues throughout the entire policy-action process (Ham and Hill 1994). Such a situation reflects the importance of the rules of the game that surround planning, policy and implementation as "the definition of the alternatives is the supreme instrument of power" (Schattsneider 1960: 66). As (Schattsneider 1960: 71) commented,

> All forms of political organisation have a bias in favour of the exploitation of some kinds of conflict, and the suppression of others, because organisation is the mobilisation of bias. Some issues are organised into politics while some others are organised out.

Issues surrounding how climate change research and its results are constructed scientifically are clearly significant for understanding the relationship between human security at the individual and community level to environmental change and the debate surrounding that relationship for several reasons (Hall 2013a, 2013c). First, they help explain why anthropogenic climate change has been primarily defined as an environmental rather than a political or economic problem, or one that requires framing in terms of the imperatives of the capitalist economic system and its alternatives. Second, even though there has been a call for greater social science information to be brought into the climate change assessment process, this has been assessed primarily in terms of neoclassical economic contributions (e.g. Stern 2007), with the need for action to minimize the effects of climate change also dominated by formal modelling (Dietz and Stern 2008). Yet such models contain numerous major weaknesses with respect to predicting behavioral responses to climate change (Gössling and Hall 2006). Furthermore, the neoclassical economic utilitarian view of value has been subjected to several philosophical and moral critiques as to the way people engage with their physical and social environment and actually behave (Demeritt and Rothman 1999), and this issue will be returned to in more detail below.

Also of significance is the way climate change is widely understood through strategic cyclical scaling (Root and Schneider 1995), with small-scale, detailed case studies informing and being informed by large-scale, comprehensive statistical and simulation studies. Such an approach reflects a reductionist perspective, in which the properties of wholes are always found among the properties of their parts, or a mechanistic perspective, in which properties of wholes are of the same kind or type of those parts, based on the same ontological assumptions. However, such ontological positions with respect to the relationship between the parts and the whole are only two of several potential philosophical positions with respect to knowledge of ecological entities (Blitz 1992; Keller and Golley 2000; Hall 2013c). For example, an emergent ontological position suggests that there is at least one property of some wholes not possessed by any of their parts. This means that parts can exist independently of the whole, and novel properties of wholes can be lost via submergence when a system is reduced to its parts. A holistic approach differs from reductionism still further. Epistemologically, holism means that knowledge of the parts is neither necessary nor sufficient to understand the whole. Ontologically, holism suggests that the emergent novel properties of the whole can be understood without further consideration of the parts and their relationships (Blitz 1992).

The ontological and epistemological bases of different systems perspectives are of critical importance in trying to understand how, in human ecological terms, individuals interact with larger socio-political groupings such as communities, regions and nations in responding to environmental change; how change at one level may or may not affect change at another; and the assumptions upon which planning interventions that seek to change tourist or community behaviors rest. Moreover, they highlight the issue that there is more than one way of describing a system and its constituent parts and their interactions. On what basis, therefore, is one approach utilized over another? Although the focus of human security is the individual (Barnett and Adger 2007), the way in which individuals are regarded as being affected by different larger-scale processes and therefore respond and adapt to them, including governance regimes at various scales, will depend on the way in which such multiscalar relationships are framed.

Recognition of the relationship between disaster risk reduction and environmental change adaptation (O'Brien et al. 2008; IPCC 2012) has been profound for the framing of human security (O'Brien et al. 2010b). As opposed to research and policy formulation on climate change adaptation that focuses on biophysical impacts, disaster risk research has tended to recognize the broader socioeconomic causes and consequences of what are otherwise presented as "natural disasters," including poverty, inequality, market failures and policy failures (Barnett and Adger 2007). As a result of the recognition of the merits of a disaster risk research approach for highlighting certain facets of human security issues, the relationships between environmental change, and climate change in particular, and sustainable development have been greatly strengthened (Swart *et al.* 2003; Halsnæs *et al.* 2008; Adger *et al.* 2009b; IPCC 2012), particularly with respect to poverty reduction initiatives, and ameliorating the human consequences of climate change (United Nations Development Program 2008). The latter issues are supposedly high on the agenda of institutions such as the United Nations World Tourism Organization (Hall *et al.* 2013). As O'Brien *et al.* (2008: 5) observe, "Enhancing human security in the 21st century is about responding to climate change and disaster risks in ways that not only reduce vulnerability and conflict, but also create a more equitable, resilient and sustainable future." Indeed, as the IPCC (2012: 20) concluded, "A prerequisite for sustainability in the context of climate change is addressing the underlying causes of vulnerability, including the structural inequalities that create and sustain poverty and constrain access to resources." However, as suggested above, such an approach clearly raises fundamental political-economic questions that other ways of framing climate and environmental change may either choose to ignore or posit differently.

The multilevel nature of human security responses to climate change

The relationship between sustainable development and vulnerability – the propensity or predisposition to be adversely affected (IPCC 2012) – provides a springboard to examining responses to tourism planning, environmental change and human security. However, difficulties in progressing and operationalizing the concept of sustainable development also points to some of the challenges facing tourism planners in responding to environmental change.

Figure 6.2 illustrates the multilevel nature of climate change, human security and sustainable development. It suggests that environmental change as an issue for sustainable development and security requires attention at all scales from global and national to the local and the individual; with interactions among the various scales being an important aspect of the policy and planning response (O'Brien *et al.* 2004; Wilbanks 2007). However, given that the effects of environmental change are geographically variable, and the capacity to manage risks and adapt to change is also unevenly distributed within and across nations, regions, communities and households, "stresses upon and strategies for sustainable development are often most usefully considered in a place-based context, where an integrated view of complex interrelationships is more tractable and strategies for action can be made more tangible" (Wilbanks 2003: S147). This is especially the case given difficulties in achieving clear global, national and even tourism industry strategies to combat environmental change.

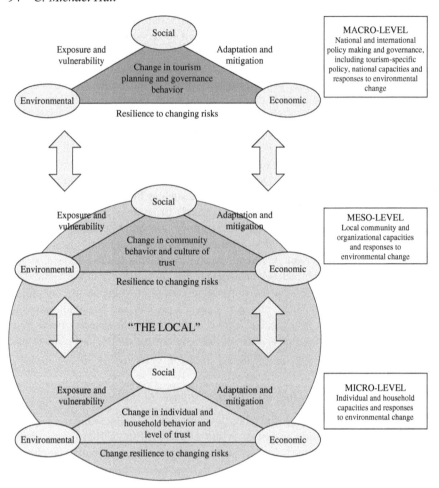

Figure 6.2 Multilevel aspects of environmental change, human security and sustainable development

Trust and the challenge of the local

Although "the local" is clearly of great significance in tourism planning's capacity to respond to environmental change, it is important not to romanticize it (Hall 2008). As research in the fields of resource management and planning indicates, communities are not the embodiment of innocence (Millar 1996; Young 2001; Suryanata and Umemoto 2003, 2005; Joyce and Satterfield 2010);

> on the contrary, they are complex and self-serving entities, as much driven by grievances, prejudices, inequalities, and struggles for power as they are united by kinship, reciprocity, and interdependence. Decision-making at the

local level can be extraordinarily vicious, personal, and not always bound by legal constraints.

(Millar and Aiken 1995: 629)

Such observations reinforce O'Brien *et al.*'s (2008: 18) observation "that risk reduction and adaptation strategies must be carefully tailored to individual, house-hold and community needs. Approaches that treat communities as homogeneous (i.e., able to adapt or reduce risks as a group) are prone to failure."

Change is a normal part of the human experience. However, environmental change, especially in the context of increased frequency of high-magnitude weather events and "natural disasters" (IPCC 2012), may hasten rates of change above those that are "comfortable" for many people. Rapid or sudden place change can dramati-cally alter the web of relations that residents and visitors have with place (Connor *et al.* 2004; Albrecht *et al.* 2007; Hanna *et al.* 2011; Biggs *et al.* 2012), and sub-stantially affect personal, household and community wellbeing and thus directly impact senses of security and trust. As Millar and Aiken (1995: 620) commented,

> Conflict is a normal consequence of human interaction in periods of change, the product of a situation where the gain or a new use by one party is felt to involve a sacrifice or changes by others. It can be an opportunity for creative problem solving, but if it is not managed properly conflict can divide a com-munity and throw it into turmoil.

A substantial body of literature addresses appropriate community-level approaches and strategies to engage communities in seeking to improve their resilience and well-being and lessen their vulnerabilities and risks (e.g. Paton and Johnston 2001; David *et al.* 2003; Hall 2008, 2013a; Ensor and Berger 2009; Comfort *et al.* 2010). Such approaches have also been long identified as signifi-cant for sustainability practices (Kelly 2009). Yet despite awareness of appropri-ate community practices in academic literature and reports (O'Brien *et al.* 2008; IPCC 2012), knowledge is not necessarily translated into action (White *et al.* 2001). Indeed, the four possible explanations provided by White *et al.* (2001) as to why more is lost while more is known are more pertinent than ever in exam-ining individual, community and destination response to environmental change:

1 Knowledge continues to be flawed by areas of ignorance.
2 Knowledge is available but not used effectively.
3 Knowledge is used effectively but takes a long time to have effect.
4 Knowledge is used effectively in some respects but is overwhelmed by increases in vulnerability and in population, wealth, and poverty.

A key issue in both acceptance and effective use of knowledge in communities is the issue of trust. Trust as a form of social capital is extremely important for knowledge acquisition, and there is substantial evidence that trust also facilitates the diffusion of new technologies (Huang *et al.* 2003). These, of course, may be extremely important in mitigating and adapting to environmental change.

The social functions of trust are at least two fold. First, and as discussed in more depth below given that it provides the usual focus for the value of trust in tourism planning (Hall 2008), trust makes social cooperation easier and functions as a "lubricant" in social and economic transactions (Arrow 1971). Second, trust provides the capacity to make novel social and environmental actions possible and to facilitate innovation and change.

Trust and responses to change

Adaptation to and mitigation of tourism-related environmental change requires appropriate policy and behavioral and technical innovation (Hall 2010, 2011b). However, innovation can be risky because of three properties. First, it is risky because it often involves the allocation of resources that in some cases may be highly restricted or constitute an opportunity cost. These include economic, social, political, human and psychological resources. Second, innovation involves doing of new things in which there is always a lack of specific behavioral information involved. Third, innovation, especially for environmental reasons, has a significant time component in the sense that only the future will show whether the changes brought about via the implementation of the innovation will return a payoff since their novelty precludes the exact evaluation of possible advantages and disadvantages.

Trust is essential to the adoption of innovations, because trust structures expectations and reduces the perception of potential risks and uncertainties (Bornschier and Volken 2005). New actions become more likely and the scope of possible actions is increased if prior trustworthy experiences can be projected into the future. Moreover, trust facilitates change by allowing actions "on the part of the trustee that would not have been possible otherwise" (Coleman 1994: 97). Furthermore, trust is important to innovation because it enhances the flow and the credibility of information and knowledge (Yli-Renko *et al.* 2001), and trust makes the diffusion of innovation easier in weak but extended ties of social networks (Granovetter 1973). A better and more extensive flow of information reduces the level of uncertainty, which prevents agents from adopting new ideas and practices (Bornschier and Volken 2005). However, a significant issue for levels of trust in the adoption of new practices and technologies is that trust reflects a basic sense of optimism and control and is most likely to emerge (and is most rational) when one is optimistic about the future as opposed to the pessimism that negative environmental change may bring (Uslaner 2000). Finally, no person is an island. Trust is also affected by socialization and the situatedness of people in their social, cultural and institutional context. Therefore, the next section examines trust in a community context.

Trust and cooperation at the community level

Where trust as a form of social capital is absent, cooperative or voluntary collective action is impossible, particularly in "commons" situations that rely on the "curbing of opportunistic impulses toward individual exploitation" (Millar 1996: 207). Trust, therefore, provides for a sufficient number of reciprocal and cooperative actions to occur such that there will be a greater return to all stakeholders than would be forthcoming through individual exploitation (Brann and Foddy 1987). Trust requires a sufficiently common set of values among community members in order to operate. Therefore, attention in many community tourism planning exercises needs to be given to the social and political context within which human security occurs and value conflict arises. As Millar and Aitken (1995: 623–624) noted:

> we must be more concerned with how the local society and resource base are organized . . . communities exist within a web of kinship, physical interdependency, and social obligation, and . . . cannot be separated from the social issues of property and morality.

Trust in relation to environmental change, and especially climate change, is arguably more significant than many other tourism planning issues given the role of climate change sceptics in the media and politics (Scott *et al.* 2012). Although there is widespread agreement within the science community on the urgency of action to deal with climate change, agreement does not necessarily exist with political interests or at the community level (Gössling *et al.* 2012b). Such a situation reflects the importance of recognizing that relevant information is individually and socially contextualized and actioned. "Concepts and tools do not necessarily motivate behavior change where individuals are not motivated to change or perceive barriers to doing so" (Whitmarsh *et al.* 2011: 58). This is something that may have significant repercussions in responding to the human security dimensions of climate change.

Climate change poses major challenges to communicators and educators, because "it is a risk 'buried' in familiar natural processes such as temperature change and weather fluctuations . . . and has low salience as a risk issue because it cannot be directly experienced" (Whitmarsh *et al.* 2011: 57). Some evidence supports this observation given that research suggests that attitudes change when people experience weather events that they believe are associated with climate change (Tervo-Kankare *et al.* 2012). Although changes in attitudes may be encouraging, if communities wait for an event to "make them believe," then the prospects for engendering more sustainable and secure communities before something happens are not good. Communications are therefore rightly highlighted as extremely important, "which suggests an emphasis on presenting knowledge in a community's own language, through innovative media, and in understandable non-scientific terms" (O'Brien *et al.* 2008: 20). However, as already noted, the acceptance of such new knowledge will in great part depend on trust in the source *and* the message.

Although public participation is seen as a standard mechanism to deal with community planning issues, simply hosting a public meeting or forum, a common consultation strategy, will not by itself make it more likely that inaction or conflicts will be resolved. Indeed, they may serve to reinforce rather than change positions. "Public meetings may help to identify conflicts, but they cannot resolve or manage them. While it is true they allow everyone to have his or her say, the root causes . . . are often neglected" (Millar and Aiken 1995: 627). The problem has often been a focus on the technique – the public meeting – rather than the process and the creation of social relations and what the hoped-for outcome of the process actually is (Umemoto and Suryanata 2006; Hall 2008). Too often, processes have been interest-based rather than values-based. However, if long-term agreement and common ground among stakeholders is sought, then attention must be given to the values of those who are affected (Millar and Yoon 2000; Evans and Garvin 2009). Community strategies require appropriate communication strategies to be integrated with community engagement in a manner that is responsive to local situations (Hall 2008; van Aalst *et al.* 2008). In great part, this highlights the importance of "trusted local intermediaries who have a firm understanding of community circumstances and dynamics, basing new activities, technologies or practices on existing coping practices" (O'Brien *et al.* 2008: 20).

There appears to be considerable opportunity for reducing vulnerability at the local level via community-based adaptation. Bottom-up approaches promote locally appropriate measures and empowerment and encourage greater ownership of risk reduction and adaptation actions and strategies to increase resilience and security (O'Brien *et al.* 2008; Ensor and Berger 2009). However, despite enthusiasm for bottom-up approaches, there is also recognition that there are nontechnical limits to adaptation capacities (Adger *et al.* 2007, 2009a), many of which relate to the issues of trust noted above. For example, Ensor and Berger (2009: 227), noted "the limits that culture places on the freedom of individuals and communities to embrace change," while Adger *et al.* (2007) identified several types of nontechnical and nonecological limits to adaptation, including informational and cognitive limits, social and cultural limits, institutional political limits and financial limits. The level of trust structures how actors perceive their environment. Trust is constructed through interaction processes with social-technical context, including institutional, power and economic relationships; therefore, the social context is crucial for the possibility of change. The next section explores these ideas further through the notion of carbon capability.

Carbon capability and approaches to individual and community change

Carbon capability is "the ability to make informed judgments and to take effective decisions regarding the use and management of carbon through both individual behavior change and collective action" (Whitmarsh *et al.* 2009: 2). In seeking to understand the different modes of policy intervention in changing behaviors with respect to climate change, there is a need to understand the situated meanings associated with environmental change, sustainability and human security (Hall 2013b) – that is, how individuals translate and apply knowledge in their daily lives and decision making (Whitmarsh *et al.* 2011). Carbon capability has three dimensions:

- *Decision making/cognitive/evaluative* (technical, material and social aspects of knowledge, skills, motivations, understandings and judgments, including the role of trust).
- *Individual behavior or practices* (e.g. energy conservation, reducing risk).
- *Broader engagement with systems of provision and governance* (e.g. voting, protesting, creating alternative infrastructures of provision; practices that also have a trust dimension to them).

Under a carbon-literacy approach, which is a common aspect of tourism interventions with respect to climate change (Scott *et al.* 2012), the assumption is that as individuals gain knowledge, perhaps as a result of educational campaigns, they change individual behaviors and practices. In contrast, a carbon-capability approach argues that much behavior is inconspicuous, habitual and routine rather than the result of conscious decision making. This means that individual cognitive decisions about behavior and risk and accompanying practices are constrained by social systems of provision, socialization processes within them and the rules and resources of macro-level structures and institutions (Whitmarsh *et al.* 2009; Hall 2013b). Carbon capability does not imply that education and communication to encourage behavior change are worthless. Rather, it highlights that the capacity for individual and community behavioral change needs to be understood in a wider context, including the role of trust for the reasons noted above (Hall 2013b).

The notion of carbon capability inherently means looking beyond an understanding of behavioral change that suggests that information provision is sufficient for consumers to make "rational" and "appropriate" choices. However, it also raises the need to understand the underlying assumptions of different governance approaches to behavior change. Three major approaches can be recognized in approaching issues of decision making, behavior and sustainable consumption: utilitarian, social/psychological and systems of provision/institutional (Seyfang 2011) (Table 6.1).

The utilitarian approach to behavioral change aims to appeal to rational actors who maximize their utility with information to overcome an "information deficit" and encourage "rational behavior" and send appropriate signals to the market (Hall 2013b). However, individual responses to climate change may not be as rational as many assessments of adaptive behavior assume (Grothmann and Patt 2005). Information overload can lead to difficulties in decision making (Seyfang 2011). Also of importance is the role of social norms and routines that are not subject to rational cost-benefit calculations, including notions of community and fairness in economic outcomes. Therefore, decision making is not a unidirectional and sequential process and is instead incremental and at times multidirectional (O'Brien *et al.* 2008)

The focus on behavior in policy and planning has assumed renewed significance with respect to climate change solutions (Thynne 2008), including

Table 6.1 Approaches to understanding different planning interventions in relation to mode of governance

Approach/ paradigm	Scale	Decision- making concept	Planning interventions to achieve behavioral change	Dominant mode of governance
Utilitarian (green economics)	individual	Cognitive information processing on basis of rational utility- maximization	Green labelling, tax incentives, pricing, education	Markets (marketiza- tion; privatization of state instruments)
Social and psychological (behavioral economics; green consumerism; ABC model)	individual	Response to psychological needs, behavior and social contexts Dominant paradigm of ABC: attitude, behavior and choice	Nudging – making better choices through manipulating the behavioral environment Social marketing to encourage behavioral change	Markets (marketiza- tion; privatization of state instruments) Networks (public– private partnerships)
Systems of provision/ institutions (degrowth; community- based approaches)	Community, society, network	Constrained/ shaped by socio-technical infrastructure and institutions	Trust, short sup- ply chains, local food security; developing local competencies and capacities	Hierarchies (nation- state and suprana- tional institutions) Communities (public– private partnerships, communities)

Sources: Hall (2011a, 2011b, 2013b, 2013c, 2014); Seyfang (2011); Burgess (2012); Gössling and Hall (2013).

transition management in tourism (Gössling *et al.* 2012a). It is an underlying dimension of public policy interest in "nudging" (Thaler and Sunstein 2008). The approach suggests that the goal of public policy making should be to steer citizens toward making positive decisions as individuals and for communities while preserving individual choice. Acting as "choice architects," policy makers organize the context, process and environment in which individuals make deci- sions, and, in so doing, they exploit "cognitive biases" to manipulate people's choices (Alemanno 2012). According to Bovens (2009) and Alemanno (2012), a policy instrument qualifies as a nudge when it satisfies the following criteria:

- The intervention must not restrict individual choice.
- It must be in the interest of the person being nudged.
- It should involve a change in the architecture or environment of choice.

- It implies the strategic use of cognitive biases.
- The action it targets does not stem from a fully autonomous choice (e.g. lack of full knowledge about the context in which the choice is made).

In the UK, the influence of the concept on policy initiatives, including emissions reduction, is seen in then Leader of the Opposition David Cameron reportedly making *Nudge* (Thaler and Sunstein 2008) obligatory reading for his colleagues before election (Burgess 2012), and the MINDSPACE report (Dolan *et al.* 2010), which suggests "approaches based on 'changing contexts' – the environment within which we make decisions and respond to cues – have the potential to bring about significant changes in behavior at relatively low cost" (Dolan *et al.* 2010: 8).

Both nudging and the closely related concept of social marketing recognize that decision making and consumption are multilayered phenomena that are full of meaning, including roles as signifiers of identity, cultural and social affiliations and relationships (Seyfang 2011). The potential of social marketing to influence sustainable behaviors in tourism, including in relation to climate change, has become increasingly argued (Downing and Ballantyne 2007; Truong and Hall 2013; Hall 2014). However, although social/psychological approaches to behavior change recognize the need to make major changes and social norms are often cited as driving factors, there is little scope for wondering about how needs and aspirations come to be as they are; that is, these approaches do not fundamentally question structures and paradigms and how people are socialized with respect to behaviors (Shove 2010), which is not the case with the systems of provision approach. Furthermore, the social/psychological approach may not be effective in situations of low "cultures of trust" (Hardin 2006), where individuals are more likely to deny risks, feel powerless to act, and/or have little adaptive capacity (O'Brien *et al.* 2008). Indeed, Burgess (2012) suggests that application of behavioral solutions assumes a fundamentally pliant and passive population that attaches limited value to individual liberty and autonomy in modern "risk society," something that would appear to be at odds with goals of empowerment in community-based tourism approaches (Hall 2008).

The systems of provision approach focuses on the contextual collective societal institutions, norms, rules, structures and infrastructure that constrain individual decision making, consumption and lifestyle practices. The significance of the approach is that it highlights that particular socio-technical systems constrain choice to that available within the system of provision, and can therefore lock in individuals and communities to particular ways of behaving (Lorenzoni *et al.* 2007, 2011; Maréchal 2010; Seyfang 2011). The systems of provision approach has focused on the development of alternative systems such as food networks for the enhancement of local food security and local economies (e.g. farmers' markets) and short supply chains (e.g. Fair Trade) that have a focus on increasing consumer trust in a specific socio-technical system (Gössling and Hall 2013). Such initiatives emphasize the potential critically of trust to the development of new forms of post-carbon communities and localism that may be essential in responding to climate and other forms of environmental change (Monaghan 2012).

The utilitarian (green labelling, tax incentives, pricing, education) and social/psychological (nudging, social marketing) approaches are grounded in an "ABC model" (Shove 2010; Hall 2013b). Social change is thought to depend upon values and attitudes (A) that are believed to drive the kinds of behavior (B) that individuals choose (C) to adopt. "The combination of A and B and C generates a clear agenda for effective policy, the conceptual and practical task of which is to identify and affect the determinants of pro-environmental behavior" (Shove 2010: 1275). ABC strategies of state intervention frame undesirable environmental change as a consequence of individual actions and assume that, given better information or incentives, individuals will choose to act and behave differently (Shove 2010; Hinkel 2011). But in so doing, they do not fundamentally question structures/paradigms and their role in influencing individual behaviors and understandings of risk and vulnerability (Hall 2013a), although there is increasing recognition of "upstream" social marketing that seeks to change institutions (Hall 2014). Indeed, this returns us to the issues raised in Figure 6.1 and the ways in which political and research interests interact with respect to the selection of planning interventions.

> Policy-makers are highly selective in the models of change on which they draw, and that their tastes in social theory are anything but random. An emphasis on individual choice has significant political advantages and in this context, to probe further, to ask how options are structured, or to inquire into the ways in which governments maintain infrastructures and economic institutions, is perhaps too challenging to be useful.
>
> (Shove 2010: 1283)

Beyond ABC? Framing individual and community response to human security and environmental change issues in tourism

This chapter has suggested that trust is intrinsic to our understanding of the ways in which individuals and communities respond to environmental change. However, rather than focusing on the role of trust for cooperation, which is often the main focus for research on trust in tourism planning (Hall 2008), it has sought to use the notion of human security to emphasize the ways in which trust affects the acceptability of knowledge and information by communities and individuals and how it then affects their capacities to adapt to environmental change. It has also highlighted the way in which different modes of problem definition as well as problem "solution," in the form of selection of different interventions, are not politically neutral and have implications for the "rules of the game" in which tourism planning with respect to environmental change occurs.

Indeed, a key point of this chapter is the need to acknowledge such rules in the first place. Without facing up to the implications of structure and institutions, the likelihood of being locked in to particular socio-technical systems of provision, which, in the case of tourism, is unsustainable at the global scale (Scott *et al.*

2012; Hall *et al.* 2013), is greatly increased. Furthermore, different concepts of behavioral change are also linked to different modes of governance (Hall 2011b, 2013b); that is, different sets of rules of the game are based on different conceptualizations of how behavior occurs (and therefore should be analyzed), and predicates the selection of particular planning instruments.

Different conceptualizations of governance are related to the use of particular sets of policy instruments and approaches to policy implementation and state intervention (Hall 2009, 2011b). It is not really possible to say what came first – the mode of governance or the intervention mechanism that implements public policies. But what is important is that the mode of governance and the manner of intervention become mutually reinforcing. One cannot be adequately understood without the other (Hall 2011a). Yet mutual reinforcement between modes of governance and intervention creates a path dependency in which solutions to increased human security in response to environmental change in tourism are primarily identified within "green growth" arguments for greater efficiency and market-based solutions, and an ideology that frames the problem of sustainable development, vulnerability and risk reduction in terms of individual decision making and responsibility (Hall 2013b), without either sufficient appreciation of the role of trust in making such solutions acceptable or useful or the role of sociotechnical systems in determining capacities to act.

One of the appeals of behavioral economics and social marketing approaches for policy making, such as nudging, is the promise of cost-effectiveness. The practical emphasis is on "smart" solutions that supposedly do not involve more resources; an imperative in recessionary times with many governments committed to reducing spending (Burgess 2012) and that have clear indicators. However, the cause-and-effect relations of even seemingly straightforward nudge proposals are not nearly as predictable or measurable as expected (Hinkel 2011), and the approach may be incapable of solving "wicked problems" such as tourism-related sustainable consumption and environmental change "in which multiple systems, operating with different norms and at different scales, interact with one another to produce emergent behavior that can be exceptionally difficult, if not impossible, to predict" (Selinger and Powys White 2012: 29), such as rebound and backfire effects (Hall *et al.* 2013b).

Another significant and complicating problem is that "given that the ABC is the dominant paradigm in contemporary environmental policy, the scope of relevant social science is typically restricted to that which is theoretically consistent with it" (Shove 2010: 1280). Therefore, the construction of the rules of the game affects not only the definition of environmental problems and tourism planning solutions and interventions but also the political acceptability of research and funding opportunities. This is, therefore, a critical issue in seeking to respond to tourism-related issues of human security and environmental change. Lock-in to particular socio-technical systems of provision is a major constraint to avoidance of dangerous environmental change (Bailey and Wilson 2009; Maréchal 2010). Such lock-ins occur at multiple scales of governance. In such a situation, policy learning is extremely difficult (Hall 2011a), with changes often occurring only at the margin in a way that does not challenge the basic growth paradigm and/or ways of doing. As Shove (2010: 1283) suggests,

> paradigms and approaches which lie beyond the pale of the ABC are doomed to be forever marginal no matter how interactive or how policy-engaged their advocates might be. To break through this log jam it would be necessary to reopen a set of basic questions about the role of the state, the allocation of responsibility, and in very practical terms the meaning of manageability, within climate-change policy.

This situation creates a very real problem for individuals (including academics) and communities seeking to do "other" and highlights the difficulties of mainstreaming adaptation into tourism planning and development, even though it would contribute to community and destination-related human security. If enhancing human security in the twenty-first century is, as O'Brien *et al.* (2008) suggest, about responding to environmental change in ways that not only reduce vulnerability and conflict but also create a more equitable, resilient and sustainable future, then it is also about finding ways to respond politically and deal with issues of power and the role of trust in responding to communication, knowledge and interventions. Nevertheless, highlighting problems such as "lack of equity" (O'Brien *et al.* 2008), "repression" (IPCC 2012: 572), and "structural inequality" (IPCC 2012: 20) with respect to human security, risk and vulnerability is a statement about the nature of current systems of provision and their inadequacy. It is as much a statement that such concepts and considerations are rarely seen in the tourism planning literature, where the role of trust has usually been understood in facilitating the development of collaborative networks and relationships – without necessarily interrogating the associated norms and values of such social structures (Hall 1999).

Networks can contribute just as much to poor environmental outcomes as they can to good. A focus on trust and collaboration in tourism planning without considering the paradigms of governance within which they are situated has also consequently contributed to

> possibilities for the privatization of environmental governance in some areas or the increasing use of market mechanisms. . . . at the same time it has made trade-offs much more difficult because it denies that they may be necessary among values of efficiency, economic growth, corporate freedom, and environmental protection.
>
> (Bernstein 2002: 14)

These represent real problems not only for the reduction of the impacts of tourism contribution to environmental change but, just as importantly given the need for policy learning (Hall 2011a), they are significant challenges to the tourism academic community that works on tourism and environmental change issues to continue to speak out on the continued promotion of economic growth strategies in policy documents and academic reports and the essential value of critical social science within the scientific community.

References

Adger, W. N., Agrawala, S., Mirza, M.M.Q., Conde, C., O'Brien, K., Pulhin, J., Pulwarty, R., Smit, B. and Takahashi, K. (2007) 'Assessment of adaptation practices, options, constraints and capacity', in M. Parry, O. Canziani, J. Palutikof, P. van der Linden and C. Hanson (eds) *Climate Change 2007: Impacts, Adaptation and Vulnerability. Contribution of Working Group II to the Fourth Assessment Report of the Intergovernmental Panel on Climate Change,* Cambridge: Cambridge University Press.

Adger, W. N., Dessai, S., Goulden, M., Hulme, M., Lorenzoni, I., Nelson, D., Naess, L., Wolf, J. and Wreford, A. (2009a) 'Are there social limits to adaptation to climate change?' *Climatic Change,* 93: 335–354.

Adger, W. N., Lorenzoni, I. and O'Brien, K. (eds) (2009b) *Adapting to Climate Change: Thresholds, Values, Governance,* Cambridge: Cambridge University Press.

Albrecht, G., Sartore, G-M., Connor, L., Higginbotham, N., Freeman, S., Kelly, B., Stain, H., Tonna, A. and Pollard, G. (2007) 'Solastalgia: The distress caused by environmental change', *Australasian Psychiatry,* 15(S1): 95–98.

Alemanno, A. (2012) 'Nudging smokers – The behavioral turn of tobacco risk regulation', *European Journal of Risk Regulation,* 1/2012: 32–42.

Alkire, S. (2003) *A Conceptual Framework for Human Security,* CRISE Working Paper 2, Oxford: Queen Elizabeth House.

Antoniades, A. (2003) 'Epistemic communities, epistemes and the construction of (world) politics', *Global Society,* 17(1): 21–38.

Arrow, K. (1971) *Essays in the Theory of Risk Bearing,* Chicago: Markham.

Bachrach, P. and Baratz, M. (1962) 'Two faces of power', *American Political Science Review,* 56: 947–952.

Bailey, I. and Wilson, G. (2009) 'Theorising transitional pathways in response to climate change: Technocentrism, ecocentrism, and the carbon economy', *Environment and Planning A,* 41: 2324–2341.

Barnett, J. (2001a) *The Meaning of Environmental Security: Ecological Politics and Policy in the New Security Era,* London: Zed Books.

Barnett, J. (2001b) *Security and Climate Change,* Tyndall Centre Working Paper No. 7, Norwich: Tyndall Centre for Climate Change Research, University of East Anglia.

Barnett, J. and Adger, W. N. (2007) 'Climate change, human security and violent conflict', *Political Geography,* 26: 639–655.

Bernstein, S. (2002) 'Liberal environmentalism and global environmental governance', *Global Environmental Politics,* 2(3): 1–16.

Biggs, D., Hall, C. M. and Stoeckl, N. (2012) 'The resilience of formal and informal tourism enterprises to disasters – reef tourism in Phuket', *Journal of Sustainable Tourism,* 20: 645–665.

Blitz, D. (1992) *Emergent Evolution: Qualitative Novelty and the Levels of Reality,* Boston: Kluwer.

Bornschier, V. and Volken, T. (2005) 'Trust and the disposition to change in cross-national perspective: A research note', *Electronic Journal of Sociology.* Available online at www.sociology.org/content/2005/tier1/trustchange.pdf.

Bovens, L. (2009) 'The ethics of nudge', in T. Grüne-Yanoff and S. Ove Hansson (eds) *Preference Change: Approaches from Philosophy, Economics and Psychology,* Berlin: Springer.

Brann, P. and Foddy, M. (1987) 'Trust and the consumption of a deteriorating common resource', *Journal of Conflict Resolution,* 31: 615–630.

Burgess, A. (2012) ' "Nudging" healthy lifestyles: The UK experiments with the behavioral alternative to regulation and the market', *European Journal of Risk Regulation,* 1: 3–16.

Calgaro, E. and Lloyd, K. (2008) 'Sun, sea, sand and tsunami: Examining disaster vulnerability in the tourism community of Khao Lak, Thailand', *Singapore Journal of Tropical Geography,* 29: 288–306.

Church, A. and Coles, T. (eds) (2007) *Tourism, Power and Space,* London: Routledge.

Coleman, J. (1994) *Foundations of Social Theory*. Cambridge, MA: Belknap Press of Harvard University Press.

Comfort, L., Birkland, T., Cigler, B. and Nance, E. (2010) 'Retrospectives and prospectives on Hurricane Katrina: Five years and counting', *Public Administration Review*, 70: 669–678.

Connor, L., Albrecht, G., Higginbotham, N., Freeman, S. and Smith, W. (2004) 'Environmental change and human health in Upper Hunter communities of New South Wales, Australia', *EcoHealth*, 1(2, Supplement): SU47–SU58.

David, R. G., Brody, S. and Burby, R. (2003) 'Public participation in natural hazard mitigation policy formation: Challenges for comprehensive planning', *Journal of Environmental Planning and Management*, 46: 733–754.

Dawson, J., Scott, D. and McBoyle, G. (2009) 'Analogue analysis of climate change vulnerability in the US Northeast ski tourism', *Climate Research*, 39(1): 1–9.

Demeritt, D. (2001a) 'The construction of global warming and the politics of science', *Annals of the Association of American Geographers*, 91: 307–337.

Demeritt, D. (2001b) 'Science and the understanding of science: A reply to Schneider', *Annals of the Association of American Geographers*, 91: 345–348.

Demeritt, D. (2006) 'Science studies, climate change and the prospects for constructivist critique', *Economy and Society*, 35: 453–479.

Demeritt, D. and Rothman, D. (1999) 'Figuring the costs of climate change: An assessment and critique', *Environment and Planning A*, 31: 389–408.

Dietz, S. and Stern, N. (2008) 'Why economic analysis supports strong action on climate change: A response to the Stern review's critics', *Review of Environmental Economics and Policy*, 2: 94–113.

Dolan, P., Hallsworth, M., Halpern, D., King, D. and Vlaev, I. (2010) *MINDSPACE: Influencing Behavior through Public Policy*. London: Cabinet Office and Institute for Government.

Downing, P. and Ballantyne, J. (2007) *Tipping Point or Turning Point? Social Marketing and Climate Change*. London: Ipsos MORI Social Research Institute.

Ensor, J. and Berger, R. (2009) 'Community-based adaptation and culture in theory and practice', in W. N. Adger, I. Lorenzoni and K. O'Brien (eds) *Adapting to Climate Change: Thresholds, Values, Governance*, Cambridge: Cambridge University Press.

Evans, J. and Garvin, T. (2009) '"You're in oil country": Moral tales of citizen action against petroleum development in Alberta, Canada', *Ethics Place and Environment*, 12: 49–68.

Füssel, H.-M. (2007) 'Vulnerability: A generally applicable conceptual framework for climate change research', *Global Environmental Change*, 17: 155–167.

Füssel, H.-M. and Klein, R. (2006) 'Climate change vulnerability assessments: An evolution of conceptual thinking', *Climatic Change*, 75: 301–329.

Gössling, S. and Hall, C. M. (2006) 'Uncertainties in predicting tourist flows under scenarios of climate change', *Climatic Change*, 79(3–4): 163–73.

Gössling, S. and Hall, C. M. (2013) 'Sustainable culinary systems: An introduction', in C. M. Hall and S. Gössling (eds) *Sustainable Culinary Systems: Local Foods, Innovation, and Tourism and Hospitality*, Abingdon: Routledge.

Gössling, S., Hall, C. M., Ekström, F., Brudvik Engeset, A. and Aall, C. (2012a) 'Transition management: A tool for implementing sustainable tourism scenarios?' *Journal of Sustainable Tourism*, 20: 899–916.

Gössling, S., Scott, D., Hall, C. M., Ceron, J. and Dubois, G. (2012b) 'Consumer behavior and demand response of tourists to climate change', *Annals of Tourism Research*, 39: 36–58.

Granovetter, M. S. (1973) 'The strength of weak ties', *American Journal of Sociology*, 78: 1360–1380.

Greenberg, M. R. and Williams, B. (1999) 'Geographical dimensions and correlates of trust', *Risk Analysis*, 19: 159–169.

Grothmann, T. and Patt, A. (2005) 'Adaptive capacity and human cognition: The process of individual adaptation to climate change', *Global Environmental Change, Part A*, 15: 199–213.

Haas, P. M. (1989) 'Do regimes matter? Epistemic communities and Mediterranean pollution control', *International Organization*, 43: 377–403.

Haas, P. M. (1992) 'Epistemic communities and international policy coordination', *International Organization*, 46: 1–35.

Hall, C. M. (1999) 'Rethinking collaboration and partnership: A public policy perspective,' *Journal of Sustainable Tourism*, 7: 274–289.

Hall, C. M. (2007) 'Tourism, governance and the (mis-)location of power', in A. Church and T. Coles (eds) *Tourism, Power and Space*. London: Routledge.

Hall, C. M. (2008) *Tourism Planning*, 2nd ed., Harlow: Pearson Prentice Hall.

Hall, C. M. (2009) 'Archetypal approaches to implementation and their implications for tourism policy', *Tourism Recreation Research*, 34: 235–245.

Hall, C. M. (2010) 'Changing paradigms and global change: From sustainable to steady-state tourism', *Tourism Recreation Research*, 35(2): 131–145.

Hall, C. M. (2011a) 'Policy learning and policy failure in sustainable tourism governance: From first and second to third order change?' *Journal of Sustainable Tourism*, 19: 649–671.

Hall, C. M. (2011b) 'A typology of governance and its implications for tourism policy analysis', *Journal of Sustainable Tourism*, 19: 437–457.

Hall, C. M. (2013a) 'Climate change and human security: The individual and community response', in M. R. Redclift and M. Grasso (eds) *Handbook on Climate Change and Human Security*. Cheltenham: Edward Elgar.

Hall, C. M. (2013b) 'Framing behavioral approaches to understanding and governing sustainable tourism consumption: Beyond neoliberalism, "nudging" and "green growth"?' *Journal of Sustainable Tourism*. doi:10.1080/09669582.2013.815764

Hall, C. M. (2013c) 'The natural science ontology of environment', in A. Holden and D. Fennell (eds) *The Routledge Handbook of Tourism and the Environment*, Abingdon: Routledge.

Hall, C. M. (2014) *Tourism and Social Marketing,* Abingdon: Routledge.

Hall, C. M., Scott, D. and Gössling, S. (2013) 'The primacy of climate change for sustainable international tourism', *Sustainable Development*, 21(2): 112–121.

Hall, C. M., Timothy, D. J. and Duval, D. (2003) 'Security and tourism: Towards a new understanding', *Journal of Travel and Tourism Marketing*, 15: 1–18.

Halsnæs, K., Shukla, P. and Garg, A. (2008), 'Sustainable development and climate change: Lessons from country studies', *Climate Policy*, 8: 202–219.

Ham, C. and Hill, M. J. (1994) *The Policy Process in the Modern Capitalist State,* 2nd ed., New York: Prentice Hall.

Hanna, E. G., Bell, E., King, D. and Woodruff, R. (2011) 'Climate change and Australian agriculture: A review of the threats facing rural communities and the health policy landscape', *Asia-Pacific Journal of Public Health*, 23(2, Supplement): 105S–118S.

Hardin, R. (2006) 'The street-level epistemology of trust', in R. M. Kramer (ed.) *Organizational Trust: A Reader*, Oxford: Oxford University Press.

Hinkel, J. (2011) 'Indicators of vulnerability and adaptive capacity: Towards a clarification of the science–policy interface', *Global Environmental Change,* 21: 198–208.

Huang, H., Keser, C., Leland J. and Shachat J. (2003) 'Trust, the Internet and the digital divide', *IBM Systems Journal*, 42: 507–518.

Intergovernmental Panel on Climate Change (IPCC) (2012) *Managing the Risks of Extreme Events and Disasters to Advance Climate Change Adaptation. A Special Report of Working Groups I and II of the Intergovernmental Panel on Climate Change*, eds C. B. Field, V. Barros, T. F. Stocker, D. Qin, D. J. Dokken, K. L. Ebi, M. D. Mastrandrea, K. J. Mach, G.-K. Plattner, S. K. Allen, M. Tignor, and P. M. Midgley, Cambridge: Cambridge University Press.

Joyce, A. L. and Satterfield, T. A. (2010) 'Shellfish aquaculture and First Nations' sovereignty: The quest for sustainable development in contested sea space', *Natural Resources Forum,* 34: 106–123.

Keller, D. R. and Golley, F. B. (eds) (2000) *The Philosophy of Ecology. From Science to Synthesis*, Athens: University of Georgia Press.

Kelly, E. D. (2009) *Community Planning: An Introduction to the Comprehensive Plan*, 2nd ed., Washington, DC: Island Press.

Lorenzoni, I., Nicholson-Cole, S. and Whitmarsh, L. (2007) 'Barriers perceived to engaging with climate change among the UK public and their policy implications', *Global Environmental Change*, 17: 445–459.

Lorenzoni, I., Seyfang, G. and Nye, M. (2011) 'Carbon budgets and carbon capability: Lessons from personal carbon trading', in I. Whitmarsh, S. O'Neill and I. Lorenzoni (eds) *Engaging the Public with Climate Change: Behavior Change and Communication*, London: Earthscan.

Majone, G. (1989) *Evidence, Argument, and Persuasion in the Policy Process*, New Haven, CT: Yale University Press.

Maréchal, K. (2010) 'Not irrational but habitual: The importance of "behavioral lock-in" in energy consumption', *Ecological Economics*, 69: 1104–1114.

Meijerink, S. (2005) 'Understanding policy stability and change. The interplay of advocacy coalitions and epistemic communities, windows of opportunity, and Dutch coastal flooding policy 1945–2003', *Journal of European Public Policy*, 12: 1060–1077.

Millar, C. (1996) 'The Shetland way: Morality in a resource regime', *Coastal Management*, 24: 195–216.

Millar, C. and Aiken, D. (1995) 'Conflict resolution in aquaculture: A matter of trust', in A. Boghen (ed.) *Coldwater Aquaculture in Atlantic Canada*, 2nd ed., Moncton: Canadian Institute for Research on Regional Development.

Millar, C. and Yoon, H. (2000) 'Morality, goodness and love: A rhetoric for resource management', *Ethics, Place and Environment*, 3: 155–172.

Monaghan, P. (2012) *How Local Resilience Creates Sustainable Societies: Hard to Make, Hard to Break*, London: Routledge.

O'Brien, K., Eriksen, S., Nygaard, L. P. and Schjolden, A. (2007) 'Why different interpretations of vulnerability matter in climate change discourses', *Climate Policy*, 7: 73–88.

O'Brien, K. L., St Clair, A. L. and Kristoffersen, B. (eds) (2010a) *Climate Change, Ethics, and Human Security*, Cambridge: Cambridge University Press.

O'Brien, K. L., St Clair, A. L. and Kristoffersen, B. (2010b) 'Towards a new science on climate change', in K. O'Brien, A. L. St Clair and B. Kristoffersen (eds) *Climate Change, Ethics, and Human Security*, Cambridge: Cambridge University Press.

O'Brien, K., Sygna, L. and Haugen, J. E. (2004) 'Vulnerable or resilient? A multi-scale assessment of climate impacts and vulnerability in Norway', *Climatic Change*, 64: 193–225.

O'Brien, K., Sygna, L., Leichenko, R., Adger, W. N., Barnett, J., Mitchell, T., Schipper, L., Tanner, T., Vogel, C. and Mortreux, C. (2008) *Disaster Risk Reduction, Climate Change Adaptation and Human Security*, Report prepared for the Royal Norwegian Ministry of Foreign Affairs by the Global Environmental Change and Human Security (GECHS) Project, GECHS Report 2008:3, Oslo: Ministry of Foreign Affairs.

Page, E. and Redclift, M. (eds) (2002) *Human Security and the Environment: International Comparisons*, Cheltenham: Edward Elgar.

Parker, D., Tapsell, S. and McCarthy, S. (2007) 'Enhancing the human benefits of flood warnings', *Natural Hazards*, 43: 397–414.

Paton, D. and Johnston, D. (2001) 'Disasters and communities: Vulnerability, resilience and preparedness', *Disaster Prevention and Management*, 10: 270–277.

Root, T. L. and Schneider, S. H. (1995) 'Ecology and climate: Research strategies and implications', *Science*, 26(5222): 334–341.

Schattsneider, E. (1960) *Semi-sovereign People: A Realist's View of Democracy in America*. New York: Holt, Rinehart and Wilson.

Scheyvens, R. and Momsen, J. (2008) 'Tourism in small island states: From vulnerability to strengths', *Journal of Sustainable Tourism*, 16: 491–510.

Schmidt, F. N. and Gifford, R. (1989) 'A dispositional approach to hazard perception: Preliminary development of the environmental appraisal inventory', *Journal of Environmental Psychology*, 9: 57–67.

Schneider, S. H. (2001), 'A constructive deconstruction of deconstructionists: A response to Demeritt', *Annals of the Association of American Geographers*, 91: 338–344.

Scott, D., Gössling, S. and Hall, C. M. (2012) *Tourism and Climate Change: Impacts, Adaptation and Mitigation*, Abingdon: Routledge.

Sebenius, J. K. (1992) 'Challenging conventional explanations of international cooperation: Negotiation analysis and the case of epistemic communities', *International Organization*, 46: 323–365.

Selinger, E. and Powys White, K. (2012) 'Nudging cannot solve complex policy problems', *European Journal of Risk Regulation*, 1: 26–31.

Seyfang, G. (2011) *The New Economics of Sustainable Consumption: Seeds of Change*. Basingstoke: Palgrave Macmillan.

Shove, E. (2010) 'Beyond the ABC: Climate change policy and theories of social change', *Environment and Planning A*, 42: 1273–1285.

Stern, N. (2007) *The Economics of Climate Change: The Stern Review*, Cambridge: Cambridge University Press.

Suryanata, K. and Umemoto, K. N. (2003) 'Tension at the nexus of the global and local: Culture, property, and marine aquaculture in Hawaii', *Environment and Planning A*, 35: 199–214.

Suryanata, K. and Umemoto, K. (2005) 'Beyond environmental impact: Articulating the "intangibles" in a resource conflict', *Geoforum*, 36: 750–760.

Swart, R., Robinson, J. and Cohen, S. (2003) 'Climate change and sustainable development: Expanding the options', *Climate Policy*, 3(Supplement 1): S19–S40.

Tervo-Kankare, K., Hall, C. M. and Saarinen, J. (2012), 'Christmas tourists' perceptions of climate change in Rovaniemi, Finnish Lapland', *Tourism Geographies*, 15: 292–317.

Thaler, R. H. and Sunstein, C. R. (2008) *Nudge: Improving Decisions about Health, Wealth and Happiness*. New Haven, CT: Yale University Press.

Thynne, I. (2008) 'Symposium introduction – climate change, governance and environmental services: Institutional perspectives, issues and challenges', *Public Administration and Development*, 28: 327–339.

Troung, V. D. and Hall, C. M. (2013) 'Social marketing and tourism: What is the evidence?' *Social Marketing Quarterly*, 19(2): 110–135.

Turnpenny, J., Jones, M. and Lorenzoni, I. (2010) 'Where now for post-normal science? A critical review of its development, definitions, and uses', *Science Technology Human Values*, doi: 10.1177/0162243910385789.

Umemoto, K. and Suryanata, K. (2006), 'Technology, culture, and environmental uncertainty considering social contracts in adaptive management', *Journal of Planning Education and Research*, 25: 264–274.

United Nations Development Program (1994) *Human Development Report 1994*, New York: Oxford University Press for UNDP.

United Nations Development Program (2008) *Fighting Climate Change: Human Solidarity in a Divided World, 2007/2008 Human Development Report*, New York: Oxford University Press for UNDP.

Uslaner, E. M. (2000) 'Producing and consuming trust', *Political Science Quarterly*, 115: 569–590.

van Aalst, M. K., Cannon, T., and Burton, I. (2008) 'Community level adaptation to climate change: The potential role of participatory community risk assessment', *Global Environmental Change,* 18: 165–179.

Wainwright, J. (2010) 'Climate change, capitalism, and the challenge of transdisciplinarity', *Annals of the Association of American Geographers*, 100: 983–991.

White, G. F., Kates, R. W. and Burton, I. (2001) 'Knowing better and losing even more: The use of knowledge in hazards management', *Global Environmental Change Part B: Environmental Hazards,* 3: 81–92.

Whitmarsh, L., O'Neill, S., Seyfang, G. and Lorenzoni, I. (2009), *Carbon Capability: What Does It Mean, How Prevalent Is It, and How Can We Promote It?* Tyndall Working Paper 132, Norwich: Tyndall Centre for Climate Change Research, University of East Anglia.

Whitmarsh, L., Seyfang, G. and O'Neill, S. (2011) 'Public engagement with carbon and climate change: To what extent is the public "carbon capable"?' *Global Environmental Change,* 21: 56–65.

Wilbanks, T. J. (2003) 'Integrating climate change and sustainable development in a place-based context', *Climate Policy,* 3(Supplement 1): S147–S154.

Wilbanks, T. J. (2007), 'Scale and sustainability', *Climate Policy,* 7(4): 278–287.

Yearley, S. (2009) 'Sociology and climate change after Kyoto: What roles for social science in understanding climate change?' *Current Sociology,* 57: 389–405.

Yli-Renko, H., Autio, E. and Sapienza, H. (2001) 'Social capital, knowledge acquisition, and knowledge exploitation in young technology-based firms', *Strategic Management Journal,* 22: 587–613.

Young, E. (2001) 'State intervention and abuse of the commons: Fisheries development in Baja California Sur, Mexico', *Annals of the Association of American Geographers,* 91: 283–306.

7 Centrally formulated tourism development plans

Evaluations, attitudes, and behaviors of excluded community members

Atila Yüksel, Fisun Yüksel, Osman Culha,
Berrin Güzel, and Ceren İşçi

Sustainable tourism development is a long-term approach that cultivates economically viable tourism without harming residents' environment or society while simultaneously ensuring fair distribution of costs and benefits (Assante *et al.* 2012). Strategic tourism planning – a process aimed to optimize the benefits of tourism so that the result is a balance of the appropriate quality and quantity of supply with the proper level of demand, without compromising either the locale's socio-economic and environmental developments or its sustainability – lies at the very heart of sustainable development (Edgell *et al.* 2008). For a tourism-related strategy to sustain itself, residents must be willing partners in the process (Ko and Stewart 2002). Communities must be involved in the planning, and their attitudes toward tourism and perceptions of its impact on community life must be continually assessed (Allen *et al.* 1988).

Community involvement in decision making for a tourism plan can play a significant role in the plan's successful implementation – for example, by increasing the local community's sense of ownership of the project (Brandon 1993). This involvement can make the local community more supportive, confident and productive (Eber 1992). Local participation may ensure that greater benefits remain in the community. "The act of allowing individual citizens within a community to take part in the formulation of policies and proposals on issues that affect the whole community" (McEwan 2003: 472) is imperative for successful formulation and implementation of tourism plans (Adomokai and Sheate 2004; Tosun 2000; Yüksel 2003). There is growing consensus that long-term success can be achieved only when planners have a thorough knowledge of the views of the host population (Haywood 1988; Pearce *et al.* 1996; Tosun 2006; van Harssel 1994). Direct and meaningful participation in tourism plan decision-making processes may generate a sense of ownership over the resulting decisions (Murphy 1985; Williams *et al.* 1998). Plan objectives resulting from shared decision-making processes are more likely to be implemented than those taken through conventional planning models (Williams *et al.* 1998).

Lack of community participation has been noted as one of the factors leading to the high rate of tourism plan failures (Burns 1999; Morah 1996; Narayan 2001; Pearce *et al.* 1996; Pizzorno 1992; Yüksel 2003; Yüksel and Yüksel 2007).

Facilitators and inhibitors of community participation, however, have been rarely studied in the tourism literature (Narayan, 2001; Pearce *et al.* 1996; Pizzorno 1992; Yüksel 2003; Yüksel and Yüksel 2007, 2008). There might be several operational, structural or cultural obstacles to community participation in policy or administration (see Tosun 2000, 2006; Komito, 2006; Yüksel and Yüksel 2007 for an extensive discussion). A lack of capacity among the majority of citizens to respond meaningfully to the complex matters of governance may account for nonparticipation (Tosun 2006). Another cause may be a lack of information about the policy decisions that are to be made and a lack of information about how to have input into such decisions (Komito 2006). Another reason may be a lack of desire for greater policy input; if people are content with the existing system, they see no reason for greater participation. Lack of conviction that their policy input would have an impact, as well as a lack of knowledge about how to convey their opinions may lead to greater alienation from the policy process (Komito 2006). Yet another cause may be a distrust of the impartiality and fairness of those making decisions, so that citizens do not believe their interventions would be effective (Komito 2006). In addition to the above factors, residents' perceptions about the intensity of corruption and clientelist relations engaged in by the local authority may prevent active participation of the public in tourism development issues (Yüksel and Yüksel 2007). Practice of governance that allows people greater access to the resources of the state only through the help of political parties and their officers at local levels may alienate active participation of citizens in governmental issues (Yüksel 2003).

Whether a community participates is determined by a variety of factors (Aref 2011). Key elements of this vital step in planning include mutual respect and trust, which are essential in community building and, ultimately, in establishing (pro) active community involvement and commitment to the process of change brought by the plan (Aref 2011). Community members are more likely to participate when they are more supportive of or committed to authorities and the institutions the authorities represent (Brockner *et al.* 1997). Bronfman *et al.*'s study (2009) demonstrates that people rely on their trust in institutions before making judgments about the acceptability of a project. Lack of trust in institutions can make a planning activity unacceptable to people and make them more prone to influence from opponents (Bronfman *et al.* 2009). The literature further suggests that participants will invest their energy in an activity only if they are informed about benefits that are entailed (Butterfoss *et al.* 1993: 322). An individual's desire to join and continue a commitment to a planning effort depends more on this benefit-cost ratio (Wandersman *et al.* 1987). Estimation of the ratio undoubtedly requires awareness (i.e., knowledge) about the plan objectives, the trust the individual holds in institutions, emotional bond to the place, attitude toward further development and prevailing administrative culture.

Previous tourism research has generally focused on tourism planning and development issues and on tourism impact assessments (Yüksel and Yüksel 2000b). However, despite its central effect on the success of the planning activity and development of the tourism industry, limited attention has been paid to tourism administration systems' effect on citizens' institutional trust and their attitudes and behaviors and to the systems' efficiency, effectiveness and potential limitations and implications on tourism plan formulation and implementation processes (Yüksel 2003). Two opposing administrative frameworks, the centralized and decentralized administrative structures, have generally been exercised in tourism management. In general, the centralized form supports the notion of a central steering agency having all information, resources and solutions at its disposal (Kickert *et al.* 1997). The decentralized form involves the transference of power from central agency to local governments and takes the interests of local actors as the point of departure (Turner and Hulme 1997). The centralist approach is generally adopted by developing countries where there is no system that would allow decisions to be taken by the people most immediately affected by them, as tourism usually is considered to be an industry of national concern that should be centrally planned and controlled (Wahab 1997).

The centralist approach results in local tourism development decisions being taken by central rather than by local authorities, and decisions are inevitably made at a distance from the location of local administrative units. This physical distance can impact the willingness of local stakeholders to participate in the decision-making process. Barry (1965: 56) points out that "if bureaucracies are too large or too distant from the people affected by decisions then people become alienated." When individuals do not have access to decision making, this brings about a substantive breakdown in the flow of communication. This alienation from participation, whether as a result of distance or bureaucracy, may impair the legitimacy of the resulting centrally determined policy decisions (Almond and Powell 1966; Barry 1965). Tourism plans developed by a mono-actor form of centralized administration, generally overlook the knowledge, skills and goals of local tourism organizations, both public and private, in their design phase, and subsequently there may be resistance from the implementing bodies, such as from local government and local people (Yüksel and Yüksel 2000a, 2000b). The centralist model appears to neglect the values and interests of implementing bodies, fails to utilize the resources and capacities of local actors and promotes the bureaucratization of the public sector, which therefore diminishes management effectiveness and efficiency (Kickert *et al.* 1997). The main characteristics of centralism – such as coercive decision making, ambiguous balances between responsibility and authority, a distant bureaucracy, limited local participation, uneven power relations, leaving locals with no option other than to accept centrally determined plans – are among the potential reasons thwarting the effectiveness of tourism development substantially (Yüksel and Yüksel 2000a). Mistrust of local people in their elected and appointed representatives who appear to have failed to satisfy local people and an over-centralization of governance in general in a country may thwart participation (Tosun 2006).

Focusing on developing countries, which are characterized by highly centralized planning, this chapter begins by presenting the concepts of clientelism and corruption and their effects on local people's trust and participation intentions in tourism development issues. Attention is particularly drawn to the communication gap between centrally determined plans and locals who are to be affected by the plan's implementation. Because current literature presents a largely Western perspective and deals with the hows of stakeholder inclusion in plan formulation, this chapter takes the perspective of excluded local people in centralist countries as the departing point and discusses likely determinants in locals' evaluations, attitudes and behaviors when they are faced with an implementation stage of an already determined plan by the central institutions.

Based on this gap, the chapter introduces a model that presents the role of community attitudes toward long-term (i.e., strategic) planning as a significant determinant in affecting their evaluations of a centrally determined plan and their intentions for participation in and support for tourism development projects. The role of trust the public holds in public institutions – responsible for governing tourism development, particularly in highly centralized countries – is explained next. The elements of trust – including dependability, reliability, transparency, accountability and accessibility of institutions – are discussed under the concept of good governance, and likely effects of trust on evaluation of a centrally determined plan are explicated. Potential linkages among community power to influence tourism, place attachment, attitudes toward tourism development and how excluded local people in centralist countries find plan proposals are discussed next to contribute to an understanding of community support for sustainable tourism projects, particularly in developing countries governed by centralism.

Administrative culture, clientelism and tourism development

Many planning approaches generally reflect Western perspectives. One is likely to encounter formidable challenges in putting the principles behind these approaches into practice in developing countries, which arguably have dissimilar administrative procedures and cultures. In most developing countries, the large majority of implementing bodies are either relatively weak or have yet to acquire many years of experience in checks and balances. Administrative control presents a particular problem to successful implementation in developing countries (Morah 1996).

> Rampant bureaucratic and political corruption is frequently among the weaknesses presented by this lack of administrative control culture. In these countries affluent opponents of a specific policy who lose in the policy formulation stage often find bribery in the execution stage an especially easy way to neutralize undesirable policy intents . . . Remedying the problem of implementation becomes primarily a question of controlling discretion and maximizing routine and compliance in the bureaucracy, through incentives and sanctions, with the limits to control tending to depend on the statutory power and amount of resources an organization possesses vis-à-vis those it is seeking to influence.
>
> (Morah 1996: 82)

Plan implementation may suffer from the misuse of resources, a lack of accountability, nontransparency in decision making, excessive rules and regulations, priorities that are inconsistent with appropriate development, a high concentration of political power or incompetent administration. All stakeholders may not be on an equal footing at the planning table, and not all participants may work cooperatively to achieve common goals. Some stakeholders might be unwilling to share their entrenched power (Williams *et al.* 1998). Many stakeholders are involved in tourism plans, each pursuing interests that might not be easy to reconcile (UN 1980). The issue of control power in a bureaucracy is perhaps the oldest and most prevalent explanation for the implementation problem (Morah 1996). According to Downs (1967), the traditionally recalcitrant behavior of lower-level bureaucrats not carrying out the instructions of higher-level officials originates from the leakage of authority inside a bureaucracy, which often occurs because implementing officials have different goals, and each official uses his or her discretion in translating orders from above into commands going to those lower in the hierarchy (Morah 1996: 82). In the implementation environment found in many developing countries, flexibility in policy implementation is viewed as part of a deliberate technique for policy-wide accommodation and conflict resolution (Morah 1996). This is often related to the fact that ethnic ties and factions, nepotism and an extended family network system and personal coalitions and patron–client relations form the basis of political activities in these countries and are well-suited to individualized interventions at the execution stage. From the point of view of government officials, community control may be seen as a loss of both their power and their control over the planning process. Thus, the level of public involvement in tourism planning may be limited to a form of tokenism where decisions have already been made by the government (Hall 1998).

Clientelism – a form of social organization common in many developing regions characterized by patron–client relationships in which relatively powerful and rich patrons promise to provide relatively powerless and poor clients with jobs, protection, infrastructure and other benefits in exchange for votes and other forms of loyalty, including labor – severely obstructs the processes of implementing true sustainability (Kermath 2005). A generally negative image of clientelism permeates scholarly analyzes (Henry and Nassis 1999). The view of most researchers (Henry and Nassis 1999; Roniger 1994) is that clientelism undermines development; politicians target the poor for clientelist payoffs, taking advantage of their need for immediate benefits and of their limited information and autonomy. Clientelism discourages the provision of public goods; it deters the entry of challengers, and hence is associated with local political monopolies and pockets of authoritarianism in transitional democracies. It keeps voters' incomes below what they would be if politics were competitive; and because it feeds on poverty, clientelism creates an interest among politicians in economic stagnation. It is the politics of the self-enclosed village, controlled by patrons and notables. Central and/ or local governments misuse the mandate of welfare improvement that have been entrusted to them, while creating funds and/or allocating resources over which they have control, to favor third parties with whom they have political interest networks (Adaman and Carkoglu 2000). "In the absence of a coherent political ideology to motivate and mobilise the electorate on non-patronage based politics, it becomes rational for voters to vote for those which they perceive to be providing them special favors" (Adaman and Carkoglu 2000: 4). Patronage relations prosper when loyalty and support, instead of efficiency, become the benchmark for economic decisions. In terms of resource allocation, clientelism defines the criteria for inclusion and exclusion (Gunes-Ayata 1994).

Clientelism can impede residents' participation in tourism planning projects (Humphreys 1999). Clientelist actions of organization(s) (e.g., local government) and their perceived credibility by residents may be a determining factor, directly or indirectly affecting residents' participation intentions in a tourism planning context (Yüksel and Yüksel 2008, 2007). Such power relations, founded on direct and/or indirect support of one's own people, may adversely influence the degree of trust that the citizens hold for local authorities (Adaman 2000). A low level of confidence is likely to bring about nonparticipation by the majority (Yüksel and Yüksel 2007, 2008). In line with this contention, Tosun (2006) states that mistrust of local people in their elected and appointed representatives who appear to have failed to satisfy local people and an over-centralization of governance in general in the country may thwart participation. In a recent report on sustainable tourism development, the European Union commission warns that clientelism can harm the people's respect for local authority (Dreher *et al.* 2004).

The noncooperation of locals in formal plan preparation, their noncompliance with regulations and implementation and, consequently, their reliance on informal social networks in Crete were reported to have resulted from the dominance of individualism, familism and political clientelism and the consequent mistrust in government (Briassoulis 2003). Other studies report that due to clientelism, the needs of local indigenous communities in some tourist destinations have been ignored so as to serve dominant business interests. For example, in the case of Varna, Bulgaria (a resort town on the Black Sea), in the early 1990s, while residents of the town suffered cuts in electricity supply, the hotels were unaffected (Harrison 1994; cf. Tosun 2000). Building on a study conducted in Turkey, Tosun and Jenkins (1996: 527) point out that

> the Ministry of Tourism and bodies responsible for the authorisation of tourism investment and incentives are accessible to a rich and educated elite and not to the majority of indigenous people in tourist regions. In this sense, there is a big communication gap between communities and decision-makers.

Different forms of clientelism – including friendship, buying of votes, abuse of authority, engaging in campaigning and electioneering while employed in the public service, use of influences and deviation of subsidies – are reported to affect public confidence in political institutions in Colombia (Uruena 2004). Clientelism was reported to have weakened citizens' confidence in the political system and made them nonparticipative in the implementation of government programs (Uruena 2004). Irresponsible conduct of officials, bureaucratic intemperance and clientelism have been shown to be responsible for delays in service provision of public organizations in Bangladesh (Zafarullah and Siddiquee 2001).

Clientelism is seen as defying the modern notion of representation and legal order through appropriation and manipulation of resources by placing "friends" in the strategic positions of power and mechanisms of control (Roniger 1994). The conditions under which political clientelism is expected to flourish are defined in the literature as follows: (1) the existence of a strong state controlling a considerable proportion of the economy; (2) a lack of consensus concerning the operationalization of objective measures of social justice; and (3) a lack of public confidence in the objectivity of measures and processes employed in resource allocation, such as political intervention on more partial grounds is accepted as legitimate and/or inevitable (Henry and Nassis 1999). Patrons and clients are not interested in the generality of equality and legal rules. Rather, they are interested in resources, and they are on the lookout for situations that are to their disadvantage on the basis of favoritism (Roniger 1994). Such networks are used to divert public resources to consolidate power and private gains. They can constrain the enactment of universalistic policies and discourage the development of community participation and support contingent general policy implementation (Gunes-Ayata 1994). Needless to say, the existence of patron–client networks in the public sphere is usually conducive to widespread bribery and corruption. There might be cases where government agents sell "government property for personal gain" (see Adaman and Carkoglu 2000). Government officials may engage in malfeasant behavior, such as giving illegal passage through customs, provided, of course, they have discretion over the provision of government property (as in the case of controlling the customs), whenever the agent's "superiors are either privy to the deal themselves or else cannot monitor the agent's behavior adequately" (Rose-Ackermen 1987: 28). Although an ideal officer should make decisions on the basis of objective, meritocratic criteria, under bribery, a willingness-to-pay procedure will dominate the public sphere, creating losses of welfare and trust (Adaman and Carkoglu 2000). With specific reference to Turkey, OECD (2008) notes that declining trust and confidence in public institutions is rampant. A recent study about the ethical perceptions and outlooks of citizens in Turkey reports that there are more and more complaints of Turkish public officials of local authorities (Adaman and Carkoglu 2000: 38). In fact, unethical behavior and corruption throughout public institutions has become one of the essential problems of Turkish governance. "The implication of clientelism on political culture has been an understanding of democracy that allows people greater access to the resources of the state through the help of political parties" (Sunnar 1994: 77). As a result, active participation of citizens in nongovernmental political and social organizations has remained very low (Sunnar 1994).

Corruption and tourism development

While some authors (e.g., Adaman and Carkoglu 2000) use the terms *corruption* and *clientelism* interchangeably, the literature points out significant differences between clientelism and corruption in terms of resources employed (votes versus money), actors involved (voters–patron/broker versus civil servants), presence of power (asymmetry versus equality), legality versus illegality and public versus secret. Although resources employed are different (votes for favors in clientelism versus money for favors in corruption), two factors provide continuity between clientelism and corruption: (1) both are based on the *direct exchange* of material benefits; and (2) both are built around domination *networks* (Máiz and Requejo 2002; Pizzorno 1992). Often, the presence of one signals the presence of the other.

Corruption, bribery and patron–client relationships may be related to the deficiencies of the political system (Dreher *et al.* 2004). Social and cultural factors (e.g., religion) may shape social attitudes toward social hierarchy and family values and thus may determine the acceptability, or otherwise, of corrupt practices. Economic factors may restrict trade and impose controls on capital flows. This creates rents and hence enhances the incentives to engage in corrupt activities. The significant role of the public sector in the economy affords public officials some degree of discretion in the allocation of goods and services provided, and this increases the likelihood of corruption (Dreher *et al.* 2004). Corruption, bribery and patron–client relations may offer greater gain to officials who exercise control over the distribution of the rights to exploit natural resources.

Corruption, defined as "wrongdoing by those in a special position of trust" (Gildenhuys 2004), "a dishonest or illegal behavior, especially of people in authority" (Oxford Advanced Learner's Dictionary 2000), "the abuse of public power for personal ends" (Frisch 1996), "efforts to secure wealth or power through illegal means – private gain at public expense" (Lipset and Lenz 2000) and "the misuse of public power for private profit" (Smelser 1971) is a self-benefiting behavior exhibited by public officials and all those dedicated to public services (Nazario 2007; Tina and Nnabuko 2012). Political corruption happens when the politicians and political decision makers, who are entitled to formulate, establish and implement the laws in the name of the people, are themselves corrupt. Political corruption takes place when policy formulation and legislation are tailored to benefit politicians and legislators (Nazario 2007). Political corruption is sometimes seen as similar to "corruption of greed" because it affects the manner in which decisions are made; it manipulates political institutions and rules of procedure and distorts the institutions of government (Nazario 2007). Local governments may be more susceptible to corruption because interactions between private individuals and officials happen at higher levels of intimacy and with more frequency at more decentralized levels (Kılınc *et al.* 2009). Bureaucratic corruption is the kind of corruption residents encounter daily at places like hospitals, schools, local licensing offices and police stations. Bureaucratic petty corruption, which is seen as similar to "corruption of need," occurs when one obtains a business from the public sector through inappropriate procedure (Nazario 2007).

Corrupt practices did not begin in modern times; their history is as old as the world. Thus, corruption has been ubiquitous in complex societies from "ancient Egypt, Israel, Rome, and Greece down to the present" (Lipset and Lenz 2000: 112). This does not, however, mean that the magnitude of corruption is equal in every society (Nazario 2007). Corruption, the abuse of public office for private gain, robs citizens' expectations for improvements in service deliveries, undermines trust in public institutions, particularly in the judiciary and security forces, and hinders investments by increasing the cost of doing business and distrust in investment security (Nazario 2007). There are clear correlations between corruption levels and a country's or region's degrees of social, economic and political development; for example, nations with higher perceived levels of corruption also have lower levels of development (Nazario 2007). Corruption is often the manifestation of multifaceted, systemic weakness that requires a broad program of governance, public sector reform and consistent accountability throughout a society and government (World Bank 1992; cf. Nazario 2007). Corruption is destructive of governmental structures and capacity, destroys the legitimacy of the government and makes governance ineffective. It may alienate modern-oriented civil servants and cause them to reduce or withdraw their service and to leave a country (Tina and Nnabuko 2012). Mauro (1997) contends that corruption negatively impacts economic growth and reduces public spending on education. Cooksey (1999) notes that corruption reduces the size of a nation's economic cake, thereby exposing some segments of the population to poverty.

Corruption is one of the biggest challenges that developing countries face when planning for future generations' growth and progress, because it eats away development opportunities (Nazario 2007). Corruption and clientelism have also been part of Western economic development; mafiosi exist in the West as well (Holland 2000). Corruption – even the perception of it – undermines essential cohesiveness in Caribbean countries (Nazario 2007). According to Collier (2002), "the Caribbean has a real political corruption problem that is significantly retarding the region's development." Swanson *et al.* (2001) identified several barriers to implementing environmental management initiatives in the Asian context, including inadequate technology, low finances, limited human resources, poor public environmental awareness, lack of information, lack of skills to collect data, organizational conflict and corruption. Graci's research (2008) identified five themes outlining the main barriers to implementing sustainable tourism initiatives in Indonesia: inadequate resources, particularly funds and information; lack of momentum from business owners; island culture and the isolation of sustainability issues from all other business aspects of the destination/organization; government bureaucracy and corruption; and physical attributes such as infrastructure impediments. Graci (2009) further notes that

> the disparity of policies on the island is dependent upon personal relationships, bribes and government corruption. This has led to frustration on the island especially in terms of volunteering time and money to implement sustainable tourism initiatives. Many initiatives are funded independently and many stakeholders feel powerless to oppose the current structure for fear of making their own lives difficult and negatively affecting their business.

Pointing to the reluctance of public participation in a Brazilian tourism development case, de Araujo and Bramwell (1999) report that some government projects in Brazil have suffered from intense political competition, problems of control and accountability in the bureaucracy, scarcity of funding and other resources, and corruption. Braun (2008) reports barriers in the Honduras tourism development context as corruption, planning, lack of participation, length of process, lack of government and management. Tourism development projects in Honduras suffered from severe corruption because many funds allocated for the project did not reach the project (Braun 2008; Ives 2007). Gutsul (2011) reports lack of planning and policy, corruption and bureaucracy as the major obstacles to sustainable tourism development in Ukraine. According to Gunfadurdoss *et al.* (2012), Tunisia's tourism suffered from severe corruption at the highest levels of power. Duffy (2002: 556) notes that "the links between the public and private sector, local elites and external capital constitute a shadow state, and this is nowhere more apparent than in the inability of the formal state apparatus to enforce environmental legislation in the ecotourism industry" in Belize. Tina and Nnabuko (2012) identify corruption being the greatest challenge of tourism in Nigeria for decades and a major impediment for tourism development. In the context of the Canary Islands, Bianchi (2004: 495) observes that

> the legacy of uneven development and the entrenched power of regional economic and political élites, is likely to undermine the prospects for a just model of sustainable tourism, and in particular, consolidate the continuing privatisation of space and increase socio-spatial inequalities across the region.

Zafarullah and Siddiquee (2001) indicate that bribery, rent seeking and misappropriation of funds, irresponsible conduct of officials, bureaucratic intemperance, patronage and clientelism adversely affect performance of public organizations in Bangladesh. Holland (2000) notes that corruption and clientelism inhibit the development of trust within and between communities, limiting the capacity of individuals or groups to take risks in the marketplace, a characteristic essential to the natural growth of a market economy. "Inadequate social capital, together with the historical determinants at play in southern Albania, seriously challenged the opportunity to develop 'deep' sustainable tourism" (Holland 2000: 511). Corruption is a daunting obstacle to sustainable tourism development, and it results in a major loss of public funds needed for appropriate development, both in developed and developing countries (Lambsdorff 2004). With specific reference to Kusadası case in Turkey, Yüksel and Yüksel (2007, 2008) found that that corruption and clientelism (i.e., social networks) played an important role in tourism development, as resource allocation decisions are prone to manipulation by local/central patrons or clients, and such relations are likely to put off participatory/collaborative tourism development. They suggest that, considering other factors remain the same (*ceterus paribus*), the nature and intensity of patronage relations and corruption are likely to determine the perceived efficiency of local government services. This in turn will have implications for tourism development through the erosion of community trust in public institutions, which is likely to result in the local community isolating itself from the tourism development process (Yüksel and Yüksel 2008).

The proposed model

Carried out in a wider political, social and economical environment, planning is a communication-intensive process with multiple phases involving engagement with a community not only in formulation but also during the implementation stage. Several examples demonstrate that engagement with community almost never exists particularly in the developing world or comes to an end once the plan is formulated. Engagement with the community, however, needs to be continual to inform all stakeholders and get their support for the centrally determined plan. Understanding the likely precedents of support by initially excluded community members can promote sustainable tourism because authorities and practitioners can assess these precedents to predict the level of support by their residents (Lee 2013). The stakeholder theory suggests that the various groups can and should have a direct influence on managerial decision making (Jones 1995). As Freeman (1984: 46) succinctly puts it, "to be an effective strategist, you must deal with those groups that can affect you, while to be responsive (and effective in the long run) you must deal with those groups that you can affect." As such, effective management demands synchronous attention to the genuine interests of all appropriate stakeholders (Donaldson and Preston 1995). Clarkson (1995) underlines this premise and warns that failure to retain participation of even a single primary stakeholder group will result in the failure of the organization (Sautter and Leisen 1999).

Among many other reasons for limited community support and hence implementation failures, the proposed model assumes that in cases where community members do not trust each other and/or government institutions as result of the intensity of corruption and clientelism in centralized countries, their level of attachment to their place is low, they do not hold positive attitudes toward tourism development, their willingness and power to influence tourism development is low, their attitudes toward long-term planning are unfavorable and they are likely to be or reluctant to participate. Under such circumstances, even the best plans formulated by central institutions are destined to come to a standstill. In addition to determinants suggested by previous studies – including community attachment, community concern, environmental sensitivity, perceived benefits and costs (Gursoy *et al.* 2002), community attachment and community involvement (Lee 2013), institution trust, neighborhood conditions, power to influence and community satisfaction (Nunkoo and Ramkissoon 2011) – borrowing a consumer-behaviorist perspective, the model introduces tourism administration system and community attitudes toward long-term planning as a determinant of understanding and addressing of community support for centrally determined tourism development projects (see Figure 7.1).

Although many studies have sought to understand the importance of attitudes by focusing on local attitudes and perceptions toward mass tourism development, a review of the literature suggests that community attitudes (or community orientation) toward long-term planning is much less common. Community members may differ in their long-term planning attitude, and an examination of local attitudes toward long-term planning may help authorities and practitioners

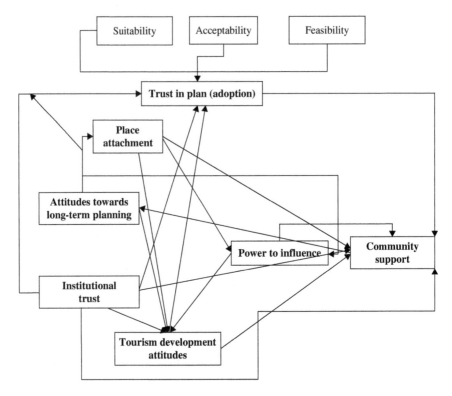

Figure 7.1 Determinants of excluded community members' evaluation and support of a centrally determined plan

understand how community members feel about utilizing long-term planning as a means to balance conservation and development (Lai and Nepal 2006). Community attitudes toward tourism development are determined mainly by a set of salient beliefs that represent the information that individuals possess about development (Lai and Nepal 2006).

In addition to reasons such as economic benefits generated from tourism – including employment opportunities, tourism revenues, infrastructure improvement, foreign exchange, education and awareness, relationship with authorities, history and length of local involvement in tourism and proximity to protected areas, all of which can drive local communities to or not to endorse tourism development – community attitude toward long-term planning is another element that may explain why a community supports tourism development. In other words, a strong community attitude toward long-term planning is likely to determine whether a centrally determined tourism development project is to be embraced by the local community and whether the community members are willing to invest their personal resources (time, energy) to realize the centrally determined tourism plan within their community. The more a person believes that long-term planning is needed to maximize one's personal well-being and own interests and to maintain stability, diversity and harmony of the ecosystem, the more likely that person will support implementation of a centrally determined tourism development plan. Limited empirical evidence suggests that residents' value orientations toward nature strongly affect residents' community attachment levels, attitudes toward tourism impacts and perceptions of desirable tourism development options (Doh 2006).

The proposed model presumes that in cases where there is a high public trust in institutions in charge of tourism, a community is more likely to accommodate a plan proposal or a predetermined plan developed by these institutions and support its implementation. In line with the literature (see Nunkoo and Ramkissoon 2011), the model considers that trust in central institutions in charge of tourism develop-ment is likely to strengthen one's attachment to the community and to surround-ing landscapes, and this may influence how residents perceive potential impacts of a growing tourism industry (Banks 2010; McCool and Martin 1994; Sheldon and Var 1984; Um and Crompton 1987; Williams *et al.* 1998). Despite the lack of interest groups associated with many environmental policies, there is increasing recognition among scholars that a sense of local context – the way in which an individual relates to and perceives the natural environment – is important to the level of environmental concern and action (Morison and Brown 2011). According to Mesch (1996), more attached residents tend to dislike environmental disruption and avoid attempts to change the physical nature of an area. It has been claimed that attachment to a place involves care and concern for the place (Relph 1976), which denotes that members with a strong attachment to a place probably will oppose environmental and social degradation (Vorkinn and Riese 2001). Because place attachment has proven to influence both the perception of and response to actual changes in the environment, it could be expected that the values reflected through place attachment also would influence the attitudes toward specific pro-posed changes (Vorkinn and Riese 2001). The more attached residents feel to a community, the more interest they will have in getting involved in community change efforts and the more favorably they will regard the ability of the commu-nity to deal with change (Ayres and Potter 1980; Smaldone *et al.* 2005).

Previous studies have demonstrated that residents' attitudes toward tourism may be related directly to the degree or stage of development within the host community (e.g., Butler 1980; Doxey 1975). Drawing on social exchange theory, previous research has indicated that the perceived benefits strongly affect the level of support for tourism development (Gursoy *et al.* 2002; Gursoy and Kendall 2006; Gursoy and Rutherford 2004; Kaltenborn *et al.* 2008; Nicholas *et al.* 2009), whereas the perceived costs significantly and negatively influence support for tourism development (Gursoy *et al.* 2002; Gursoy and Kendall 2006; Gursoy and Rutherford 2004; Lee 2013; Nicholas *et al.* 2009; Nunkoo and Ramkissoon 2011). Based on social exchange theory, Lee (2013) found perceived benefits and costs were effective predictors of the support for sustainable tourism development. Thus, attitudes toward tourism development are expected to influence the extent to which the centrally determined plan is found more or less suitable, feasible and acceptable by the initially excluded community members. Moreover, the personal power to influence tourism-related issues should be carefully taken into account, because this is likely to determine how the community will react to a centrally determined planning activity. Increasing the perceived control that the host community members have over community decisions regarding tourism development increases pro-tourism attitudes (Ap 1992; Gursoy *et al.* 2002). Favorable attitudes toward tourism development and a higher degree of individual power to influence tourism are likely to enhance community participation and support for tourism developments.

Attitudes toward long-term planning

An understanding of community attitudes is essential in planning. Ritchie and Inkari (2006) suggest that the perceptions and attitudes of residents toward the impacts of any proposed model of tourism development should be considered in the creation of tourism policies and plans. Community attitudes toward tourism development have long been studied. Community beliefs and attitudes about long-term planning, however, need to be integrated into tourism planning. Basically, beliefs – a person's judgment about what he or she considers true or false – form his or her attitudes, which are strongly predictive of behavior and form an individual's consistent tendency to respond favorably or unfavorably toward an object, concept or individual (Ajzen and Fishbein 1980). "Attitude is a psychological tendency that is expressed by evaluating a particular entity with some degrees of favor or disfavor . . . evaluating refers to all classes of evaluative responding, whether overt or covert, cognitive, affective, or behavioral" (Eagly and Chaiken 1993: 1). A better understanding of the relationship between residents' long-term planning beliefs, attitudes and participation behavior may help managers and practitioners develop better ways to address, identify and engage residents in plan formulation and implementation.

The importance of the natural and social environment to the community and the perceived need for better planning are likely to vary among community members, and this will influence their cognitions and evaluations (Williams and Lawson 2001). Sirakaya *et al.* (2008) reported that a large segment in a community is likely to value a long-term planning approach to tourism development. Residents' values and preferences for preservation and utilization of resources may vary based upon their attitude about humans' relationship to the natural environment (Gursoy *et al.* 2002). Researchers suggest that residents with ecocentric values are likely to prefer that resources be allocated to protect and preserve the environment, while those with anthropocentric inclinations favor transforming the environment to fulfill human needs and desires (Jurowski *et al.* 1995; Uysal *et al.* 1994). As a result, each community member may hold a different attitude toward long-term planning.

Long-term planning concern is thought to be positively related to community participation and support for tourism development activities. Strategic planning may be viewed by some community members as a time-consuming, unnecessary and bureaucratic process. Absence of a positive attitude toward long-term planning may have consequences on overall quality of tourism development in a community. This lack of support may be shaped by both direct and indirect experiences of the individual with tourism development in his or her community. In particular, when negative impacts of tourism are experienced, community members may consider long-term planning as a necessity to alleviate developmental problems. When positive impacts are dominant, community members may believe that long-term planning is a prerequisite to sustain and enhance positive impacts. Moreover, culture – the values, beliefs and behaviors that people hold in common, transmit across generations and use to interpret their experiences – may play a significant role in whether a community participates in a planning process.

Along with other factors, including trust in institutions, the extent to which the community members think that the future must be planned is likely to affect their overall evaluations about and their reactions to what is going on in terms of tourism development. Negative community attitudes toward long-term tourism planning raise concern that community-driven tourism planning may be an unachievable ideal. Gursoy *et al.* (2002) suggest that the "level of concern" residents feel about their community may influence their willingness to support tourism. They argue that community perceptions are influenced by residents' concern for their community, their emotional attachment to it, the degree to which they are environmentally sensitive and the extent to which they use the same resource base that tourists use. The more concern residents have for their community, the more likely they are to perceive that the local tourism economy needs assistance in terms of planning (Gursoy *et al.* 2002). This, in turn, is likely to mediate how they perceive the costs and benefits of the industry. If they feel that new investments are needed to be planned in their region, they are likely to evaluate the benefits more positively and minimize the negative impacts (Gursoy *et al.* 2002). Duran and Ozkul's (2012) research indicates that residents' support is likely to be strongly affected especially by "long-term planning need" for sustainability. Hence, we purpose *the attitude toward long-term planning* as an exogenous construct in determining community intentions for supporting tourism development projects.

Proposition 1: The higher the perceived need for long-term planning, the more likely it is that residents will approve of a centrally determined plan.

Trust in leading institutions and their plans

A growing research effort is devoted to the definition of trust, and to distinguishing forms of trust and examining in what situations trust might be relevant and why (Höppner 2009). In its simplest form, trust refers to a person's beliefs in or expectations toward another party (Höppner, 2009). Trust can be general or context-specific. The individual's evaluation of one's competence, reliability, openness, honesty, caring, consistency and fairness contribute to trust judgment (Butler 1991). The building of trust has been considered as a goal and indicator of success criteria in participatory planning projects (Höppner 2009). Numerous studies have proposed that locals are more likely to accept proposals, outcomes or measures if they trust the responsible decision-making body (e.g., Connick and Innes 2003; Webler and Tuler 2002; White 2001). "Even unpopular measures are more effectively 'sold' if the body in charge is perceived as trustworthy" (Höppner 2009: 1047). Trust in responsible authorities is likely connected to people's perception of the planning process (Höppner 2009). It has been emphasized that to trust the actors who rule the game means to have confidence in the procedure and the quality of engagement (Lauber and Knuth 1999; Parkins and Mitchell 2005; Smith and McDonough 2001; Webler and Tuler 2002). In particular, the perception of fair participation is considered to be influenced by the public's perception of the decision-making body (Illsley 2003).

The study of trust in various contexts has contributed the belief that trust is necessarily related to cooperative behavior. Moreover, it is not only cooperation in the implementation of measures that is regarded as hinging on trust, but also people's intention to participate in planning processes in general. Locals were found to trust the planning committee if its members were perceived as competent, honest, open, fair, reliable, reciprocating, respectful and committed to fulfilling locals' personal interests (Höppner 2009). Trust in the planning committee was directly and positively related to the acceptance of the planning process and confidence in its outcomes (Höppner 2009). Jongeneel *et al.* (2008) found that trust in the government is an important explanatory factor for participation in nature conservation and tourism.

Political economy suggests that government has a central role in tourism planning and regulation of the sector (Bramwell 2011). Thus, trust is conceptualized as residents' trust in government actors (also referred to as political trust or citizens' trust in institutions) involved in tourism development (Nunkoo and Smith 2013). Political trust is the belief that the political system or some of it will produce preferred outcomes even in the absence of constant scrutiny (Miller and Listhaug 1990; Shi 2001). It is vital for good governance, sustainability of the political system and democratic consolidation (Nunkoo *et al.* 2012).

Political trust depends on the government's ability, in the eyes of the people, to deliver effective polices (Wong *et al.* 2011). Nunkoo *et al.* (2012) found that economic performance and political performance of institutions are positively correlated with trust. This suggests that the more positive citizens' evaluations are of both the economic and political performance of tourism institutions, the higher their level of political trust. Positive perceptions about the political performance of tourism institutions indicate existence of effective and democratic tourism governance, which is necessary for furthering the objectives of sustainable tourism (Bramwell and Lane 2011). Public trust in tourism institutions may have wide-ranging positive consequences for tourism development (Nunkoo *et al.* 2012). Residents' support for tourism is a prerequisite for the sustainable development of the industry (Nunkoo and Ramkissoon, 2011) and may be used as an indicator of good tourism governance. Nunkoo *et al.*'s (2012) research provides empirical support for the argument that s higher trust in tourism institutions results in higher support for tourism development. This finding is consistent with the argument that political trust is important for gaining support for development (Norris 1999; Nunkoo and Ramkissoon 2011).

Given that participation in tourism planning is a process of social interaction involving different actors, trust represents a crucial aspect in structuring mutual relationships. Trust may foster and facilitate open dialogue and dynamic, productive cooperation among actors as well as influence public support for decisions and projects (Hassan *et al.* 2011; Höppner 2009; Nunkoo and Smith 2013). In a political context, trust ties citizens to institutions that are intended to represent them (Bianco 1994; Höppner 2009). Because participation is a process of social interaction involving different actors, trust represents a crucial aspect in structuring mutual relationships (Hassan *et al.* 2011). Usually the perception of trust-related attributes or dimensions of trust – such as transparency, openness, competence and reliability – are assessed as empirical indicators for trust (Hassan *et al.* 2011). Openness and transparency play a role in trust in institutional arrangements. Through openness and transparency, understanding and predictability are able to grow (de Vos and van Tatenhove 2011). Höppner (2009) found that people who believed that the planning authority treats them in a reciprocal, reliable, respectful and equal manner, is honest, performs competently and informs transparently were more likely to have positive views of the planning process.

The proposed model assumes that because the majority of community members would not be able to participate in development stage of a plan in highly centralized countries, limited or no information may result in hesitations and reservations about the central plan and what it brings. Limited time and other resources, as well as skepticism by groups that have been involved in conflict over tourism development, may make potential participants wary about joining and supporting (Jamal and Getz 1995). Thus, communication with the public at large is a requisite to enable them to comprehend the planning intentions in detail.

Johnson *et al.* (2011) suggest evaluating strategic options based on three key criteria: suitability, feasibility and acceptability. Suitability deals with the overall rationale of the strategy and its fit with the organization's mission. Strategic choices should be suitable and compatible within the current and expected local environment. Feasibility is concerned with whether the organization has the resources it needs to implement the strategy. Acceptability is concerned with stakeholder expectations and the expected outcomes of implementing the strategy. The requirement of strategy suitability relates to the ability of planning that can specifically affect the composition and usage of resources by a series of measures in accordance with the conditions of the macro- and micro-environment.

The requirement of acceptability focuses on the satisfaction of the key stakeholders through the development of demand for tourism in the destination. Finally, the requirement of the strategy feasibility is aimed at creating conditions for strategy implementation (Martin and Tomas 2012). How excluded community members assess a centrally determined plan and support its implementation represents a dilemma. Nevertheless, if they are given a chance to self-assess a centrally determined plan's contents, the model assumes that the excluded community members are likely to judge the plan's suitability to the local needs, the extent to which the plan outcomes can fulfill the community expectations and the efficiency of measures taken to secure successful implementation. The model considers these three dimensions – suitability, acceptability and feasibility – as essential components of trust for the centrally determined plan. This plan evaluation and resulting feeling of trust for the plan itself cannot be separated from individuals' general attitudes toward planning, attitudes toward tourism development and institutional trust. According to the proposed model, the extent to which individuals find the leading institutions trustworthy will affect how they evaluate the plan proposed by the institution (i.e., whether they find the plan suitable, feasible and acceptable). Depending on the outcome of their evaluation, locals may support or reject implementation, or they may decide nothing to do with implementation.

> *Proposition 2: The more the leading institutions related to tourism development are perceived as transparent, reliable and dependable, the higher the likelihood that individuals will find satisfactory the centrally determined plan developed by these institutions.*

Public trust in institutions is important for gaining political support for development (Klingemann 1999; Norris 1999; Nunkoo and Ramkissoon 2011). Trust in government institutions also affects the level of trust in other domains of life (Lovell 2001; Nunkoo and Ramkissoon 2011). The level of trust that the community holds for leading institutions is likely to determine the extent to which an individual feels happy in living in a community. Grzeskowiak *et al.*'s (2003) study on residents of Genesee County, Michigan, demonstrated that the residents' level of institutional trust was a good determinant of their overall satisfaction with the community. Thus, trust in local institutions contributes significantly to residents' attachment to their community. Widgery's (1982) research also reveals that residents' trust in government and the political system are significant predictors of community-wide satisfaction. Residents with high levels of trust were found to be more satisfied with their community than residents with low levels of trust (Widgery 1982; Nunkoo and Ramkissoon 2011). The effect of institutional trust on overall community satisfaction was found to be statistically significant by Nunkoo and Ramkissoon (2011), suggesting that the level of trust residents have in their institution is a good predictor of their overall satisfaction with the community. Losses of trust and not trusting the system were found to damage attachment and connectivity among community members (Curry and Fisher 2012). Residents who feel government effectively manages tourism will be more positive toward the environmental impacts of tourism (Assante *et al.* 2012). Based on the above reviewed literature, the model proposes that:

> *Proposition 3: The more the central institutions are perceived as transparent, reliable and dependable, the higher the likelihood that individuals will develop more favorable attitudes toward tourism development.*
>
> *Proposition 4: Because government institutions can influence residents' quality of life, the more transparent, reliable and dependable the institutions are perceived to be, the higher the likelihood that individuals will develop attachment to their place.*

Proposition 5: The more the central institutions are perceived as transparent, reliable and dependable, the higher the likelihood that individuals will invest more of their personal resources to influence tourism development.

Proposition 6: The more the central institutions are perceived as transparent, reliable and dependable, the higher the likelihood that individuals will intend to participate in tourism development activities.

Power to influence

Power denotes the ability of one actor to influence policy decisions that affect others (Nunkoo and Ramkissoon 2011; Thibaut and Kelley 1959; Wrong 1979). Previous research has shown that residents' perception of impacts depends on their perceived level of power in relation to the tourism sector or the level of personal influence over tourism (Nunkoo and Ramkissoon 2011). Kayat's (2002) research demonstrates that powerful residents had positive attitudes and strongly supported future development. Madrigal (1993) also highlights that favorable attitudes were positively related to perceived personal influence over tourism development but negatively related to perceived business influence over tourism. Nunkoo and Ramkissoon (2011) found that residents who perceived themselves as having enough power to influence development viewed the impacts positively. Less powerful residents viewed the sector as resulting in several costs (Nunkoo and Ramkissoon 2011).

Community participation increases people's sense of control over issues that affect their lives and promotes self-confidence and self-awareness (Aref *et al.* 2010). Community participation provides a sense of community to take responsibility for oneself and others and a readiness to share and interact (Aref *et al.* 2010). Community members who believe that they are able to influence policy decisions are likely to be more supportive of tourism and to have more favorable intention to participate in tourism development issues. Under the effect of their perceived trust to the leading institutions, personal stance on long-term planning, level of attachment and attitude toward tourism development, the community members may be willing to influence tourism development within their community. They will try to influence tourism development by exchanging views in meetings with community leaders and planning authorities or by devoting personal time and energy to follow occasions to contribute to tourism development.

Proposition 7: The more power an individual has to influence tourism, the more likely the individual is to support the proposed plan and participate in official planning exercises.

Community attachment

An important consideration in tourism planning is the impact of changes brought by new development. Several studies have suggested that attachment to the community and place is one factor that affects people's perception and support of tourism impacts (Gursoy and Rutherford 2004; Um and Crompton 1987). Hence, the level of attachment that a community member feels toward her place and community may hold significance in understanding whether plans can be adopted and hence supported by those who were not involved in its development. Etzioni's (1996: 304) "responsive community" concept suggests that "community members are members of one another, that people are ontologically embedded in a social existence." This suggests that the thinner the community bonds, the more alienated and unreasonable members tend to be (Nunkoo *et al.* 2012). Hence, it is essential for tourism institutions to engage in policies and activities that help in developing affective bonds among community members, because this is likely to promote general interpersonal trust in the society (Nunkoo *et al.* 2012). "They should support social, community, and other civic organizations that can help community members to interact. Such interactions generate social capital and improve interpersonal trust which is likely to spill over to political institutions" (Nunkoo *et al.* 2012: 1557).

As Frederickson and Anderson (1999: 22) point out, "it is through one's interactions with the particulars of a place that one creates their own personal identity and deepest-held values." If people's identities and values are indeed informed by places they deem significant, then it follows that people's bonds with those places will shape their engagement in such places, whether to maintain or improve them, respond to changes within them or simply to stay in that place (Pretty *et al.* 2003). For example, proposed tourism development projects can be perceived by some community members as a threat to place attachments because they will change the physical fabric of the neighborhood. Those who feel their relationships to their community places are threatened by new development may consequently resist a proposal regardless of its potential value. To adequately understand and respond to such reactions, it is critical to uncover and address these latent place and community attachments. Nunkoo and Ramkissoon (2010) considered community satisfaction, a precondition for community attachment, to be a determinant of residents' attitudes that reveals the former to be a good predictor of community responses to development. Residents who were satisfied with their community were more likely to perceive tourism as having positive impacts (Nunkoo and Ramkissoon 2010).

A sense of community and participation are the main factors that can affect tourism development (Aref 2011). Bopp *et al.* (2000: 113) define sense of community as: "the quality of human relationship that makes it possible for people to live together in a healthy and sustainable way." The emotional connection plays an important role, because this connection can motivate community members to participate in neighborhood improvement planning efforts (Manzo and Perkins 2006) and may enhance long-term sustainability as a broad basis for tourism development planning (Mair *et al.* 2005: 175–176). Especially in the participatory planning that requires the active participation of community in all stages of planning, a sense of community is of vital importance as a factor affecting the level of participation.

The lack of a sense of community has been reported as one of the reasons that people do not participate in development activities (Aref 2011; Tsai 1996).

Without community participation and a sense of community, tourism development could not be achieved. Developing a sense of community contributes to participation by enabling people to feel connected and motivated to live in harmony and work together toward common goals (Aref 2011). A sense of community can be seen as the capacity of the local people to participate in development activities (Cupples 2005; cf. Aref *et al.* 2010). Another example of empirical evidence supporting the link between levels of community attachment and participation in projects is reported by Kyle *et al.* (2004), who found that mountain climbers create place attachment through participating in activities and affect the attitude that climbers have toward mountain climbing. Li and Wang (2008) believe that place attachment can affect residents' tourism cognition, attitude and tourism experience. Brown *et al.* (2003) found that place attachments and sense of community play a significant role in neighborhood revitalization efforts. Rivlin's (1987) study of a Brooklyn neighborhood reported that attachment to the neighborhood was a precondition for the development of a sense of community among neighbors.

McCool and Martin (1994) discussed residents' attachment to their community and investigated whether those with strong feelings were more negative toward tourism than those who were less attached. In their study of Montana, they found that those with stronger attachment did have stronger views relating to both positive and negative impacts, and those with more attachment were more informed and hence more concerned. The findings of Williams *et al.* (1995) suggest that residents are likely to react differently depending on their length of residency and the source of attachment to or identification with the region. Jurowski *et al.* (1997) found that residents who are more attached to their community display more positive attitudes toward the economic and social impacts of tourism.

Previous studies have reported that the more attached people are to their community, the more likely they are to perceive that the local economy needs assistance (Gursoy *et al.* 2002). This is likely to mediate how they perceive the costs and benefits of a proposed plan. If they feel that new investments are needed in their region, they are likely to evaluate the benefits more positively and minimize the negative impacts (Gursoy and Rutherford 2004; Gursoy *et al.* 2002). Walker and Ryan (2008) found that place attachment strongly influenced residents' willingness to engage in conservation and land use planning strategies in the rural landscape in a small but fast-growing town in Maine, New England. Community attachment and place attachment were significantly correlated with resident attitudes toward tourism, especially in the areas of economic benefit and urbanization or overcrowding. Residents with higher levels of both community attachment and place attachment were more likely to agree that tourism was causing overcrowding in their community (Banks 2010). Sense of place, however, does not necessarily lead to better management strategies without continuous and proactive community involvement (Aref 2011; Nunkoo and Ramkissoon 2011).

Proposition 8: The higher the level of place attachment, the more receptive and participative the individual will become to what is going on, in terms of proposed development activities, in the community.

Proposition 9: The higher the level of place attachment, the more likely the individual will develop positive attitudes toward development opportunities brought by tourism.

Attitudes toward tourism development

Not all individuals support tourism development to the same extent. Variations in the level of support are often due to variations in community members' dependence on tourism. While some may view tourism as offering greater benefits than costs, others may refuse tourism development due to concerns about its so-called devastating effects on the society, economy and ecology. Thus, how community members view tourism development plays a significant role in their subsequent evaluations, intentions and behaviors. We think that attitudes toward long-term planning, attachment to the place and trust in government institutions in general are likely to influence development of attitudes toward tourism. The greater support for long-term planning is expected to result in more favorable attitudes toward tourism development within the community.

Research on resident attitudes indicates that residents' opinions on tourism development within a community can vary greatly. For example, several studies have shown that people who benefit from tourism perceive greater economic but lesser social or environmental impact from tourism than those who do not (Lankford and Howard 1994; Milman and Pizam 1988; Pizam 1978; Prentice 1993). Other studies suggest a positive relationship between residents' perceptions of the positive impacts and support (Gursoy and Rutherford 2004; Lee *et al.* 2010; Nunkoo and Ramkissoon 2010). Studies indicate that a higher perception of negative impacts leads to lower support (Gursoy and Rutherford 2004). Sustained low trust in public institutions challenges regime legitimacy (Hetherington 1998; Miller and Listhaug 1999) and may hinder the acceptability of tourism in a region. Residents' trust in tourism planning institutions is likely to influence attitudes toward the industry (Nunkoo and Ramkissoon 2011).

Proposition 10: The more favorable attitudes are to development, the higher the individuals' readiness for taking action for tourism development will be.
Proposition 11: The more favorable attitudes are to development, the higher the likelihood that the individuals will adopt the centrally determined plan.
Proposition 12: The more favorable attitudes are to development, the higher the individuals' support for implementation.

Conclusion

A review of planning literature in tourism suggests that failure is more common than success. Several factors may account for why most planning efforts end in disappointment. Among other reasons frequently highlighted by previous research, we believe that the views, attitudes and reactions, shaped by the administrative culture of initially excluded community members, must be taken into account. This is because even the best plan formulation cannot include all the community members. Thus, an understanding of how excluded community members react to a centrally determined plan is warranted. Based on the concepts discussed above, it could be stated that the success of planning increasingly relies on the effectiveness, efficiency and dependability of the institutions, the administrative framework and the community's receptiveness to long-term planning. A trustable framework that promotes participative decision making, delineates clear balances between responsibility and authority and effectively coordinates the fragmented activities carried out by different public and private sector agencies and organizations undoubtedly enhances the chances of success (Yüksel 2003).

A framework fostering coercive decision making, resulting in ambiguous balances between responsibility and autonomy and inducing a distant bureaucracy and uneven power relations between public and private agencies, can undermine the legitimacy of policy decisions and their implementation (Yüksel 2003). Thus, successful tourism planning and development requires a process that supports a democratic and transparent participation system in decision making, promotes greater accountability of institutions to those people they are instituted to serve, improves the availability of information and optimizes the use of resources by clarifying responsibilities, authority and standards (Yüksel 2003). This will increase public trust in public institutions; therefore, their participation in planning will increase.

Research suggests that institutional trust is a complex variable comprising honesty, integrity, transparency and competence (Johnson 1999; Lang and Hallman 2005). Effective governance is central to the creation and maintenance of an environment that fosters strong and equitable development, and it is essential to the achievement of social and economic objectives. In general, governance is described as "the manner in which power is exercised in the management of a country's economic and social resources for development" (World Bank 1992). It is a process that includes the legislative, administrative and judicial functions of government (or the governing body within the subsystem) and the role of non-government institutions and individuals in relation to them (Government and Institutions Department [GID] 1993). Effective governance is concerned with the legitimacy, accountability and competency of the process by which the governing body instills trust in citizens. *Legitimacy* is the concept where "there is a range of institutions outside government which represent other interests and provide a counterweight to the power of government; in other words healthy civil society" (GID 1993: 5). *Accountability* is the driving force that

> generates the pressure for key actors involved to be responsible for and to ensure good public service performance. It may focus on regularity where public servants are expected to follow the formal rules and regulations of a bureaucratic type of organisation.
>
> (Paul 1991: 5)

Accountability entails transparency of decision making and relationships, availability of information, including freedom of the press, and some means of holding to account those who have responsibilities (GID 1993: 5). Accountability is established "where rulers readily delegate authority, where subordinates confidently exercise their discretion, where the abuse of power is given its proper name, and is properly punished under a rule of law which stands above political faction" (Londsdale 1986: 135, in World Bank 1992). *Competency* means the capacity needed to formulate policies and strategies and to make timely decisions both on long-term and immediate issues, implement policy decisions and manage the delivery of services (GID 1993).

The model presented in this chapter proposes that community members' perception of how the central institution(s) perform determines the individuals' evaluations, intentions and behaviors in a planning context. The extent to which the leading institution is perceived to be dependable, transparent, reliable, competent, accountable, democratic, participative, constructive and accessible is likely to influence the (re)action of community members to the propositions and projects coming from these institutions. The model extends place attachment theory, which can help us understand how particular preferences, perceptions and emotional connections to place relate to community social cohesion, organized participation and community development.

Often the focus in community development and planning is on economic, political or social dynamics both within the community and between the community and public agencies (Aref 2011). However, the unique qualities and meanings of the specific physical setting in which community planning and development take place can play a vital role in the process as well. Thoughts, feelings and beliefs about local community places – what psychologists call "intra-psychic" phenomena – affect behaviors toward such places, thus influencing whether and how one might participate in local planning efforts. Moreover, both sense of community and place attachment are likely to manifest themselves behaviorally in participation (Aref 2010, 2011).

Unfortunately, many studies have ignored these country-based administrative culture and place-based psychological ties to the community, but these can make critical contributions to effective community development and planning efforts, because they are a source of community power and collective action (Aref 2011).

As the current literature largely deals with hows of stakeholder inclusion in plan formulation, the model takes initially excluded local people as the departing point and introduces likely determinants in their evaluations, attitudes and behaviors when they face a centrally determined plan. The model presents the role of community attitudes toward long-term planning as a significant determinant in affecting community members' evaluations of a centrally determined plan and intentions for participation in and support for tourism development projects. The role of trust the public holds in public institutions, responsible for governing tourism development particularly in highly centralized countries, lies at the heart of the model. The model recognizes that elements of trust – including dependability, reliability, transparency, accountability and accessibility of institutions – are likely to determine how the public evaluates a centrally determined plan. Several factors are likely to intervene in why some initially excluded community members find the centrally determined plan more acceptable, suitable and feasible than others. Potential linkages among community power to influence tourism, place attachment, attitudes toward tourism development and how initially excluded local people find a centrally determined plan need to be examined to contribute to an understanding of community support for sustainable tourism projects.

References

Adaman, F. (2000) 'Halk kime güveniyor' [Public trust], *Gorus*, 5(November): 40–46.

Adaman, F. and Carkoglu, A. (2000, June) 'Reforming the public services delivery mechanisms in Turkey: Challenges and opportunities ahead', *Report of Euro-Mediterranean Forum of Economic Institutes*, Amman, Jordan: Euro-Mediterranean Forum of Economic Institutes, 1–54.

Adomokai, R. and Sheate, W. R. (2004) 'Community participation and environmental decision-making in the Niger Delta', *Environmental Impact Assessment Review*, 24(5): 495–518.

Ajzen, I. and Fishbein, M. (1980) *Understanding Attitudes and Predicting Social Behavior*, Englewood Cliffs, NJ: Prentice Hall.

Allen, L. R., Long, P. T. Perdue, R. R. and Kieselbach, S. (1988) 'The impact of tourism development on residents' perception of community life', *Journal of Travel Research*, 27(1): 16–21.

Almond, G. A. and Powell, G. B. (1966) *Comparative Politics: A Developmental Approach*, Boston: Little, Brown.

Ap, J.(1992) 'Residents' perceptions on tourism impacts', *Annals of Tourism Research*, 19(4): 665–690.

Aref, F. (2010) 'Residents' attitudes towards tourism impacts: A case study of Shiraz, Iran', *Tourism Analysis*, 15(2): 253–261.

Aref, F. (2011) 'Sense of community and participation for tourism development', *Life Science Journal*, 8(1): 20–25.

Aref, F., Redzuan, M. and Gill, S. S. (2010), 'Dimensions of community capacity building: A review of its implications in tourism development', *Journal of American Science*, 6(1): 172–180.

Assante, L. M., Wen, H. I. and Lottig, K. J. (2012) 'An empirical assessment of residents' attitudes for sustainable tourism development: A case study of Oahu, Hawaii', *Journal of Sustainability and Green Business*, 1. Online: www.aabri.com/manuscripts/10602.pdf (accessed 17 May 2013).

Ayres, J. and Potter, H. (1980) 'Attitudes toward community change: A comparison between rural leaders and residents', *Journal of the Community Development Society*, 20(1): 1–18.

Banks, C. E. (2010) 'Disentangling the influence of community and place attachment on resident attitudes toward tourism development', unpublished master thesis, North Carolina State University, Raleigh, North Carolina.

Barry, B. (1965) *Political Argument: A Reissue with a New Introduction*, Berkeley, California: University of California Press.

Bianchi, R. V. (2004) 'Tourism restructuring and the politics of sustainability: A critical view from the European periphery (The Canary Islands)', *Journal of Sustainable Tourism*, 12(6): 495–529.

Bianco, W. T. (1994) *Trust: Representatives and Constituents*, Ann Arbor: University of Michigan Press.

Bopp, M., GermAnn, K., Bopp, J., Baugh Littlejohns, L. and Smith, N. (2000) *Assessing Community Capacity for Change*. Online: www.k4health.org/sites/default/files/ACCC_complete_document.pdf (accessed 12 July 2012).

Bramwell, B. (2011) 'Governance, the state and sustainable tourism: A political economy approach', *Journal of Sustainable Tourism*, 19(4–5): 459–477.

Bramwell, B. and Lane, B. (2011) 'Critical research on the governance of tourism and sustainability', *Journal of Sustainable Tourism*, 19(4–5): 411–421.

Brandon, K. (1993). 'Basic steps towards encouraging local participation in nature tourism projects.' In K. Lindberg and D. E. Hawkins (eds) *Ecotourism: A Guide for Planners and Managers*, North Bennington, VT: The Ecotourism Society.

Braun, J. (2008) 'Community-based tourism in northern Honduras: Opportunities and barriers', unpublished honors thesis, University of Manitoba Winnipeg, Manitoba.

Briassoulis, H. (2003) 'Crete: Endowed by nature, privileged by geography, threatened by tourism?' *Journal of Sustainable Tourism*, 11(3): 97–115.

Brockner, J., Siegel, P. A., Daly, J. P., Tyler, T. and Martin, C. (1997) 'When trust matters: The moderating effect of outcome favorability', *Administrative Science Quarterly*, 42(3): 558–583.

Bronfman, N. C., Vazquez, E. L. and Dorantes, G. (2009) 'An empirical study for the direct and indirect links between trust in regulatory institutions and acceptability of hazards', *Safety Science*, 47(5): 686–692.

Brown, B. B., Perkins, D. and Brown, G. (2003) 'Place attachment in a revitalizing neighborhood: Individual and block levels of analysis', *Journal of Environmental Psychology*, 23(3): 259–271.

Burns, P. (1999) 'Paradoxes in planning tourism elitism or brutalism?' *Annals of Tourism Research*, 26(2): 329–348.

Butler, J. K., Jr. (1991) 'Toward understanding and measuring conditions of trust: Evolution of a conditions of trust inventory', *Journal of Management*, 17(3): 643–663.

Butler, R. W. (1980) 'The concept of a tourism areas cycle of evaluation: Implications for management of resources', *Canadian Geographer*, 24(1): 5–12.

Butterfoss, F. D., Goodman, R. M. and Wandersman, A. (1993) 'Community coalitions for prevention and health promotion', *Health Education Research*, 8(3): 315–330.

Clarkson, M. A. (1995) 'A stakeholder framework for analyzing and evaluating corporate social performance', *Academy Management Review*, 20(1): 92–117.

Collier, M. W. (2002) 'The effects of political corruption on Caribbean development', paper prepared for the Caribbean Studies Association annual conference, 27 May to 2 June, Nassau, Bahamas.

Connick, S. and Innes, J. E. (2003) 'Outcomes of collaborative water policy making: Applying complexity thinking to evaluation', *Journal of Environmental Planning and Management*, 46(2): 177–197.

Cooksey, J. (1999) 'Corruption and poverty: What are the linkages?' paper presented at the Technical Review Workshop on the Socio-economic Consequences of Poverty and Corruption, International Centre for Economic Growth, Nairobi, Kenya.

Cupples, J. (2005) *What Is Community Capacity Building?* Online: www.ccwa.org.uk/v2/ downloads/cms/1121303664.pdf (accessed 3 March, 2008).

Curry, N. and Fisher, R. (2012) 'The role of trust in the development of connectivities amongst rural elders in England and Wales', *Journal of Rural Studies*, 28(4): 358–370.

de Araujo, L. M. and Bramwell B. (1999) 'Stakeholder assessment and collaborative tourism planning: The case of Brazil's Costa Dourada project', *Journal of Sustainable Tourism*, 7(3–4): 356–378.

de Vos, B. I. and van Tatenhove, J.P.M. (2011) 'Trust relationships between fishers and government: New challenges for the co-management arrangements in the Dutch flatfish industry', *Marina Policy*, 35(2): 218–225.

Doh, M. (2006) 'Change through tourism: Resident perceptions of tourism development', unpublished doctoral dissertation, Texas A&M University, Lubbock, Texas.

Donaldson, T. and Preston, L. E. (1995) 'The stakeholder theory of the corporation: Concepts, evidence and implications', *Academy of Management Review*, 20(1): 65–91.

Downs, A. (1967) *Inside bureaucracy*. Online: www.rand.org/content/dam/rand/pubs/papers/2008/P2963.pdf (accessed 10 July 2012).

Doxey, G. V. (1975) 'A causation theory of visitor-resident irritants' methodology and research inferences', paper presented at the Sixth Annual Conference of the Travel Research Association, San Diego, California.

Dreher, A., Kotsogiannis, C., and McCorriston, S. (2004) 'Corruption around the world: Evidence from a structural model', unpublished manuscript, Department of Economics, School of Business and Economics, University of Exeter.

Duffy, R. (2002) *A Trip Too Far: Ecotourism, Politics and Exploitation*, London: Earthscan.

Duran, E. and Ozkul, E. (2012) 'Residents' attitudes toward tourism development: A structural model via Akcakoca sample', *International Journal of Human Sciences*, 9(2): 500–520.

Eagly, A. H. and Chaiken, S. (1993) *The Psychology of Attitude*, Orlando, FL: Harcourt Brace Jovanovich.

Eber, S. (1992) *Beyond the Green Horizon: Principles for Sustainable Tourism*, Surrey, UK: World Wide Fund for Nature.

Edgell, D., Allen, M. Smith G. and Swanson, J. (2008) *Tourism Policy and Planning: Yesterday, Today and Tomorrow*, Oxford, UK: Elsevier.

Etzioni, A. (1996) 'Positive aspects of community and the dangers of fragmentation', *Development and Change*, 27(2): 301–314.

Frederickson, L. M. and Anderson, D. H. (1999) 'A qualitative exploration of the wilderness experience as a source of spiritual inspiration', *Journal of Environmental Psychology*, 19(1): 21–39.

Freeman, R. E. (1984) *Strategic Management: A Stakeholder Approach*, Cambridge, MA: Ballinger.

Frisch, D. (1996) 'The effects of corruption on development', *The Courier,* ACP-EU No. 158, July–August.

Government and Institutions Department (1993) 'Taking account of good government', Technical Note, No. 10, October.

Graci, S. (2008) 'What hinders the path to sustainability? A study of barriers to sustainable tourism development in Gili Trawangan, Indonesia', *Pacific News*, No. 29, January/February.

Graci, S. (2009) *Do Hotels Accommodate Green? Examining the Factors That Influence Environmental Commitment in the Hotel Industry*, Frankfurt: Verlag.

Grzeskowiak, S., Sirgy, M. J. and Widgery, R. (2003) 'Residents' satisfaction with community services: Predictors and outcomes', *Journal of Regional Analysis and Policy*, 33(2): 1–36.

Gildenhuys, J.S.H. (2004) *Ethics and Professionalism: The Battle Against Public Corruption*, Stellenbosch: Sun Press.

Gunes-Ayata, A. (1994) 'Roots and trends of clientelism in Turkey', in L. Roniger and A. Gunes-Ayata (eds) *Democracy, Clientelism and Civil Society,* London: Lynne Rienner.

Gunfadurdoss, A., Hanna, H., Salhab, J. and Tarabay, D. (2012) 'Improving the competitiveness of the tourism cluster in Tunisia' microeconomics of competitiveness', student project. Online: www.isc.hbs.edu/pdf/Student_Projects/2012%20MOC%20Papers/MOC_Tunisia_Tourism_Final.pdf (accessed 26 July 2013).

Gursoy, D., Jurowski, C. and Uysal, M. (2002) 'Resident attitudes: A structural modeling approach', *Annals of Tourism Research*, 29(1): 79–105.

Gursoy, D. and Kendall, K. W. (2006) 'Hosting mega events – modeling locals support', *Annals of Tourism Research*, 33(3): 603–623.

Gursoy, D. and Rutherford, D. G. (2004) 'Host attitudes toward tourism – an improved structural model', *Annals of Tourism Research*, 31(3): 495–516.

Gutsul, D. (2011) 'Strategic analysis of domestic tourism development in Ukraine', unpublished master thesis, Eastern Mediterranean University, North Cyprus.

Hall, C. M. (1998) *Tourism Development, Dimensions and Issues*, South Melbourne: Addison Wesley Longman.

Harrison, D. (1994) 'Learning from the old south by the new south? The case of tourism', *Third World Quarterly*, 15(4): 707–721.

Hassan, G. F., Hefnawi, A. E. and Refaie, M. E. (2011) 'Efficiency of participation in planning', *Alexandria Engineering Journal*, 50(2): 203–212.

Haywood, K. M. (1988) 'Responsible and responsive tourism planning in the community', *Tourism Management*, 9(2): 105–118.

Henry, P. I. and Nassis, P. (1999) 'Political clientelism and sport policy in Greece', *International Review for the Sociology of Sport*, 34(1): 43–58.

Hetherington, M. J. (1998) 'The political relevance of political trust', *American Political Science Review*, 92(4): 791–808.

Holland, J. (2000) 'Consensus and conflict: The socioeconomic challenge facing sustainable tourism development in Southern Albania', *Journal of Sustainable Tourism*, 8(6): 510–524.

Höppner, C. (2009) 'Trust – a monolithic panacea in land use planning?' *Land Use Policy*, 26(4): 1046–1054.

Humphreys, F. (1999) *Main Findings from the Country Report*. Online: www.metla.fi/eu/cost/e19/Humphreys.ppt (accessed 22 June 2004).

Illsley, B. M. (2003) 'Fair participation – a Canadian perspective', *Land Use Policy*, 20(3): 265–273.

Ives, A. (2007) 'Cayos Cochinos, Honduras and the areas of influence', report sponsored by the Nature Conservancy, New York.

Jamal, T. B. and Getz, D. (1995) 'Collaboration theory and community tourism planning', *Annals of Tourism Research*, 22(1): 186–204.

Johnson, B. B. (1999) 'Exploring dimensionality in the origins of hazard related trust', *Journal of Risk Research*, 2(4): 325–354.

Johnson, G., Whittington, R. and Scholes, K. (2011) *Exploring Strategy*, Harlow: FT Prentice Hall.

Jones, T. M. (1995) 'Instrumental stakeholder theory: A synthesis of ethics and economics', *Academy of Management Review*, 20(2): 404–437.

Jongeneel, R. A., Nico, B. P., Polman, N.B.P. and Slangen, L.H.G (2008) 'Why are Dutch farmers going multifunctional?' *Land Use Policy*, 25(1): 81–94.

Jurowski, C., Uysal, M. and Williams, R. (1997) 'A theoretical analysis of host community resident reactions to tourism', *Journal of Travel Research*, 36(2): 3–11.

Jurowski, C., Uysal, M., Williams, D. R. and Noe, F. P. (1995) 'An examination of preferences and evaluations of visitors based on environmental attitudes: Biscayne Bay National Park', *Journal of Sustainable Tourism*, 3(2): 73–86.

Kaltenborn, B. P., Andersen, O., Nellemann, C., Bjerke, T. and Thrane, C. (2008) 'Resident attitudes towards mountain second-home tourism development in Norway: The effects of environmental attitudes', *Journal of Sustainable Tourism*, 16(6): 664–680.

Kayat, K. (2002) 'Power, social exchanges and tourism in Langkawi: Rethinking resident perceptions', *International Journal of Tourism Research*, 4(3): 171–191.

Kermath, B. (2005) 'What is clientelism?' Online: www.uwsp.edu/cnr/gem/ambassador/what_is_clientelism.htm (accessed 12 March 2005).

Kickert, W.J.M., Klinj, E. H. and Koppenjan, J.F.M. (1997) 'Introduction: A management perspective on policy networks', in W.J.M. Kickert, E. H. Klinj, and J.F.M. Koppenjan (eds) *Managing Complex Networks: Strategies for the Public Sector*, London: Sage.

Kılınc, G., Özgür, H. and Genc, F. N. (2009) 'Planning ethics at local level', *Academic Research Report for Ethics for the Prevention of Corruption in Turkey* (TYEC), funded by the European Commission and implemented by the Council of Europe in co-operation with the Council of Ethics for the Public Service of the Republic of Turkey, 1–108.

Klingemann, H. D. (1999) 'Mapping political support in the 1990s: A global analysis', in P. Norris (ed.), *Critical Citizens: Global Support for Democratic Governance*, Oxford: Oxford University Press.

Ko, D. W. and Stewart, W. P. (2002) 'A structural equation model of residents' attitudes for tourism development', *Tourism Management*, 23(5): 521–530.

Komito, L. (2006) 'E-governance in Ireland: New technologies, public participation, and social capital.' Online: www.ucd.ie/lkomito/e_governance_ireland.htm (accessed 20 December 2006).

Kyle, G., Graefe, A., Manning, R., and Bacon, J. (2004) 'Effects of place attachment on users' perceptions of social and environmental conditions in a natural setting', *Journal of Environmental Psychology*, 24(2): 213–225.

Lai, P. H. and Nepal, S. K. (2006) 'Local perspectives of ecotourism development in Tawushan Nature Reserve, Taiwan', *Tourism Management*, 27(6): 1117–1129.

Lambsdorff, G. (2004) 'Global corruption barometer.' Online: www.transparency.org/working_papers/lambsdorff/lambsdorff_eresearch.htm (accessed 19 July 2012).

Lang, J. T. and Hallman, W. K. (2005) 'Who does the public trust? The case of genetically modified food in the United States', *Risk Analysis*, 25(5): 1241–1252.

Lankford, S. V. and Howard, D. R. (1994) 'Developing a tourism impact attitude scale', *Annals of Tourism Research*, 21(1): 121–139.

Lauber, T. B. and Knuth, B. A., (1999) 'Measuring fairness in citizen participation: A case study of moose management', *Society and Natural Resources*, 12(1): 19–37.

Lee, C., Kang, S. K., Long, P. and Reisinger, Y. (2010) 'Residents' perceptions of casino impacts: A comparative study', *Tourism Management*, 31(2): 189–201.

Lee, T. H. (2013) 'Influence analysis of community resident support for sustainable tourism development', *Tourism Management*, 34: 37–46.

Li, J. Q. and Wang, L. (2008) 'Study on visitor attraction competitiveness based on place attachment theory', *Human Geography*, 23(4): 79–83.

Lipset, S. M. and Lenz, G. S. (2000) 'Corruption, culture, and markets', in L. E. Harrison and S. P. Huntington (eds) *Culture Matters*, New York: Basic Books.

Lovell, D. W. (2001) 'Trust and the politics of postcommunism', *Communist and Post-Communist Studies*, 34(1): 27–38.

Madrigal, R. (1993) 'A tale of two cities', *Annals of Tourism Research*, 20(2): 336–353.

Mair, H., Reid, D. G. and George, W. (2005) 'Globalization, rural tourism and community power', in D. R. Hall, I. Kirkpatrick, and M. Mitchell (eds) *Rural Tourism and Sustainable Business*, Bristol, UK: Channel View Publications.

Máiz, S. R. and Requejo, F. (2002) *Democracy, Nationalism and Multiculturalism*, London: Routledge.

Manzo, L. C. and Perkins, D. D. (2006) 'Finding common ground: The importance of place attachment to community participation and planning', *Journal of Planning Literature*, 20(4): 335–350.

Martin, L. and Tomas, K. (2012) 'Tourism destination benchmarking: Evaluation and selection of the benchmarking partners', *Journal of Competitiveness*, 4(1): 99–116.

Mauro, P. (1997) 'The effects of corruption on growth, investment, and government expenditure: A cross-country analysis', in K. Elliott (ed.) *Corruption and the Global Economy*, Washington, DC: Institute for International Economics.

McCool, S. F. and Martin S. R. (1994) 'Community attachment and attitudes toward tourism development', *Journal of Travel Research*, 32(3): 29–34.

McEwan, C. (2003) 'Bringing government to the people: Women, local governance and community participation in South Africa', *Geoforum*, 34(4): 469–481.

Mesch, G. S. (1996) 'The effect of environmental concerns and government incentives on organized action in local areas', *Urban Affairs Review*, 31(3): 346–366.

Miller, A. H. and Listhaug, O. (1990) 'Political parties and confidence in government: A comparison of Norway, Sweden and the United States', *British Journal of Political Science*, 20(3): 357–386.

Miller, A. H. and Listhaug, O. (1999) 'Political trust and institutional trust', in P. Norris (ed.) *Critical Citizens: Global Support for Democratic Governance*, Oxford: Oxford University Press.

Milman, A. and Pizam, A. (1988) 'Social impact of tourism on Central Florida', *Annals of Tourism Research*, 15(2): 208–220.

Morah, E. U. (1996) 'Obstacles to optimal policy implementation in developing countries', *Third World Planning Review*, 18(1): 79–105.

Morison, P. J. and Brown, R. R. (2011) 'Understanding the nature of publics and local policy commitment to water sensitive urban design', *Landscape and Urban Planning*, 99(2): 83–92.

Murphy, P. E. (1985) *Tourism: A Community Approach*, New York: Routledge.

Narayan, P. K. (2001) 'Fiji's sugar, tourism and garment industries: A survey of performance, problems and potentials', *Fijian Studies*, 1(1): 4–27.

Nazario, O. (2007) 'A strategy for fighting corruption in the Caribbean', paper presented at the Conference on the Caribbean: A 20/20 Vision, Washington, DC, 19–21 June.

Nicholas, L., Thapa, B. and Ko, Y. (2009) 'Residents' perspectives of a world heritage site – the Pitons Management Area, St. Lucia', *Annals of Tourism Research*, 36(3): 390–412.

Norris, P. (1999) 'Institutional explanations for political support', in P. Norris (ed.), *Critical Citizens: Global Support for Democratic Governance*, Oxford: Oxford University Press.

Nunkoo, R. and Ramkissoon, H. (2010) 'Community perceptions of tourism in small island states: A conceptual framework', *Journal of Policy Research in Tourism, Leisure & Events*, 2(1): 51–65.

Nunkoo, R. and Ramkissoon, H. (2011) 'Developing a community support model for tourism', *Annals of Tourism Research*, 38(3): 964–988.

Nunkoo, R., Ramkissoon, H. and Gursoy, D. (2012) 'Public trust in tourism institutions', *Annals of Tourism Research*, 39(3): 1538–1564.

Nunkoo, R. and Smith, S.L.J. (2013) 'Political economy of tourism: Trust in government actors, political support, and their determinants', *Tourism Management*, 36: 120–132.

OECD (2008) *OECD Annual Territorial Reviews*. Online: www.oecd.org/publishing/corrigenda (accessed 12 June 2012).

Oxford Advanced Learner's Dictionary (2000) 'Definition of corruption.' Online: http://oald8.oxfordlearnersdictionaries.com/dictionary/corruption (accessed 19 July 2013).

Parkins, J. R. and Mitchell, R. E. (2005) 'Public participation as public debate: A deliberative turn in natural resource management', *Society and Natural Resources*, 18(6): 529–540.

Paul, S. (1991) 'Accountability in public service; Exit, voice and capture', *Policy Research and External Affairs Working Papers*, WPS 614, World Bank.

Pearce, P. L., Moscardo, G. and Ross, G. F. (1996) *Tourism Community Relationships*, Oxford: Pergamon.

Pizam, A. (1978) 'Tourism's impacts: The social costs of the destination community as perceived by its residents', *Journal of Travel Research*, 16(4): 8–12.

Pizzorno, A. (1992) '*La corruzione nel sistema político: Introduzione a della Porta Lo scambio occulto cit*' [Corruption in the political system], European Consortium for Political Research, Paper Archive – Joint Sessions of Workshops, Workshop 16, Corruption, Scandal and the Contestation of Governance in Europe, Grenoble, France, 1–18. Online: www.essex.ac.uk/ecpr/events/jointsessions/paperarchive/grenoble/ws16/maiz_requejo.pdf (accessed 19 January 2005).

Prentice, R. (1993) 'Community-driven tourism planning and resident preferences', *Tourism Management*, 14(3): 218–227.

Pretty, G. H., Chipuer, H. M. and Bramston, P. (2003) 'Sense of place amongst adolescents and adults in two rural Australian towns: The discriminating features of place attachment, sense of community and place dependence in relation to place identity', *Journal of Environmental Psychology*, 23(3): 273–287.

Relph, E. (1976) *Place and Placelessness*, London: Pion.

Ritchie, B. and Inkari, M. (2006) 'Host community attitudes toward tourism and cultural tourism development: The case of the Lewes district Southern England', *International Journal of Tourism Research*, 8(1): 27–44.

Rivlin, L. (1987) 'The neighborhood, personal identity and group affiliation', in I. Altman and A. Wandersman (eds) *Neighborhood and Community Environments*, New York: Plenum.

Roniger, L. (1994) 'Conclusions: The transformation of clientelism and civil society', in L. Roniger and A. Gunes-Ayata (eds) *Democracy, Clientelism and Civil Society*, London: Lynne Rienner.

Rose-Ackerman, S. (1987) *Bribery in the New Palgrave: A Dictionary of Economics*, London: Macmillian.

Sautter, E. T. and Leisen, B. (1999) 'Managing stakeholders a tourism planning model', *Annals of Tourism Research*, 26(2): 312–328.

Sheldon, P. J. and Var, T. (1984) 'Resident attitudes to tourism in North Wales', *Tourism Management*, 5(1): 40–7.

Shi, T. (2001) 'Cultural values and political trust: a comparison of the People's Republic of China and Taiwan', *Comparative Politics*, 33(4): 401–419.

Sirakaya, E., Ekinci, Y. and Kaya, A. G. (2008). 'An examination of the validity of SUSTAS in cross-cultures', *Journal of Travel Research*, 46(4): 414–421.

Smaldone, D., Harris, C. C., Sanyal, N. and Lind, D. (2005) 'Place attachment and management of critical park issues in Grand Teton National Park', *Journal of Park and Recreation Administration*, 23(1): 90–114.

Smelser, N.J. (1971) 'Stability, instability, and the analysis of political corruption', in B. Bernard and I. Alex (eds) *Stability and Social Change*, Boston: Little, Brown.

Smith, P. D. and McDonough, M. (2001) 'Beyond public participation: Fairness in natural resource decision making', *Society and Natural Resources*, 14(3): 239–249.

Sunar, İ (1994) 'The politics of state interventionism in "populist" Egypt and Turkey', in A. Öncü, Ç. Keyder and S. E. İbrahim (eds) *Developmentalism and Beyond: Society and Politics in Egypt and Turkey*, Cairo: The American University in Cairo, 94–107.

Swanson, K. E., Kuhn, R. G. and Xu, W. (2001) 'Environmental policy implementation in rural China: A case study of Yuhang, Zhejiang', *Environmental Management*, 27(4): 481–491.

Thibaut, J. W. and Kelley, H. H. (1959) *The Social Psychology of Groups*, New York: Wiley.

Tina, C. A. and Nnabuko, J. O. (2012) 'Corruption and tourism: Restructuring Nigeria's image for development using public relations strategies', *Kuwait Chapter of Arabian Journal of Business and Management Review*, 2(4): 10–26.

Tosun, C. (2000) 'Limits to community participation in the tourism development process in developing countries', *Tourism Management*, 21(6): 613–633.

Tosun, C. (2006) 'Expected nature of community participation in tourism development', *Tourism Management*, 27(3): 493–504.

Tosun, C. and Jenkins, C. L. (1996) 'Regional planning approaches to tourism development: The case of Turkey', *Tourism Management*, 17(7): 519–531.

Tsai, C. H. (1996) 'Community awareness and community development', *Social Welfare*, 124: 21–26.

Turner, M. and Hulme, D. (1997) *Governance, Administration and Development*, London: Macmillan.

Um, S. and Crompton, J. L. (1987) 'Measuring residents' attachment levels in a host community', *Journal of Travel Research*, 25(3): 27–29.

United Nations (UN) (1980) *Public Administration Institutions and Practices in Integrated Rural Development Programmes*, New York: United Nations Publications.

Uruena, N. (2004) *Citizen Participation as a Means of Controlling Corruption in Columbia*. Online: www.kus.uu.se/pdf/publications/Nubia Thesis.pdf (accessed 11 September 2004).

Uysal, M., Jurowski, C., Noe, F. P. and Mcdonald, C. D. (1994) 'Environmental attitude by trip and visitor characteristics', *Tourism Management*, 15(4): 284–294.

van Harssel, J. (1994) *Tourism: An Exploration*, Upper Saddle River, NJ: Prentice Hall.

Vorkinn, M. and Riese, H. (2001) 'Environmental concern in a local context: The significance of place attachment', *Environment and Behavior*, 33(2): 249–263.

Wahab, S. (1997). 'Sustainable tourism in the developing world', in S. Wahab and J. J. Piagram (eds) *Tourism, Development and Growth: The Challenge of Sustainability*, London: Routledge.

Walker, A. J. and Ryan, R. L., (2008) 'Place attachment and landscape preservation in rural New England: A Maine case study', *Landscape and Urban Planning*, 86(2): 141–152.

Wandersman A., Florin P., Friedmann R. and Meier R. (1987) 'Who participates, who does not, and why? An analysis of voluntary neighborhood organizations in the United States and Israel', *Sociological Forum*, 2(3): 534–555.

Webler, T., and Tuler, S. (2002) 'Unlocking the puzzle of public participation', *Bulletin of Science, Technology and Society*, 22(3): 179–189.

White, S. S. (2001) 'Public participation and organizational change in Wisconsin land use management', *Land Use Policy*, 18(4): 341–350.

Widgery, R. (1982) 'Satisfaction with quality of urban life: A predictive model', *American Journal of Community Psychology*, 10(1): 37–48.

Williams J., and Lawson, R. (2001), 'Community issues and resident opinions of tourism', *Annals of Tourism Research*, 28: 269–290.

Williams, D. R., McDonald, C. D., Riden, C. M. and Uysal, M. (1995). 'Community attachment, regional identity and resident attitudes toward tourism', paper presented at the 26th annual Travel and Tourism Research Association Conference, Wheat Ridge, CO: Travel and Tourism Research Association.

Williams, P. W., Penrose, R. W. and Hawkes, S. (1998) 'Shared decision-making in tourism land use planning', *Annals of Tourism Research*, 25(4): 860–889.

Wong, T. K., Wan, P. and Hsiao, H. M. (2011) 'The bases of political trust in six Asian societies: Institutional and cultural explanations compared', *International Political Science Review*, 32(3): 263–281.

World Bank (1992) *Governance and Development*, Washington, DC: World Bank.

Wrong, D. H. (1979) *Power: Its Forms, Bases and Uses*, New York: Harper & Row.

Yüksel, F. (2003) 'Interorganizational relations and central-local interactions in tourism planning in Belek, Turkey', unpublished doctoral dissertation, Sheffield Hallam University, Sheffield, UK.

Yüksel, F. and Yüksel, A. (2007) 'Clientelist relationships: Implications for tourism development in the declining coastal resort of Kusadasi, Turkey', in S. Agarwal and G. Shav (eds) *Managing Coastal Tourism Resorts: A Global Perspective*, Clevedon, UK: Channel View Publications.

Yüksel, F. and Yüksel, A. (2008) 'Perceived clientelism: Effects on residents' evaluation of municipal services and their intentions for participation in tourism development projects', *Journal of Hospitality and Tourism Research*, 32(2): 187–208.

Yüksel, F. and Yüksel, A. (2000a) 'Decentralised tourism administration: Is it the way forward?' paper presented at the First International Joint Symposium on Business Administration, Challenges for Business Administration in the New Millennium, Karvina, Czech Republic.

Yüksel, F. and Yüksel, A. (2000b) 'Tourism plan formulation and implementation: The role of interorganizational relations', paper presented at the First International Joint Symposium on Business Administration, Challenges for Business Administration in the New Millennium, Karvina, Czech Republic.

Zafarullah, H. and Siddiquee, N. (2001) 'Dissecting public sector corruption in Bangladesh: Issues and problems of Contro', *Public Organization Review*, 1(4): 465–486.

8 Correlates of political trust and support for tourism

Development of a conceptual framework

Robin Nunkoo

Introduction

Citizens' trust in government institutions and their political support for development are important preconditions for a democratic and sustainable form of development. In the context of tourism, it is important that residents of a destination endorse development and tourism policies of government to ensure sustainability and good governance of the sector. Recognition that communities are central to tourism development and one of the most important groups of stakeholders has led researchers to conduct numerous studies on residents' support for tourism development and its antecedents. Whereas early studies on this topic were of an atheoretical nature, researchers have increasingly made use of theories such as social exchange theory (SET), originally drawn from sociology, to understand the ways in which residents react to tourism development and the circumstances that prompt them to do so. On one hand, use of SET has strengthened the theoretical base of and has made significant contributions to this area of research; on the other hand, some researchers found the theory to lack predictive power in explaining residents' support for tourism development. This is probably because researchers failed to consider important variables of the theory simultaneously in an integrative framework. Key constructs such as power and trust have been left out by most studies on this topic. It is also important that SET complement other theoretical approaches so that new insights are uncovered in this area of study. For example, institutional theory of political trust and cultural theory of political trust are valuable perspectives to consider because they provide contrasting, but valuable, insights on the potential determinants of political trust in tourism development.

Grounded in political economy, this study develops a theoretical framework (Figure 8.1) using key variables from SET, institutional theory of political trust, and cultural theory of political trust. Using these theories as basis, the framework considers the key determinants of political trust in tourism development. Based on the postulates of the three theories (SET, institutional theory of political trust, and cultural theory of political trust), perceived economic and political performance of government actors involved in tourism development, residents' perceived level of power in tourism, interpersonal trust among society members, and residents'

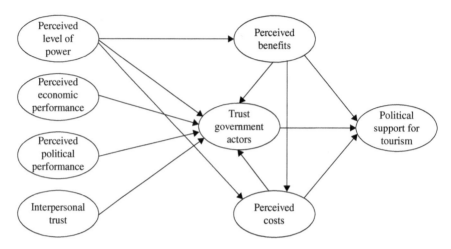

Figure 8.1 Conceptual framework linking political trust and its determinants to support for tourism development

perceived benefits and costs of tourism development are proposed to influence political trust. In addition, the framework considers trust as a central variable in a tourism exchange process between residents of a destination and government. The conceptual framework further proposes that political trust, together with residents' perceived benefits and costs of tourism influence their level of support for tourism.

Political economy of state intervention in tourism development

Political economy, a broad social theory that has been widely used in social science, is concerned with the political nature of decision making and with how politics affects choices in a society. It encompasses a wide variety of approaches to studying the relationship between the economy and its noneconomic (i.e. political, socio-cultural, psychological, and geographical) and provides an understanding of structures and social relations that form societies in order to evoke social change toward more equitable and democratic conditions (Mosedale, 2011). Political economy provides a useful perspective to study tourism development and governance processes, yet it has been an uncommon approach in tourism studies (Bramwell, 2011). Nevertheless, some researchers have successfully applied it to study tourism development (e.g. Bianchi, 2009; Hall, 2006; Mosedale, 2011). Williams (2004) noted that important theoretical developments in political economy have been largely neglected in tourism studies. Mosedale (2011) argued that "political economy (in its various guises and transfigurations) still has much to offer tourism analyzes and should not be ignored or indeed written off in favor of a more fashionable approach to studying and analyzing tourism" (p. 7).

The political economy approach considers that the state has an influential role in managing and promoting tourism development (Webster *et al.*, 2011). Although some researchers argue that the role of government in tourism has been declining, its role in the sector's development and regulations should in no circumstances be neglected (Bramwell, 2011; Newman and Clarke, 2009). In fact, government is the principal actor in the political process of tourism development (Bramwell, 2011; Hall, 1994) and has usually adopted a more interventionist approach in tourism development than in other sectors (Ruhanen, 2013). Government controls the industry through formal ministries and other institutions (Elliot, 1997) and intervenes in tourism development for environmental, political, and economic reasons (Nyaupane and Timothy, 2010). Hall (2005) is of the view that governments have seven functions in tourism development: coordination, planning, legislation and regulation, entrepreneurship, stimulation, social tourism, and public interest protection.

Traditionally economic gains in the form of tax revenues, income, and employment were the principal reasons for government to intervene in tourism by developing infrastructure and services and committing considerable funds to destination marketing and promotion (Bramwell, 1994; Charlton and Essex, 2000). Over time, the negative effects of tourism development and local residents' opposition and reluctance to accept tourism have meant that government's roles in the sector have extended beyond economic considerations to address environmental and social consequences of development (Inskeep, 1988; Ruhanen, 2013). The diffusion of the sustainable development concept in the 1980s has also led governments to assume greater roles and responsibilities in tourism planning and development (Ruhanen, 2013). Governments now usually attempt to secure a balance between economic priorities, the environment, and the local society to gain political support for tourism development (Bramwell, 2011). Wearing and Neil (2009) asserted that only governments and public authorities can coordinate efforts to achieve sustainable tourism.

Political economy focuses not only on government intervention in tourism development, but this approach also emphasizes on the importance of the state's relationship with society. Jessop (2008) argued that political economy "starts from the proposition that the state is a social relation" and is "socially embedded" (pp. 1, 5). Government's responsiveness to its citizens is a key issue in political economy (Besley and Burgess, 2002). Bramwell (2011) argued that the state is well placed to work in the interests of the citizens who may often hold it accountable for policy decisions. The public can also call upon the government to improve coordination on a range of issues on policy making for sustainable tourism. Thus, a politically stable relationship between the state and the citizens is important to maintain political legitimacy and effective authority (Purcell and Nevins, 2005) and to ensure the state's ability to reflect the popular will (Bramwell, 2011).

O'Neil (2007) distinguished among four types of political economy, each characterized by varying roles and degree of intervention of government in tourism. His view provides a useful basis to study tourism development and governance processes across different societies. The four political economic systems and their characteristics are described in Table 8.1.

Table 8.1 Political economic systems and their characteristics

	Liberalism	*Social democracy*	*Communism*	*Mercantilism*
Role of government	Little; minimal welfare state	Some government regulation; large welfare state	Total state ownership; extensive welfare state	Much state ownership; small welfare state
Role of the market	Paramount	Important but not sacrosanct	None	Limited
Government autonomy	Low	Moderate	Very high	High
Importance of equality	Low	High	High	Low
How is policy made?	Pluralism	Corporatism	Government/ party	Government
Possible flaws	Inequality; monopolies	Expense of the welfare state; inefficiency	Authoritarianism and inefficiency	Can tend toward authoritarianism; can distort market
Examples	United States, United Kingdom, Canada	Germany, Sweden, Finland	Cuba, Soviet Union, China	Japan, South Korea, India

Note: Adapted from O'Neil (2007).

The liberal model is characterized by minimal welfare state, low state involvement in tourism, and high levels of social and economic inequality. This political economic system is based on the assumption that the market is the best mechanism to allocate tourism resources among society members in the best possible and most efficient ways. However, the drawbacks of such an economic system are that it leads to an unequal distribution of wealth and other resources among tourism actors and it has weak institutions to deal with the tourism sector (Webster *et al.*, 2011). In contrast to liberal regimes, the communist model is characterized by total state ownership, extensive welfare state, and an emphasis on social and economic equality. In such an economic system, almost no emphasis is placed on market forces as a mechanism for resource allocation. Private ownership of resources is also minimized to allow for greater equality in economic and social outcomes among tourism actors (Webster *et al.*, 2011).

Mercantilist political economies allow for private ownership of resources, but with a great deal of state intervention and low emphasis on equality (Webster *et al.*, 2011). In such an economic system, political leadership largely influences the ways in which the market is managed and resources are allocated. Although such an economic system ensures that the country is strong economically and militarily, some degree of inequality among social actors is evident. The social democratic model is characterized by some level of government intervention in the economy, the existence of a large welfare state, and a focus on equality. Mercantilists and social democratic political economies tend to have stronger public agencies to deal with the challenges of the tourism sector than other political economic systems. Mercantilist states is also characterized by a high tendency toward privatization of tourism services, whereas social democratic political economies focus on how tourism development can result in benefits for the society (Webster *et al.*, 2011).

Webster *et al.* (2011) argued that few economies would fit completely into any one category, and some overlaps may exist. Nevertheless, the researchers noted that the ways in which governments respond to tourism development is largely influenced by the type of political economic system prevailing. They argued that "organizational responses to tourism are inherently political decisions dealing with quantity and quality of regulation that the state will have upon the tourism industry" (p. 60).

While political economy is a broad theory that provides a valuable perspective to study state's activities in tourism development, distribution of tourism benefits among society members, power relationships among tourism stakeholders, citizens' trust in government actors and its determinants, and political support for tourism (Bramwell, 2011; Mosedale, 2011; Wang and Bramwell, 2012), SET, institutional theory of political trust, and cultural theory of political trust enable an empirical testing of the relationships among the key concepts of political economy. In doing so, these theories shed light on the relationship between government actors and residents in tourism development.

Political trust in tourism development

Political trust is a useful concept to understand citizens' relationships with government actors. Citizens' trust in government actors is often referred to as political trust or institutional trust (Luhiste, 2006). Political trust is an important, but overlooked ingredient of the politics of tourism, although it remains an important area of research in the political science literature (*e.g.* Backstrom and Edlund, 2012; Rohrschneider and Schmitt-Beck, 2002; Wong *et al.*, 2011). Research on political trust is driven by the importance of linking citizens to institutions, the desire to achieve good governance and legitimacy of government, and the need to gain public support for development (Luhiste, 2006; Scheidegger and Staerkle, 2011). Political trust is important because it conveys a message to the governing elites about whether their policy decisions conform to the normative expectations of the governed (Citrin and Luks, 2001).

Although states' intervention in tourism and addressing sustainable development concerns is widely supported by the political economy approach (Godfrey, 1998; Hall, 1998; Weaver, 2006), governments may not always promote democracy, ensure equitable outcomes, work in the best interests of the society, and further the objectives of sustainable tourism (Bramwell, 2011). Governments have been criticized for implementing tourism policies that are short-term and lack overall direction and coordination (Madrigal, 1995; Vogel and Swanson, 1988), for imposing tourism planning on the local communities, particularly in developing countries (Keogh, 1990), for adopting top-down tourism planning and decision making, and for exercising excessive power in tourism policy and planning (Bramwell, 2011; Moscardo, 2011). Some researchers also criticize governments for not overtly releasing statements and providing complete and accurate information on their hidden political agendas (Nyaupane and Timothy, 2010). These raise suspicions and cause distrust among citizens, challenging legitimacy of governments and compromising a democratic and sustainable form of tourism development. Trust is further compromised because states' activities increasingly happen through arm's-length relationships, with a growing role for agencies and public–private sector partnerships. These threaten legitimacy of government institutions and create political and social instability, making it difficult for the government to sustain economic activities (Bramwell, 2011). It is for these reasons some researchers claim that public trust in government in the context of tourism development is declining (Bramwell, 2011).

Correlates of political trust: institutionalist approach

Studies from the political science literature suggest that a number of factors influence citizens' trust in government institutions. Political scientists have used two competing theories to explain the determinants of citizens' trust in government institutions: the institutional theory of political trust and the cultural theory of political trust. The institutional theory of political trust considers that citizens' trust in institutions is endogenous to the political system (Mishler and Rose, 2005; Wong *et al.*, 2011). It is based on the assumption that trust stems from the extent to which people perceive political institutions to work effectively. An implicit assumption of many citizens is that governmental institutions should perform satisfactorily (Hetherington, 1998). Here, trust is dependent on how people evaluate the performance of institutions with respect to their demands (Luhiste, 2006; Mishler and Rose, 2001). Citizens' trust in government institutions is rational, implying that when institutions perform well, they generate trust among the public, while those performing poorly create distrust and skepticism.

Institutionalists therefore emphasize the importance of policy outcomes and citizens' evaluation of these outcomes. From this perspective, political trust depends on the government's ability to deliver effective polices in the eyes of the people (Wong *et al.*, 2011). Thus, the performance explanation of institutional trust is based on the assumption that people trust things they perceive to be working effectively (Luhiste, 2006). This is important for tourism development because citizens often hold the government responsible for policy decisions and for improving tourism policy making, particularly in democratic societies (Bramwell, 2011). The institutional theory of political trust has received considerable support in many studies (e.g. Chen *et al.*, 1997; Luhiste, 2006; Mishler and Rose, 2001, 2005; Wang, 2005; Wong *et al.*, 2011).

Economic performance of government actors in tourism development

There is considerable debate about which aspects of institutional performance are important. However, political scientists generally agree that the economic performance of institutions has a strong impact on citizens' trust (Mishler and Rose, 2001, 2005). The economic performance hypothesis focuses on the government's ability to meet citizens' expectations in the economic domain (Luhiste, 2006). Thus, institutions are trusted based on the extent to which they produce desired economic outcomes. Political economy suggests that a key role for the government is intervention to encourage the conditions for capital accumulation and economic expansion (Bevir, 2009). In the context of tourism development, government often gives priority to economic outcomes and securing immediate economic returns, although it intervenes to protect environmental and socio-cultural resources (Bramwell, 2011; Wang and Bramwell, 2012). Priority is often given to the economy because this produces wealth for the citizens and fosters political support for development (Jessop, 2008).

A number of empirical studies confirm that a significant relationship exists between economic performance of government institutions and citizens' trust in government. For example, Wang's (2005) findings suggested that the legitimacy of political institutions in China as perceived by the citizens was largely determined by the economic performance of those institutions. Chen *et al.*'s (1997) study found a positive relationship between citizens' evaluation of economic performance of government institutions and trust in those political institutions. Wong *et al.*'s (2011) research on six Asian societies also revealed that the citizens' perceived economic performance of government institutions was a significant determinant of their trust in government. Several other studies have validated a significant positive relationship between perceived economic performance of government institutions and citizens' trust in those institutions (e.g. Brehm and Rahn, 1997; Citrin and Green, 1986; Hetherington, 1998; Miller and Borelli, 1991; Mishler and Rose, 2001). Based on the theoretical and empirical evidence from the literature, it is reasonable to extrapolate that residents' trust in government actors involved in tourism is likely to be influenced by their perceptions of the economic performance of those actors in tourism. Hence, the following proposition is developed:

> *Proposition 1: Residents' perceptions of the economic performance of government actors involved in tourism development and planning influence political trust.*

Political performance of government actors in tourism development

Political performance of government institutions is usually measured by the extent of corruption in institutions (Wong *et al.*, 2011) and government's capacity to produce procedural goods and desired output such as equal and fair treatment to citizens, protection of civil liberties, and a transparent and effective administration (Luhiste, 2006). Although tourism is often considered to be a solution for several economic and social challenges, in reality, it rarely lives up to community expectations (Moscardo, 2011). Tourism development is often accompanied by community conflict and concerns and is often criticized for marginalizing local residents in the process (Moscardo, 2011). External businesses and society's elites often derive most of the benefits from development, resulting in inequality among social actors, including local community members. These issues hinder the development of residents' trust in government actors involved in tourism, because factors such as inequality, extent of universalism of institutions, and fairness in development have been found to adversely influence citizens' trust (e.g. Freitag and Buhlmann, 2009).

In general, research suggests that citizens' positive evaluation of the political performance of government actors is positively related to citizens' trust in those actors. Luhiste's (2006) study in the Baltic States suggested that the political performance of government institutions was a significant determinant of citizens' trust in those institutions. Mishler and Rose (2005) also reported a positive relationship between the political performance of government actors and citizens' trust in those actors. Such a relationship is validated by several other studies carried out in advanced democracies (e.g. Aberbach and Walker, 1970; Citrin and Green, 1986; Hetherington, 1998; Miller and Borelli, 1991; Newton, 1999) as well as postcommunist countries (e.g. Johnson, 2005; Mishler and Rose, 1997; Rose *et al.*, 1998). Thus, based on the above review, it can reasonably be proposed that the political performance of government actors involved in tourism development is likely to be a determinant of residents' trust in those actors. Therefore, the following proposition is presented:

> *Proposition 2: Residents' perceptions of the political performance of government actors involved in tourism development and planning influence political trust.*

Level of power

Power is a central concept of SET (Emerson, 1962) and an underlying theme of political economy (Mosedale, 2011). It has been a subject of discussion in the social science literature since the days of the Ancient Greece (Hall, 2010). However, it remains elusive despite the vast number of studies on the concept. Although it is widely used in social science research, there is little agreement as to what constitutes power, how to conceptualize it, and how to operationalize the concept in the research process (Doorne, 1998). Its elusiveness is demonstrated by the disagreement with respect to the definition and locus of power between sociologists and political scientists (Bachrach and Baratz, 1962). Political scientists argue that power is widely diffused in society and among social actors, while sociologists note that power is highly centralized. Consequently, the latter group styles itself as "elitist" and the former as "pluralist." The divergent views on power have led researchers to conclude that it is an essentially contested concept.

Wolf (1999) provides an interesting perspective on power that highlights its omnipresence in society and in social relations by arguing that:

> Power is often spoken of as if it were a unitary and independent force, sometime incarnated in the image of a giant monster such as Leviathan or

Behemoth, or else as a machine that grows in capacity and ferocity by accumulating and generating more powers, more entities like itself. Yet it is best understood neither as an anthropomorphic force nor a giant machine but as an aspect of all relations among people.

(p. 4)

Dahl (1968) referred to power in modern social science as "subsets of relations among social units such that the behaviors of one or more units . . . depend in some circumstances on the behavior of other units" (p. 407). Both Wolf (1999) and Dahl (1968) consider power as a relationship construct. Their definitions highlight the manner in which power works differently in interpersonal and institutional relationships and society as a whole (Hall, 2011).

Power is ubiquitous in tourism (Cheong and Miller, 2000), and it governs the interactions among actors influencing or trying to influence the formulation of tourism policy and the ways in which it is implemented (Hall, 1994). All decisions affecting tourism development, nature of government intervention, management of tourism, and community tourism issues emerge from a political process involving the values of actors in a struggle for power (Hall, 2003). Thus, power among actors involved in tourism policy and planning is a central theme of many recent studies (e.g. Beritelli and Laesser 2011; Bramwell and Meyer, 2007). The debate on the structure of power in tourism is driven by a number of key questions: (1) What organization, group, or class in the social structure under study receives the most of what people seek and value (who benefits)? (2) What organization, group, or class is over-represented in the decision-making process (who sits)? (3) What organization, group, or class wins in the decision-making process (who wins)? (4) Who is considered to be powerful by others (who has a reputation for power)? (Domhoff, 2007).

An important, but neglected aspect of the political arrangements of government institutions is the influence of the power-sharing aspects of those institutions on the development of public trust (Freitag and Buhlmann, 2009). Issues of power and trust become important because government institutions are often distant from the daily lives of people (Gabriel and Trudinger, 2011; Hetherington and Globetti, 2002), and political outcomes and intentions of government are not always fully known to the public (Lewis and Weigert, 1985). In this context, Luhiste (2006) argued that, "in situations where one does not have full information about the intentions and outcomes of governance, one is still confident that government would not misuse its power and would not willingly harm one" (p. 478). The researcher went on to argue that trust in government is the belief that political institutions would not misuse power.

The relationship between power and trust is considered to be complementary and opposing components of social behavior (Ireland and Webb, 2007). They function as alternative ways of controlling an exchange relationship, although with different effects (Walker *et al.*, 2007). However, power is often a precondition rather than an alternative to trust (Bachman *et al.*, 2001). Power determines trust, because it influences the partners' evaluation of the relative worth of the exchange relationship and the kinds of cooperation that take place on the basis of truth (Farrell, 2004). Cook *et al*. (2005) noted that power inequalities create "fertile ground for distrust" (p. 40) and "commonly block the possibility of trust" (p. 42). Farrell (2004) argued that trust is difficult to achieve when disparity of power exists. Institutions face lack of trust from citizens if their arrangements hinder citizens' participation in decision making and if the community feels singled out from the policy processes (Gabriel *et al*., 2002). Evidence suggests that institutions characterized by power sharing and consensual decision making by integrating citizens in decision-making processes, contribute to the development of public trust (Freitag and Buhlmann, 2009). Some studies, although few, suggest that power positively influences the level of trust one actor places on the other actor in a social exchange relationship (Oberg and Svensson, 2010; Oskarsson *et al*., 2009). Based on the above review, the following proposition is presented:

> *Proposition 3: Residents' perceptions of their level of power in tourism development influence political trust.*

Correlates of political trust: culturalist approach

In contrast to the institutional theory of political trust which suggests trust is endogenous to the political system, cultural theory posits that political trust is exogenous to the political system. That is, trust originates not from within the political spheres but outside of it, in the long-standing and deeply held beliefs about people that are rooted in cultural norms and values in a society (Mishler and Rose, 2001, 2005; Wong *et al*., 2011). Cultural theorists posit that trust is a phenomenon linked to basic forms of social relationships and are shaped by cultural orientations that assign meanings and values to events (Eckstein *et al*., 1998; Mishler and Rose, 2001; Shi, 2001). Culturalists further note that trust in institutions varies across cultures and societies (Fukuyama, 1995; Inglehart, 1997). For example, Shi (2001) reported considerable variations in political trust in People's Republic of China and Taiwan, which the researcher attributed to cultural value differences between the two nations. Although proponents of cultural theory do not deny the influence of institutional variables on political trust, they argue that cultural influences on trust are deeper and more profound. They even assert that citizens' perceptions of the economic and political performance of government institutions are culturally determined (Mishler and Rose, 2005). Cultural theory of political trust has received some support in different types of economies and societies, although with some contradictions (Christensen and Laegreid, 2005; Inglehart, 1997; Norris, 1999).

Interpersonal trust

In a modern society involving interactions of people of different backgrounds, interpersonal trust is inherent to civic culture and is the basis for social connectedness, peaceful collective action, inclusiveness, trust in government, and democracy itself (Delhey *et al.*, 2011; Helliwell and Putman, 2004; Inglehart, 1999; Putman, 2000; Uslaner, 2002). Consequently, interpersonal trust has become an important topic of debate among social scientists (Delhey *et al.*, 2011). Proponents of cultural theory of political trust argue that trust is generated by nonpolitical factors such as a general disposition to trust or distrust in others (Luhiste, 2006). Culturalists argue that institutional trust is an extension of interpersonal trust learned in life, and later projected onto political institutions. From birth, individuals learn to trust or distrust others and are influenced by how others treat them, and how others, in return, react to their behaviors (Mishler and Rose, 2001). Trust starts within the immediate family, and eventually, the set of interactions extends to include, friends, colleagues, and neighbors. Over time, trust is extended in the context of the individual and political institutions. Thus, cultural theorists postulate a hierarchy of trust that first starts with an individual's interpersonal bond with the family arising through socialization. At a second level, the individual's trust is extended to other people not personally known to him/her. On a third level, the individual extends the trust to political institutions. The latter reflects the spillover effects of interpersonal trust to institutional trust. Such spillover effects underlie the relationship between interpersonal trust and political trust.

Luhiste's (2006) study findings on the Baltic States suggested that institutional trust depended on the extent to which individuals trust other people. Evidence also suggests that interpersonal trust is positively related to trust in political institutions in democratic economies (e.g. Brehm and Rahn, 1997; Newton, 2001) as well as postcommunist societies (e.g. Mishler and Rose, 2001; Dowley and Silver, 2002). However, contradicting the above observations, some studies found no significant relationship between interpersonal trust and political trust in institutions (e.g. Rohrschneider and Schmitt-Beck, 2002), while still others revealed a negative relationship between the two variables (e.g. Aberg, 2000; Kim, 2005). Based on the postulates of cultural theory of political trust and the empirical evidence from the literature, it is reasonable to suggest that interpersonal trust among residents is likely to be a determinant of their level of trust in government actors involved in tourism planning and development. The above review led to the development of the following proposition:

Proposition 4: Interpersonal trust influences political trust.

Correlates of political trust: social exchange theory

Early studies on residents' support for tourism were criticized for being atheoretical, and, as a result, it was unclear why residents perceived and responded to tourism as they did, and under what conditions they reacted to the impacts of the industry (Husbands, 1989). To address these shortcomings and provide a better explanation of residents' perceptions of and their support for tourism, researchers began to use several theoretical frameworks to guide their research.

Among these theories, SET has been instrumental in strengthening the theoretical foundation of this field of investigation. Originally developed in sociology to explain social interactions, SET has been found to be one of the most applicable and relevant theories in explaining community support for tourism development (Andereck *et al.*, 2005). Emerson (1981) noted that social exchange involves a minimum of two persons, each of whom provides some benefits to the other, contingent upon rewards from the other. A few seminal studies that have contributed to the development of SET are Homans (1958), Thibaut and Kelley (1959), Emerson (1962), and Blau (1964). Homans (1958) emphasized social behavior in the exchange process. Thibaut and Kelley (1959) discussed how actors in an exchange relationship weigh the benefits of the exchange relation. Emerson's (1961) work related to the concept of power between the actors in an exchange relationship, while Blau (1964) emphasized social interaction as an exchange process.

SET is based on the premise that human behavior or social interaction is an exchange of activity, tangible and intangible, particularly of rewards and costs (Homans, 1961). It analyzes how the structure of rewards and costs in a relationship affects patterns of interaction (Molm, 1991). SET considers exchange as the basis of human behavior (Homans, 1961). Actors in an exchange process are dependent on one another for outcomes they value. They behave in a way that increases outcomes they positively value and decreases outcomes they negatively value, and if the benefits from the exchange exceed the costs, actors engage in recurring exchanges over time (Cook *et al.*, 1993). SET posits that all individuals' decisions to engage in an interaction process are based on the use of a subjective cost-benefit analysis and the comparison of alternatives. Individuals engage in an exchange process once they have judged the rewards and the costs, and will enter relationships in which they can maximize benefits and minimize costs. Actors will engage in an exchange if the resulting rewards are of value to them and the perceived costs do not exceed the perceived benefits (Ap, 1992). Interactions are likely to continue only if both parties feel that they are benefiting more from the exchange than they are giving up.

Social exchanges differ from economic ones in several fundamental ways. Although benefits involved in economic exchanges are formal and often contractual, such benefits and their exact nature are rarely negotiated in social exchanges (Blau, 1964). Exchange of benefits is a voluntary action and entails unspecified future obligations (Konovsky and Pugh, 1994; Whitener *et al.*, 1998). Benefits do not occur on a calculated or *quid pro quo* basis (Konovsky and Pugh, 1994). There is also no guarantee that there will be a reciprocation of benefits. Thus, social exchanges involve uncertainty, particularly in the early stages of the relationship (Whitener *et al.*, 1998). Like economic exchanges, in social exchanges, there exists an expectation of some future returns for contributions between the exchange partners, although the exact nature of the returns is not known or negotiated in social exchanges (Blau, 1964). Social exchanges are also characterized by long-term fairness in contrast to short-term fairness, which underpins economic exchanges (Konovsky and Pugh, 1994). According to SET, social exchange involves benefits with economic and/or social outcomes (Cropanzano and Mitchell, 2005; Emerson, 1976; Lambe *et al.*, 2001). Whitener *et al.* (1998) noted that exchanges without any objective utility may have a significant impact on the social dimension of the relationship.

SET posits that trust between exchange partners can be generated through regular discharge of obligations and through the gradual expansion of exchanges over time (Blau, 1964). The extent to which a partner has proven to be reliable in previous social interactions with another actor determines the level of trust between them. Trust is also determined by the expectations of one partner (e.g. residents) from another (e.g. government) in a social exchange relationship (Boon and Holmes, 1991; Lewicki and Bunker, 1994) and the extent to which the partner (e.g. government) appears benign (Yamagishi and Yamagishi, 1994). An exchange partner uses several cues such as benevolence and positive and negative outcomes to assess the trustworthiness of another partner (Bhattacharya *et al.*, 1998; Sheppard and Sherman, 1998).

Positive economic and social outcomes resulting from an exchange increase the partners' trust of each other and their commitment to maintaining the relationship (Blau, 1964; Lambe *et al.*, 2001). Farrell (2004) also asserted that the economic and nonmaterial benefits resulting from an exchange relationship influence the level of truth between the actors. In a political context, Citrin (1974) suggested that cumulative outcomes between political authorities and citizens determine the level of public trust in government institutions. He further argued that institutions create policies, and in exchange, they receive trust from citizens who are satisfied with these policies and cynicism from dissatisfied individuals. Based on the theoretical postulates of SET and the arguments that positive and negative outcomes from an exchange influence trust, it is reasonable to extrapolate that residents' trust in government actors is likely to be predicted by residents' perceptions of the benefits and costs of tourism development. Perceptions of benefits are likely to lead to higher levels of trust in government actors, while perceptions of costs may adversely influence trust. Based on these arguments, the following proposition is formulated:

> *Proposition 5: Residents' perceptions of the benefits and costs of tourism development influence political trust.*

Social exchange theory and political support for tourism development

Sutton (1967) argued that the encounter between the host community and the guests "may provide either an opportunity for rewarding and satisfying exchanges, or it may stimulate and reinforce impulses to exploitation on the part of the host" (p. 221). Supporting his assertion, a number of studies (e.g. Gursoy *et al.*, 2010; Gursoy and Rutherford, 2004; Nunkoo and Gursoy, 2012; Nunkoo and Ramkissoon, 2010a, 2010c, 2011a, 2011b) found that the economic, socio-cultural, and environmental elements resulting from the host–tourism exchange process affect residents' support for tourism development. The findings of these studies suggest that the value attributed to the elements of the exchange influences the way in which residents of a destination perceive tourism and determines the level of community acceptance of tourism development. "The way that residents perceive the economic, socio-cultural and environmental elements of exchange affects the manner in which they react to tourism" (Andriotis and Vaughan, 2003, p. 173). Such reactions are manifested in residents' support for or opposition to tourism development. Findings suggest that in a host–tourism context, the elements in an exchange process include not only economic benefits and costs but social, cultural, and environmental ones.

SET is particularly appealing to study political support for tourism because it takes into account those benefits and costs to explain support. Support is defined as an "attitude by which a person orients himself to an object either favorably or unfavorably, positively or negatively" (Easton, 1965, p. 436). Here, the "object" refers to tourism development. Government requires a certain amount of political support for its policies to persist or flourish. In a tourism context, political economy suggests that it is important for government to maintain legitimacy and influence on governance processes by ensuring that the local population supports its policies (Wang and Bramwell, 2012).

Residents' support for tourism development is influenced by their perceptions of the benefits and costs of the sector (Gursoy *et al.*, 2010; Nunkoo and Gursoy, 2012; Nunkoo and Ramkissoon, 2011a, 2011b). Previous studies suggest that residents perceive tourism to result in employment opportunities, better infrastructure, more business and investment opportunities (Dyer *et al.*, 2007; Nunkoo and Ramkissoon, 2010c, 2011a), more public development, and improvement in the local economy (Latkova and Vogt, 2012). Most studies investigating the relationship between perceived economic benefits and support report a positive relationship between the two constructs (Gursoy and Rutherford, 2004; Gursoy *et al.*, 2010). The positive socio-cultural impacts of tourism as perceived by residents also are well documented. Studies suggest that tourism provides opportunities for cultural exchanges between hosts and guests (Besculides *et al.*, 2002), increases entertainment opportunities for local people (Latkova and Vogt, 2012), encourages development of cultural activities (Gursoy *et al.*, 2010), improves the image of a destination (Nunkoo and Ramkissoon, 2007), and leads to the preservation of cultural and historic sites (Nunkoo and Ramkissoon 2010c).

SET postulates that individuals are likely to support tourism development if they believe that they will gain from the development (Ap, 1992; Andereck *et al.*, 2005; Nunkoo and Ramkissoon, 2010a). In support of SET, several studies report a positive relationship between perceived benefits and support for tourism (Gursoy *et al.*, 2010; Latkova and Vogt, 2012; Nunkoo and Gursoy, 2012; Nunkoo and Ramkissoon, 2010a, 2010c, 2011a, 2011b). Based on the preceding theoretical and empirical discussion from the literature, it can logically be proposed that stronger perceptions of the benefits of tourism are likely to lead to more support for tourism development, while weaker perceptions of the benefits of tourism are likely to lead to less support for development. Hence, the following proposition is developed:

Proposition 6: Residents' perceptions of the benefits of tourism development influence political support for the sector's development.

Development of tourism also results in several costs on local communities that may threaten legitimacy of government and political support (Wang and Bramwell, 2012). Tourism has been found to increase cost of living (Liu and Var, 1986; Perdue *et al.*, 1990), prices of land and housing (Latkova and Vogt, 2012; Nunkoo and Ramkissoon, 2011a; Pizam, 1978), and prices of goods and services (Belisle and Hoy, 1980; Husbands, 1989; Jackson and Inbarakan, 2006; Pizam, 1978). Studies also suggest that tourism development often leads to a lack of economic diversification (Jackson and Inbakaran, 2006), negatively affects the occupational distribution by sector, and adversely affects a community's traditional employment pattern (Nunkoo and Gursoy, 2012). Residents also perceive that tourism destroys the natural environment, increases environmental pollution (Dyer *et al.*, 2007; Nunkoo and Ramkissoon, 2011a; Nunkoo and Ramkissoon, 2010c), causes litter, leads to overcrowding, creates traffic congestion (Dyer *et al.*, 2007; Latkova and Vogt, 2012; Nunkoo and Ramkissoon, 2010c), increases prostitution in a destination area (Dyer *et al.*, 2007; Nunkoo and Ramkissoon, 2011a), causes vandalism, changes local culture, increases pressure on local services (Dyer *et al.*, 2007), and contributes to crime and substance abuse (Nunkoo and Ramkissoon, 2010c).

SET posit that residents' who perceive tourism development to result in costs are likely to be less supportive of the sector's development. Findings of some empirical studies confirm this postulate of SET and suggest that residents' perceptions of the costs of tourism are negatively related to their support for its development (e.g. Gursoy *et al.*, 2010; Gursoy and Rutherford, 2004; Ko and Stewart, 2002; Latkova and Vogt, 2012; Nunkoo and Gursoy, 2012; Nunkoo and Ramkissoon, 2011a; Perdue *et al.*, 1990). However, some other research reveals an insignificant relationship between the two constructs (e.g. Dyer *et al.*, 2007; Gursoy and Kendall, 2006; Gursoy *et al.*, 2002). Thus, findings have generally been inconclusive, suggesting the need for further research to confirm the relationship between residents' perceptions of the costs of tourism and their support for the sector. The theoretical and empirical evidence from the literature led to the development of the following proposition:

Proposition 7: Residents' perceptions of the costs of tourism development influence political support for the sector's development.

Citizens' acceptance of government policies and decisions depends on political trust (Marien and Hooghe, 2011), because individuals rely on their trust in institutions before making judgments about the acceptability of development projects and policies (Bronfman *et al.*, 2009). Hetherington and Globetti (2002) noted that even if people are not well aware of the intricacies of government policies and strategies, they do develop a general impression about the mandate of government, and this impression acts as a decision rule for supporting or opposing government activities. Residents' trust strengthens their feelings that government institutions are acting fairly and providing equitable benefits to all citizens, and if governments are seen as acting in these ways, it engenders political trust. If people perceive the government as untrustworthy, they are likely to reject its policies, and if they consider it as trustworthy, they tend to support its policies (Bronfman *et al.*, 2009; Rudolph and Evans, 2005). Harisalo and Stenvall (2002) argued that if residents trust ministries, they tend to support governmental policies and keep their demands reasonable. Easton (1965) noted that citizens' trust in institutions affects their attitudes toward government policies.

A number of studies in political science, social psychology, and organizational theory confirm the significant influence of trust on people's acceptance of policies (Hetherington and Globetti, 2002). Tyler and Degoey's (1995) study also revealed that trust had the largest influence on people's willingness to accept decisions of management and political authorities. Hetherington and Globetti's (2002) study reported a positive relationship between trust in government and support for governmental policies. More recently, Backstrom and Edlund (2012) noted a significant positive relationship between trust in government institutions and support for welfare policies. Using SET as a theoretical base, Nunkoo and Ramkissoon's (2012) and Nunkoo *et al.*'s (2012) study revealed that residents' trust in tourism institutions positively influenced their level of support for tourism development. A number of other studies have validated the relationship between trust in government and political support for government policies (e.g. Earle *et al.*, 2007; Gabriel and Trudinger, 2011; Hetherington, 2004; Marien and Hooghe, 2011; Rudolph and Evans, 2005). Hence, the following proposition is formulated:

Proposition 8: Political trust influences support for tourism development.

Conclusion

Understanding political support for tourism development has become an important area of research since the 1980s, after diffusion of the sustainable development concept in tourism studies. It is now well recognized that residents are important stakeholders in tourism and that it is difficult to develop tourism in a sustainable way without their input and active support. This has led to a proliferation of studies that assess community support for tourism development and the antecedents of such support. Although early studies on this topic were of an atheoretical nature, researchers have increasingly made use of theories such as SET to understand the ways in which residents respond to tourism development and the circumstances that prompt them to do so. On one hand, use of SET has strengthened the theoretical base of and made significant theoretical contributions to this area of research; on the other hand, some researchers have found the theory to lack predictive power in explaining residents' support for tourism and is "an incomplete structure for understanding response to tourism phenomenon by community residents" (Andereck *et al.*, 2005, p. 1073; Ward and Berno, 2011). This is probably because researchers have failed to consider all key variables of the theory (e.g. trust and power between actors) in a single framework (Nunkoo and Ramkissoon 2012; Nunkoo *et al.*, 2012).

It is therefore important that studies make a complete use of SET to derive the full benefits offered by the theory and to be able to reach accurate conclusions about the predictive power of the theory in explaining political support for tourism. In addition, as advocated by some researchers (e.g. Andereck *et al.*, 2005), it is also important that SET is used jointly with other theories to investigate residents' support for tourism so that new perspectives on community support and its determinants can be discovered. Prompted by this notion, the study developed a comprehensive framework based on three theories: SET, institutional theory of political trust, and cultural theory of political trust. SET is derived from sociology, while the other two theories are borrowed from political science and offer contrasting views on the determinants of political trust. The framework investigates the determinants of political trust in tourism development and the relationship between the latter and political support for tourism development.

The discussion here contributes to the limited literature on residents' trust in government actors in the context of tourism development and planning. Central to our discussion, is the element of trust. "Trust relationships are fundamental to the stability of democratic societies and to the orderly conduct of social and economic affairs, and they have become a central topic of concern in the social science" (Cook, 2001, p. xxviii). Trust is also an essential component of civic culture (Marien and Hooghe, 2011) and an important mechanism for social coordination, problem solving, and functioning of modern and complex societies (Gabriel and Trudinger, 2011). In a political context, trust is important, because it ensures a democratic political system (Almond and Verba, 1963) and citizens' political support for development (Earle *et al.*, 2007; Gabriel and Trudinger, 2011; Marien and Hooghe, 2011).

However, despite the centrality of trust for the development of a modern and democratic society, little research has been conducted on political trust in tourism studies. In fact, the literature on the politics of tourism has been traditionally dominated by the concept of power, and there has been a little consideration of the vocabulary of trust. Research on residents' support for tourism also suffers from a paucity of studies on trust. Although several researchers and scholars have developed and tested different models of community support for tourism based on SET (e.g. Gursoy and Rutherford, 2004; Gursoy *et al.*, 2010; Nunkoo and Gursoy, 2012; Nunkoo and Ramkissoon, 2010a, 2010b, 2010c, 2011b; Latkova and Vogt, 2012), trust as a key variable of the theory has been omitted in most studies. Social exchange theorists describe trust as the most important of the key variables in social exchanges (Blau, 1964; Holmes, 1981; Homans, 1958). Yet the role of trust in the context of a social exchange relationship between residents and government actors in tourism is not well understood by researchers. This is despite the fact that several studies in political science suggest that residents' trust in government institutions is a strong determinant of their political support for development (e.g. Gabriel and Trudinger, 2011; Hetherington, 2004; Hetherington and Globetti, 2002; Marien and Hooghe, 2011). The implications of these studies are that existing research on this topic is based on incomplete theoretical propositions and may be lacking in predictive power. It is therefore important that these studies are enhanced and made theoretically more robust so that a more accurate analysis of residents' support for tourism can be made. The framework proposed in the present study addresses these gaps in literature.

Another noteworthy theoretical contribution of our discussion relates to the simultaneous inclusion of the concepts of trust and power in a single framework. Social scientists have been urging for more research on the relationship between power and trust than hitherto has been carried out on trust and note that, theoretically, they should be studied jointly (Oberg and Svensson, 2010). Cook *et al.* (2005) argued that "power inequalities are ubiquitous in modern societies; thus, any treatise of trust must take them seriously. They cannot be assumed away in any theory that deals with the world of social relations and social institutions" (p. 40). These researchers stressed the need for more empirical research on the relationship between power and trust, because this remains poorly investigated. However, so far, scant empirical evidence exists on the relationship between power and trust in the broader social science literature, including that of tourism. Social scientists are still unsure whether one needs to be powerful to be trusted or whether power drives out trust (Cook *et al.*, 2005; Hardin, 2004). Therefore, it is important that both constructs are considered simultaneously in a single conceptual model. This discussion addresses this gap by incorporating the concepts of power and trust in a single framework. By understanding the dynamics of power and trust in the context of tourism development, partners involved in the exchange can strategically adjust social relations to achieve mutually desired outcomes. By considering these concepts jointly, our discussion provides researchers and scholars with a better theoretical understanding of why residents are, or are not, positively or negatively disposed toward tourism development.

Finally, the theoretical basis of the framework proposed here should also be seen as a contribution to the literature. Nunkoo *et al.* (2013) reviewed 140 studies on residents' support for tourism published in *Annals of Tourism Research, Tourism Management,* and *Journal of Travel Research* and reported that the majority of studies on the topic made use of SET. The discussion here is drawn from three different theories (SET, institutional theory of political trust, and cultural theory of political trust) to explain political support for tourism development. The latter theories of political trust complement SET, which has been found to suffer from a number of weaknesses and a lack of predictive power (Fredline and Faulkner, 2000; Nunkoo *et al.,* 2010; Nunkoo and Gursoy, 2012; Pearce *et al.,* 1996; Ward and Berno, 2011). While some researchers found full support for SET (e.g. Nunkoo and Gursoy, 2012; Nunkoo and Ramkissoon, 2011a, 2011b, 2012), other studies found the theory to be partially applicable at best (e.g. Andereck *et al.,* 2005; McGehee and Andereck, 2004). Andereck *et al.* (2005) encouraged researchers to investigate community support from other theoretical perspectives because of such weaknesses. This leads to a potentially theoretically more robust framework than existing ones because our discussion embraces the concept of theoretical triangulation that involves using multiple theoretical perspectives. Benefits of such an approach are well documented in the literature (see for e.g. Decrop, 1999).

References

Aberbach, J. D., and Walker, J. L. (1970). Political trust and racial ideology. *American Political Science Review, 64*(4), 1199–1220.

Aberg, M. (2000). Putman's social capital theory goes east: A study of western Ukraine and L'Viv. *Europe-Asia Studies, 52*(2), 295–317.

Almond, G., and Verba, S. (1963). *The civic culture*. Princeton, NJ: Princeton University Press.

Andereck, K. L., Valentine, K. M., Knopf, R. C., and Vogt, C. A. (2005). Residents' perceptions of community tourism impacts. *Annals of Tourism Research, 32*(4), 1056–1076.

Andriotis, K., and Vaughan, R. D. (2003). Urban residents' attitudes toward tourism development: The case of Crete. *Journal of Travel Research, 42*, 172–185.

Ap, J. (1992). Residents' perceptions on tourism impacts. *Annals of Tourism Research, 19*, 665–690.

Bachmann, R., Knights, D., and Sydow, J. (2001). Trust and control in organizational relations [Editorial]. *Organizational Studies, 22*(2), 5–8.

Bachrach, P., and Baratz, M. S. (1962). Two faces of power. *American Political Science Review, 56*(4), 947–952.

Backstrom, A., and Edlund, J. (2012). *Understanding the link between trust in public institutions and welfare policy preferences: On the role of market institutions for uncovering a supposed relationship.* Working paper 4/2012. Umea, Sweden. Department of Sociology, Umea University.

Belisle, F. J., and Hoy, D. R. (1980). The perceived impact of tourism by residents: A case study in Santa Maria, Columbia. *Annals of Tourism Research, 7*(1), 83–101.

Beritelli, P., and Laesser, C. (2011). Power dimensions and influence reputation in tourist destination: Empirical evidence from a network of actors and stakeholders. *Tourism Management, 32*(6), 1299–1309.

Besculides, A., Lee, M. E., and McCormick, P. J. (2002). Residents' perceptions of the cultural benefits of tourism. *Annals of Tourism Research, 29*(2), 303–319.

Besley, T., and Burgess, R. (2002). The political economy of government responsiveness: Theory and evidence from India. *Quarterly Journal of Economics, 117*(4), 1415–1451.

Bevir, M. (2009). *Key concepts in governance*. London. Sage.

Bhattacharya, R., Devinney, T., and Pillutla, M. M. (1998). A formal model of trust based on outcomes. *Academy of Management Review, 23*(3), 459–472.

Bianchi, R. (2009). The "critical turn" in tourism studies: A radical critique. *Tourism Geographies, 11*(4), 484–504.

Blau, P. M. (1964). *Exchange and power in social life*. New York: John Wiley.

Boon, S., and Holmes, J. (1991). The dynamics of interpersonal trust: Resolving uncertainty in the face of risk. In R. Hindle and J. Groebel (Eds.), *Cooperation and prosocial behavior* (pp. 167–182). New York: Cambridge University Press.

Bramwell, B. (1994). Rural tourism and sustainable rural tourism. *Journal of Sustainable Tourism, 2*(1/2), 1–6.

Bramwell, B. (2011). Governance, the state and sustainable tourism: A political economy approach. *Journal of Sustainable Tourism, 19*(4/5), 459–477.

Bramwell, B., and Meyer, D. (2007). Power and tourism policy relations in transition. *Annals of Tourism Research, 34*(3), 766–788.

Brehm, J., and Rahn, W. (1997). Individual-level evidence for the causes and consequences of social capital. *American Journal of Political Science, 41*(3), 999–1023.

Bronfman, N. C., Vazquez, E. L., and Dorantes, G. (2009). An empirical study for the direct and indirect links between trust in regulatory institutions and acceptability of hazards. *Safety Science, 47*, 686–692.

Charlton, C., and Essex, S. (2000). The involvement of district councils in tourism in England and Wales. *Geoforum, 27*(2), 175–192.

Chen, J., Zhong, Y., Hillard, J., and Scheb, J. (1997). Assessing political support in China: Citizens' evaluations of governmental effectiveness and legitimacy. *Journal of Contemporary China, 6*(16), 551–566.

Cheong, S. M., and Miller, M. L. (2000). Power and tourism: A Foucauldian observation. *Annals of Tourism Research, 27*(2), 371–390.

Christensen, T., and Laegreid, P. (2005). Trust in government: The relative importance of service satisfaction, political factors, and demography. *Public Performance and Management Review, 28*(4), 487–511.

Citrin, J. (1974). Comment: The political relevance of trust in government. *The American Political Science Review, 68*(3), 973–988.

Citrin, J., and Green, D. P. (1986). Presidential leadership and the resurgence of trust in government. *British Journal of Political Science, 16*(4), 431–453.

Citrin, J., and Luks, S. (2001). Political trust revisited: Déjà vu all over again? In J. R. Hibbing and E. Theiss-Morse (Eds.), *What is it about government that Americans dislike?* (pp. 9–27). New York: Cambridge University Press.

Cook, K. S. (2001). *Trust in society.* New York: Russell Sage Foundation.

Cook, K. S., Hardin, R., and Levi, M. (2005). *Cooperation without trust?* New York: Russell Sage Foundation.

Cook, K. S., Molm, L. D., and Yamagishi T. (1993). *Exchange relations and exchange networks: Recent developments in social exchange theory.* In J. Berger and M. Zelditch, Jr. (Eds.), *Theoretical research programs: Studies in the growth of theory* (pp. 296–322). Stanford, CA: Stanford University Press.

Cropanzano R., and Mitchell, M. S. (2005). Social exchange theory: An interdisciplinary review. *Journal of Management, 31*, 874–900.

Dahl, R. A. (1968). Power. In D. L. Sills. (Ed.), *International encyclopedia of the social sciences* (Vol. 12, pp. 405–415). New York: Macmillan Free Press.

Decrop, A. (1999). Triangulation in qualitative tourism research. *Tourism Management, 20*, 157–161.

Delhey, J., Newton, K., Welzel, C. (2011). How general is trust in "most people"? Solving the radius of trust problem. *American Sociological Review, 76*, 786–807.

Domhoff, G. W. (2007). C. Wright Mills, Floyd Hunter, and 50 years of power structure research. *Michigan Sociological Review, 21*, 1–54.

Doorne, S. (1998). Power, participation and perception: An insider's perspective on the politics of the Wellington waterfront redevelopment. *Current Issues in Tourism, 1*(2), 129–166.

Dowley, K., and Silver, B. (2002). Social capital, ethnicity and support for democracy in the post-community states. *Europe-Asia Studies, 54*(4), 505–527.

Dyer, P., Gursoy, D., Sharma, B., and Carter, J. (2007). Structural modeling of resident perceptions of tourism and associated development on the Sunshine Coast, Australia. *Tourism Management, 28*(2), 409–422.

Earle, T. C., Siegrist, M., and Gutscher, H. (2007). *Trust, risk perceptions and the TCC model of cooperation. Trust in cooperative risk management: Uncertainty and skepticism on the public mind.* Earthscan.

Easton, D. (1965). *A system analysis of political life.* New York: Wiley.

Eckstein, H., Fleron, F. J., Hoffman, E. P., and Reisinger, W. M. (1998). *Can democracy take root in post-Soviet Russia? Explorations in state-society relations.* Lanham, MD: Rowman and Littlefield.

Elliot, J. (1997). *Tourism: Politics and public sector involvement.* New York: Routledge.

Emerson, R. M. (1962, February). Power-dependence relations. *American Journal of Sociological Review, 27*, 31–41.

Emerson, R. M. (1976). Social exchange theory. *Annual Review of Sociology, 2*, 335–362.

Emerson, R. M. (1981). Social exchange. In M. Rosenberg and R. Turner (Eds.), *Social psychology: Sociological perspective* (pp. 3–24). New York: Basic Books.

Farrell, H. (2004). Trust, distrust and power. In H. Russell (Ed.), *Distrust* (pp. 85–105). New York: Russell Sage Foundation.

Fredline, E., and Faulkner, B. (2000). Host community reactions: A cluster analysis. *Annals of Tourism Research, 27*(3), 763–784.

Freitag, M., and Buhlmann, M. (2009). Crafting trust: The role of political institutions in a comparative perspective. *Comparative Political Studies, 42*, 1537–1566.

Fukuyama, F. (1995). *Trust: Social virtues and the creation of prosperity.* NY: Free Press.

Gabriel, O. W., Kunz, V., Rossdeutscher, S., and Deth, J. W. (2002). *Social capital and democracy: The resources of civil society in a comparative perspective.* Vienna, Austria: WUV Universitatsverlag.

Gabriel, O. W., and Trudinger, E. M. (2011). Embellishing welfare state reforms? Political trust and the support for welfare state reforms in Germany. *German Politics, 20*(2), 273–292.

Godfrey, K. B. (1998). Attitudes toward "sustainable tourism" in the UK: A view from local government. *Tourism Management, 19*(3), 213–224.

Gursoy, D., Chi, C. G., and Dyer, P. (2010). Local's attitudes toward mass and alternative tourism: The case of Sunshine Coast, Australia. *Journal of Travel Research, 49,* 381–394.

Gursoy, D., Jurowski, C., and Uysal, M. (2002). Resident attitudes: A structural modeling approach. *Annals of Tourism Research, 29*(1), 79–105.

Gursoy, D., and Kendall, K. (2006). Hosting mega events: Modeling local's support. *Annals of Tourism Research, 33*(3), 603–623.

Gursoy, D., and Rutherford, D. G. (2004). Host attitudes toward tourism: An improved structural model. *Annals of Tourism Research, 31*(3), 495–516.

Hall, C. M. (1994). *Tourism and politics: Policy, power and place.* Chichester, UK: John Wiley.

Hall, C. M. (1998). *Tourism development, dimensions, and issues* (3rd ed.). South Melbourne: Addison Wesley Longman.

Hall, C. M. (2003). Politics and place: An analysis of power in destination communities. In S. Sing, D. J. Timothy, and R. K. Dowling (Eds.), *Tourism in destination communities* (pp. 99–113). Oxon, UK: CABI.

Hall, C. M. (2005). The role of government in the management of tourism: The public sector and tourism policies. In L. Pender and R. Sharpley (Eds.), *The management of tourism* (pp. 217–230). Thousand Oaks, CA: Sage Publications.

Hall, C. M. (2006). Urban entrepreneurship, corporate interests and sports mega-events: The thin policies of competitiveness within the hard outcomes of neoliberalism. *Sociological Review, 54,* 59–70.

Hall, C. M. (2010). Power in tourism: Tourism in power. In D.V.L. Macleod and J. G. Carrier (Eds.), *Tourism, power and culture: Anthropological insights* (pp. 199–213). Bristol, UK: Channel View Publications.

Hall, C. M. (2011). Yes, Virginia, there is a tourism class. In J. Mosedale (Ed.), *Political economy of tourism: A critical perspective* (pp. 111–125). London: Routledge.

Hardin, R. (2004). Distrust: Manifestation and management. In R. Hardin (Ed.), *Distrust* (pp. 3–33). New York: Russell Sage Foundation.

Harisalo, R., and Stenvall, J. (2002, September). *Citizens' trust in government.* Paper presented at the annual conference of the European Group for Public Administration, Retrieved from http://webh01.ua.ac.be/pubsector/potsdam/paper_potsdam_stenvall_harisalo.pdf

Helliwell, J. F., and Putman, R. D. (2004). The social context of well-being. *Philosophical Transactions of the Royal Society of London, 359,* 1435–1446.

Hetherington, M. J. (1998). The political relevance of political trust. *American Political Science Review, 92,* 791–808.

Hetherington, M. J. (2004). *Why trust matters: Declining political trust and the demise of American liberalism.* Princeton, NJ: Princeton University Press.

Hetherington, M. J., and Globetti, S. (2002). Political trust and racial policy preferences. *American Journal of Political Science, 46*(2), 253–275.

Holmes, J. G. (1981). The exchange process in close relationships: Microbehavior and macromotives. In M. J. Lerner and S. C. Lerner (Eds.), *The justice motive in social behavior* (pp. 261–284). New York: Plenum.

Homans, G. (1958). Social behavior as exchange. *American Journal of Sociology, 63*(6), 597–606.

Homans, G. (1961). *Social behavior.* New York: Harcourt, Brace & World.

Husbands, W. (1989). Social statue and perception of tourism in Zambia. *Annals of Tourism Research, 16,* 237–253.

Inglehart, R. (1997). *Modernization and postmodernization: Cultural, economic, and political change in 43 societies.* Princeton, NJ: Princeton University Press.

Inglehart, R. (1999). Trust, well-being and democracy. In M. Warren (Ed.), *Democracy and trust* (pp. 88–120). Cambridge, UK: Cambridge University Press.

Inskeep, E. (1988). Tourism planning: An emerging conceptualization. *American Planning Association Journal, 54*(3), 360–372.

Ireland, R. D., and Webb, J. W. (2007). A multi-theoretic perspective on trust and power in strategic supply chains. *Journal of Operations Management, 25,* 482–497.

Jackson, M. S., and Inbarakan, R. J. (2006). Evaluating residents' attitudes and intentions to act toward tourism development in Regional Victoria, Australia. *International Journal of Tourism Research, 8,* 355–366.

Jessop, B. (2008). *State power: A strategic-relational approach.* Cambridge, UK: Polity.

Johnson, I. (2005) Political trust in societies under transformation. *International Journal of Sociology, 35*(2), 63–84.

Keogh, B. (1990). Public participation in community tourism planning. *Annals of Tourism Research, 17,* 449–465.

Kim, J. (2005). "Bowling together" isn't a cure-all: The relationship between social capital and political trust in Korea. *International Political Science Review, 26*(2), 193–213.

Ko, D. W., and Stewart, W. P. (2002). A structural model of residents' attitude for tourism development. *Tourism Management, 23,* 521–530.

Konovsky, M. A., and Pugh, S. D. (1994). Citizenship behavior and social exchange. *Academic of Management Journal, 37*(3), 656–669.

Lambe, C. Y., Wittmann, C. M., and Spekman, R. E. (2001). Social exchange theory and research on business-to-business relational exchange. *Journal of Business-to-Business Marketing, 8*(3), 1–36.

Latkova, P., and Vogt, C. A. (2012). Residents' attitudes toward existing and future tourism development in rural communities. *Journal of Travel Research, 51,* 50–67.

Lewicki, R. J., and Bunker, B. (1994). Trust in relationships: A model of trust development and decline. In B. Bunker and J. Rubin (Eds.), *Conflict, cooperation and justice.* San Francisco: Jossey-Bass.

Lewis, D. J., and Weigert, A. (1985). Trust as social reality. *Social Forces, 63*(4), 967–985.

Liu, J., and Var, T. (1986). Residential attitudes toward tourism impact in Hawaii. *Annals of Tourism Research, 13,* 193–214.

Luhiste, K. (2006). Explaining trust in political institutions: Some illustrations from the Baltic States. *Communist and Post-Communist Studies, 39,* 475–496.

Madrigal, R. (1995). Residents' perceptions and the role of government. *Annals of Tourism Research, 22*(1), 86–102.

Marien, S., and Hooghe, M. (2011). Does political trust matter? An empirical investigation into the relation between political trust and support for law compliance. *European Journal of Political Research, 50,* 267–291.

McGehee, N. G., and Andereck, K. L. (2004). Factors predicting rural residents' support of tourism. *Journal of Travel Research, 43*(2), 131–140.

Miller, A. H., and Borelli, S. A. (1991). Confidence in government during the 1980s. *American Politics Quarterly, 19*(2), 147–173.

Mishler, W., and Rose, R. (1997). Trust, distrust and skepticism: Popular evaluations of civil and political institutions in post-communist societies. *Journal of Politics, 59*(2), 418–451.

Mishler, W., and Rose, R. (2001). What the origins of political trust? Testing institutional and cultural theories in post-communist societies. *Comparative Political Studies, 34,* 30–62.

Mishler, W., and Rose, R. (2005). What are the political consequences of trust? A test of cultural and institutional theories in Russia. *Comparative Political Studies, 38*(9), 1050–1078.

Molm, L. D. (1991). Social exchange: Satisfaction in power-dependence relations. *American Sociological Review, 56*(4), 475–493.

Moscardo, G. (2011). Exploring social representations of tourism planning: Issues for governance. *Journal of Sustainable Tourism, 19*(4), 423–436.

Mosedale, J. (Ed.). (2011). *Political economy of tourism: A critical perspective*. London: Routledge.

Newman, P., and Clarke, J. (2009). *Publics, politics and power: Remaking the public in public services*. London: Sage.

Newton, K. (1999). Social and political trust in established democracies. In P. Norris (Ed.), *Critical citizens: Global support for democratic governance* (pp. 169–187). Oxford: Oxford University Press.

Newton, K. (2001). Trust, social capital and democracy. *International Political Science Review, 22*(2), 201–214.

Norris, P. (1999). Introduction: The growth of critical citizens? In P. Norris (Ed.), *Critical citizens: Global support for democratic government* (pp. 1–30). Oxford: Oxford University Press.

Nunkoo, R., and Gursoy, D. (2012). Residents' support for tourism: An identity perspective. *Annals of Tourism Research, 39*(1), 243–268.

Nunkoo, R., Gursoy, D., and Juwaheer, T. D. (2010). Island residents' identities and their support for tourism: An integration of two theories. *Journal of Sustainable Tourism, 18*(5), 675–693.

Nunkoo, R., and Ramkissoon, H. (2007). Residents' perceptions of the socio-cultural impact of tourism in Mauritius. *Anatolia: An International Journal of Tourism and Hospitality Research, 18*(1), 138–145.

Nunkoo, R., and Ramkissoon, H. (2010a). Community perceptions of tourism in small island states: A conceptual framework. *Journal of Policy Research in Tourism, Leisure and Events, 2*(1), 51–65.

Nunkoo, R., and Ramkissoon, H. (2010b). Gendered theory of planned behavior and residents' support for tourism. *Current Issues in Tourism, 13*(6), 525–540.

Nunkoo, R., and Ramkissoon, H. (2010c). Small island urban tourism: A residents' perspective. *Current Issues in Tourism, 13*(1), 37–60.

Nunkoo, R., and Ramkissoon, H. (2011a). Developing a community support model for tourism. *Annals of Tourism Research, 38*(3), 964–988.

Nunkoo, R., and Ramkissoon, H. (2011b). Residents' satisfaction with community attributes and support for tourism. *Journal of Hospitality and Tourism Research, 35*, 171–190.

Nunkoo, R., and Ramkissoon, H. (2012). Power, trust, social exchange and community support. *Annals of Tourism Research, 39*(3), 997–1023.

Nunkoo, R., and Ramkissoon, H., and Gursoy, D. (2012). Public trust in tourism institutions. *Annals of Tourism Research, 39*(3), 1538–1564.

Nunkoo, R., Smith, S. L., and Ramkissoon, H. (2013). Residents' attitudes to tourism: a longitudinal study of 140 articles from 1984 to 2010. *Journal of Sustainable Tourism, 21*(1), 5–25.

Nyaupane, G. P., and Timothy, D. J. (2010). Power, regionalism and tourism policy in Bhutan. *Annals of Tourism Research, 37*(4), 969–988.

Oberg, P., and Svensson, T. (2010). Does power drive our trust? Relations between labor market actors in Sweden. *Political Studies, 58*, 143–166.

O'Neil, P. (2007). *Essentials of comparative politics* (2nd ed.). New York: Norton.

Oskarsson, S., Svensson, T., and Oberg, P. (2009). Power, trust, and institutional constraints: Individual level evidence. *Rationality and Society, 21*, 171–195.

Pearce, P. L., Moscardo. G., and Ross. G. F. (1996). *Tourism community relationships*. Oxford: Pergamon Press.

Perdue, R. R., Long, P. T., and Allen, L. (1990). Resident support for tourism development. *Annals of Tourism Research, 17*, 586–599.

Pizam, A. (1978). Tourism's impacts: The social costs of the destination community as perceived by its residents. *Journal of Travel Research, 16*(4), 8–12.

Purcell, M., and Nevins, J. (2005). Pushing the boundary: State restructuring, state theory, and the case of US: Mexico border enforcement in the 1990s. *Political Geography, 24*(2), 211–235.

Putman, R. D. (2000). Bowling alone: American's declining social capital. *Journal of Democracy, 6*, 65–78.

Rohrschneider, R., and Schmitt-Beck, R. (2002). Trust in democratic institutions in Germany: Theory and evidence ten years after unification. *German Politics, 11*(3), 35–58.

Rose, R., Mishler, W., and Haerpfer, C. (1998). *Democracy and its alternatives: Understanding post-communist societies.* Baltimore: John Hopkins University Press.

Rudolph, T. J., and Evans, J. (2005). Political trust, ideology, and public support for government spending. *American Journal of Political Science, 49*(3), 660–671.

Ruhanen, L. (2013). Local government: facilitator or inhibitor of sustainable tourism development? *Journal of Sustainable Tourism, 21*(1), 80–98.

Scheidegger, R., and Staerkle, C. (2011). Political trust and distrust in Switzerland: A normative analysis. *Swiss Political Science Review, 17*(2), 164–187.

Sheppard, B. H., and Sherman, D. M. (1998). The grammars of trust: A model and general implications. *Academy of Management Review, 23*(3), 422–437.

Shi, T. (2001). Cultural values and political trust: A comparison of the People's Republic of China and Taiwan. *Comparative Politics, 33*(4), 401–419.

Sutton, Jr. W. (1967). Travel and understanding: Notes of the social structure of tourism. *Journal of Comparative Sociology*, 8, 217–223.

Thibaut, J. W., and Kelley, H. H. (1959). *The social psychology of groups.* New York: John Wiley.

Tyler, T. R., and Degoey, P. (1995). Trust in organizational authorities: The influence of motive attributions on willingness to accept decisions. In R. M. Kramer and T. R. Tyler (Eds.), *Trust in organizations: Frontiers of theory and research* (pp. 331–356). Thousand Oaks, CA: Sage.

Uslaner, E. M. (2002). *The moral foundation of trust.* Cambridge, UK: Cambridge University Press.

Vogel, R. K., and Swanson, B. E. (1988). Setting agendas for community change: The community goal-setting strategy. *Journal of Urban Affairs, 10*(1), 41–61.

Walker, R., Bisset, P., and Adam, J. (2007). Managing risk: Risk perception, trust and control in a primary care partnership. *Social Science and Medicine, 64*, 911–923.

Wang, Y., and Bramwell, B. (2012). Heritage protection and tourism development priorities in Hangzhou, China: A political economy and governance perspective. *Tourism Management, 33*, 988–998.

Wang, Z. (2005). Before the emergence of critical citizens: Economic development and political trust in China. *International Review of Sociology, 15*(1), 155–171.

Ward, C., and Berno, T. (2011). Beyond social exchange theory: Attitudes toward tourists. *Annals of Tourism Research, 38*(4), 1556–1569.

Wearing, S., and Neil, J. (2009). *Ecotourism: Impacts, potential and possibilities.* Oxford: Butterworth-Heinemann.

Weaver, D. (2006). *Sustainable tourism.* Amsterdam: Elsevier.

Webster, C., Ivanov, S., and Illum, S. F. (2011). The paradigms of political economy and tourism policy. In J. Mosedale (Ed.), *Political economy of tourism: A critical perspective* (pp. 55–73). London: Routledge.

Whitener, E. M., Brodt, S. E., Korsgaard, M. A., and Werner, J. M. (1998). Managers as initiators of trust: An exchange relationship framework for understanding managerial trustworthy behavior. *Academy of Management Review, 23*(3), 513–530.

Williams, A. M. (2004). Toward a political economy of tourism. In A. A. Lew and C. M. Hall (Eds.), *A companion to tourism.* Oxford: Blackwell.

Wolf, E. R. (1999). *Envisioning power: Ideologies of dominance and crisis*. Berkeley, CA: University of California Press.

Wong, T. K., Wan, P., and Hsiao, H. M. (2011). The bases of political trust in six Asian societies: Institutional and cultural explanations compared. *International Political Science Review, 3*, 263–281.

Yamagishi, T., and Yamagishi, M. (1994). Trust and commitment in the United States and Japan. *Motivation and Emotion, 18*, 129–166.

9 Researching trust in tourism

Methodological issues and associated concerns

Mark N. K. Saunders, Fergus Lyon, and Guido Möllering

Introduction

Whether researching trust between people, trust in Organizations or trust in institutions and places, the emerging field of trust research has seen a diverse range of approaches. Methods used to research trust are, like the disciplines that research trust, wide ranging and varied. Over the past decade the rapid rise in the number of research outputs on trust, the publication of various handbooks such as Bachmann and Zaheer's (2006) *Handbook of Trust Research*, our own *Handbook of Research Methods on Trust* (Lyon *et al.*, 2012a) and the founding of the *Journal of Trust Research* have all served to demonstrate an increasing interest in trust and to highlight this diversity of methods. For those researching trust in tourism, this diversity raises practical concerns regarding choice of method or methods alongside real opportunities to draw upon experiences across a wide range of disciplines. Such choices are, invariably, driven by the research question or problem as well as each researcher's epistemological and ontological position. As pluralists, we consider a wide range of methods have a place within trust research. However, this does not negate the need to consider practical concerns associated with different methods.

In this chapter, our focus is the practical concerns and associated issues for those conducting empirical research in trust in tourism development and planning. Knowledge and understanding of methods for researching trust are dispersed across a broad multidisciplinary community of trust scholars (Lyon *et al.*, 2012b). Not surprisingly, we therefore draw upon trust research from a wide range of social science disciplines, including tourism, in our consideration of quantitative and qualitative methods, multimethod and mixed-methods designs. In so doing, we do not seek to favor one method or design over another but rather to offer insights into the practical concerns and associated issues when selecting method within trust research. We begin our chapter with issues derived from discussion regarding the nature of trust which we believe need to be considered at the outset of researching trust whatever method or methods are adopted. We then consider the practical concerns and issues associated with different methods for researching trust dynamics in the context of tourism development and planning. We adopt the tried and tested paradigmatic division of quantitative and qualitative methods followed by a brief consideration of multimethod and mixed-methods designs. We conclude with a summary of the associated issues that we believe should be addressed prior to commencing research on trust in tourism development and planning.

The nature of trust

Trust research has, to date, focused on a range of levels of analysis from the personal to the institutional (Rousseau *et al.*, 1998), reviewed in some detail by Bigley and Pearce (1998), Kramer and Lewicki (2010) and Möllering *et al.* (2004). Although these conceptualisations have resulted in wide-ranging debates and in excess of 70 definitions (Seppanen *et al.*, 2007), general agreement is now emerging regarding a definition of trust. Outlined in similar terms by scholars such as Lewicki *et al.* (1998), Mayer *et al.* (1995), and Rousseau *et al.* (1998), trust is depicted as occurring under conditions of risk which require the trusting party (the trustor) to develop favorable expectations of the intentions and behavior of the other party (the trustee), sufficient to prompt a willingness to become vulnerable to the trustee's future conduct. This definition encapsulates the trustor's assessment of the trustee's ability (her or his technical competence to carry out a given task), benevolence (his or her motives toward the trustor) and integrity (her or his adherence to principles such as fairness and honesty) (Mayer *et al.*, 1995). These beliefs inform a subsequent "intention to accept vulnerability based upon positive expectations of the intentions or behavior of another" (Rousseau *et al.*, 1998: 395) – in other words, the trustor's intent to become trusting of the trustee.

Perceived motives and intentions therefore inform how an individual evaluates her or his level of trust of the other. Consequently, the other's behaviors are an integral part of an individual's decision to trust, enabling learning about intentions through observation and interpretation. Based upon such behaviors, an individual makes a judgment about and acts upon the perceived trustworthiness of another, be it an individual, workgroup, organization or some other form (Redman *et al.*, 2011) – this 'other' being the specific focus of the trust. However, the *action* of trusting, as opposed to a *willingness* to trust, is demonstrated through a risk-taking act in which the trustor makes her or himself vulnerable to the other (trustee) (Mayer *et al.*, 1995).

Recently, researchers have started to take a closer look at trusting as a process (Möllering, 2013), not least because issues of trust development over time (Lewicki *et al.*, 2006) have, in many contexts, become issues related to trust repair processes (Kramer and Lewicki, 2010). Although this approach favors longitudinal research designs, multiple points of measurement may actually not capture process effectively per se. Rather, it is important to be able to identify mechanisms of change in the process (such as tourism development and planning) and to enable respondents to reflect on the past, present and future of their trust relationships (Möllering, 2006: 152).

According to common accounts of trust development, trust will be based initially upon rational choice, perceived positive intentions being derived from credible information about the trustee from others rather than personal experience, known as calculus-based trust (Rousseau *et al.*, 1998). Repeated positive experiences will, over time, build upon calculus-based trust to support high levels of relational trust. Inevitably, personal trust will be influenced by the institutional (and cultural) frameworks within which it operates (Saunders *et al.*, 2010; Weibel, 2003). Such frameworks offer controls that allow the focus of trust to be extended beyond a specific individual to a generalised representative (Whitener, 1997). Consequently, the other who is the focus of either trusting intentions or the trust act can take many forms (Redman *et al.*, 2011). This referent (Mayer and Davis, 1999) can take many forms, including an individual known personally such as a tourism agent (e.g. Hornby *et al.*, 2008), organizations or larger groups such as governments agencies and related tourism actors (e.g. Nunkoo and Smith, 2013) as well as tourist destinations (Etzinger and Wiedermann, 2008). For each, trust can occur within a wide range of scenarios, including, in relation to the previous examples, marketing, tourism development and safety management, respectively.

Trust research has highlighted the possibility of the determinants and consequences of trust differing, at least in part, across cultural groups (Saunders *et al.*, 2010). Drawing upon a major review of predominantly quantitative empirical research, Ferrin and Gillespie (2010) highlight that, although there is strong evidence that trust differs between national-societal cultures, there is also evidence that trust is to some extent universal across cultures. For example, whereas Mayer *et al.*'s (1995) apparently universal trustworthiness components of ability, benevolence and integrity may be universally applicable (etic), the relative importance of each has been found to be culturally specific (emic) with regard to small business owners' relationships with customers (Altinay *et al.*, 2014). This emphasises the importance of considering the cultural context in which research is undertaken with regard to the overall research design, the choice of data collection methods and the use of specific instruments to measure trust.

Our brief consideration of the nature of trust highlights four aspects that need to be clarified by the researcher of trust within tourism development and planning at the start of her or his research:

- The conceptualisation of trust to be used; in particular, whether the research is concerned with trustors' intentions (their propensity to trust), their act of trusting (trusting behavior), the trustee's trustworthiness (Dietz *et al.*, 2010) or trusting as a process.
- Whether research is cross-sectional or longitudinal; for example, rather than providing a snapshot, it is concerned with the process of trust development, or changes in trust over time, that have occurred as part of tourism development and planning.
- The referent of trustor's trust; whether the trustee (other) is a specific individual or some form of generalised representative.
- The cultural context within which trust is being researched; in particular, the likely impact this will have upon the suitability and utility of specific quantitative and specific qualitative data collection methods.

It is clarity with regard to these guidelines that helps provide a firm foundation for subsequent research.

Quantitative methods

Trust researchers adopting quantitative methods tend to collect primary data using either a survey strategy in a real-world situation or some form of experimental strategy usually involving a simulation; examples of the former being far more prevalent in tourism trust research. Much recent quantitative research on trust has its origin in experiments, often referred to as 'games' or 'dilemmas', such as the Prisoners' Dilemma (e.g. Deutsch, 1958). Within such experiments, individuals are presented with simulated scenarios in which decisions to collaborate or defect equate to the decision of whether to trust or distrust another party (Gezelius, 2007). Despite more sophisticated simulations such as the Trust Game (Berg *et al.*, 1995), this research has been criticised for over-interpreting the meanings of a simple two-way choice. However, while such experimental strategies offer a clear way of measuring quantitatively a trustor's willingness to trust a trustee and the extent to which such trust is justified, Lewicki and Brinsfield (2012) argue their feasibility for field research is limited. Consequently, in this section we focus on the survey strategy; in particular, the use of questionnaires to collect quantitative data when highlighting issues and associated concerns.

Within the survey strategy, the most common data collection approach is a questionnaire incorporating an existing scale or an adaptation of an existing scale to measure trust. Such instruments are well suited to capturing respondents' perceptions and intentions and, where pre-existing scales are used, potentially allow the replication of results (Gillespie, 2012). Nunkoo and Smith (2013), for example, surveyed a sample of 391 residents of Niagara region, Canada, to test their trust in government actors and support for tourism. In the survey they used an established trust scale consisting of four items to measure trust in government actors and an additional, slightly modified, existing three-item scale to measure interpersonal trust. Similarly, Yasamorn and Ussahawanitchakit (2011) used an established (albeit different) three-item scale to measure mutual trust in their study of strategic collaborative capability. In contrast, Kim *et al.*'s (2010) study of factors influencing Korean online tourism shoppers' trust, satisfaction and loyalty used another three-item measure of perceived trust, items for their scale being derived from a range of previous research findings.

Our brief consideration of these three tourism and trust studies highlights a potential concern for tourism trust researchers, already recognized within the field of trust research: the wide range of potential trust scales and measures available. Within trust research there is a confusing array of instruments covering differing trust dimensions that vary widely in their construct validity and the use of which is both fragmented and idiosyncratic (McEvily and Tortoriello, 2011). Recent reviews of trust measurement scales (Dietz and den Hartog, 2006; McEvily and Tortoriello, 2011) although providing a useful assessment and allowing comparison of existing scales, reveal serious limitations associated with many. These have been summarised by Gillespie (2012) and, in addition to their fragmented and idiosyncratic use, include concerns about their construct validity and differences between how trust has been conceptualised by the researcher and how it is measured.

Fragmented and idiosyncratic use of scales – in particular, the multitude (over 100) of measures of trust in existence, many of which are newly developed (McEvily and Tortoriello, 2011) – means that few have been replicated more than once. Where replication is argued by researchers to have occurred, modifications to item wording are likely to be relatively minor, often only contextual (e.g. Nunkoo and Smith, 2013). However for some replications, modifications may be so substantial as to raise doubts as to whether the revised items actually represent the original measure (Gillespie, 2012). Alternatively, the trust scale used is acknowledged as based on the work of a range of others (e.g. Moliner *et al.*, 2007) rather than a replication. In such studies, the precise derivation of individual items used in the scale often remains unclear. Invariably, this lack of common scale items and of clarity of explanation limits the possibility of research replication.

Construct validity is of vital importance for any scale, assessing how accurately the concept has been measured (Saunders *et al.*, 2012). The reviews by Dietz and den Hartog (2006) and McEvily and Tortoriello (2011) highlight how many studies developing scales to measure trust report only reliability statistics rather than provide evidence of convergent or discriminant validity. Of equal concern for trust in tourism development and planning researchers, it is assumed, often implicitly, that an instrument developed to measure trust in one situation can be adapted for use in another situation without any real check on whether it is also valid in that new situation (Gillespie, 2012). This mismatch can occur in terms of both the referent of trust – for example, line manager or tour guide – and the broader context within which trust is being researched – for example, a particular organization or resort or a different culture (Saunders *et al.*, 2010). An additional concern is where the referents used for individual items within a scale switch inappropriately (Gillespie, 2012) – for example, between a named individual and organizations in general.

We have already highlighted the difference between an individual's *willingness* to trust and his or her *action* of trusting. Linked to this is the need within research to adopt a scale that measures trust in the same way as it has been conceptualised within the research. In particular, most scales measure the trustor's *perceived trustworthiness* of the trustee, which, although a determinant of trust, does not equate to the action of trusting and the associated risk-taking behavior (Gillespie, 2012). For example, asking respondents to rate the extent to which they agree with the item "Tourism online sites are reliable" (Kim *et al.*, 2011: 262) will collect data on their perceptions of these sites' trustworthiness. In contrast, the item "Trust in local government to do what is right in tourism" measured on a five-point scale from *do not trust them at all* to *trust them very much* (Nunkoo and Smith, 2013: 125) relates to the act of trusting. It is important when looking at such items to note that, although opposites in definitional terms, trust and distrust appear to have differing expressions and manifestations (Lewicki *et al.*, 1998;

Saunders *et al.*, 2014). Consequently, a response of *strongly disagree* to a statement used to indicate trust, such as "Tourism institutions can be trusted to do what is right without our having to constantly check on them" (Nunkoo *et al.*, 2012: 1550), might indicate an absence of trust rather than distrust.

For researchers of tourism development and planning intending to research trust quantitatively, this highlights three additional concerns that need to be addressed prior to data collection:

- Where existing trust instruments are being considered, the derivation of the trust scale and the precise nature, if any, of adaptations made.
- The appropriateness of the trust scale for the research situation; in particular, whether the measure has been validated (or can be coherently argued to be valid if it is a rigorous, transparent and well-accepted measure) within the research context and for the intended referent group.
- The fit between how trust has been conceptualised for the research and the aspect or aspects of trust measured by the adopted, researcher-adapted or researcher-developed trust scale.

Qualitative methods

Qualitative methods in trust research have been and continue to be particularly important for shedding light on trust processes and theory building, allowing more in-depth exploration and the emergence of new concepts not previously found in the academic literature. As for other research foci, the use of qualitative methods in trust research invariably tends to involve less-structured data collection (Lyon *et al.*, 2012b), often within a case study or ethnographic strategy. The dominant data collection techniques within these designs are the semi-structured and in-depth interviews. Both of these allow themes related to trust to be explored in detail and participant answers to be probed further as necessary, including establishing precisely how participants define trust. For example, Yin and Zhao (2006: 10) used semi-structured interviews with 24 senior managers selected from five varied case study regional Chinese tourism alliances to explore trust-building processes. Like many, they supplemented this with documentary secondary data, including records of board meetings and annual reports. Qualitative methods allowing the collection of in-depth data, such as the critical incident technique (e.g. Münscher and Kühlmann, 2012), are particularly suited to understanding processual and narrative accounts of trust. Other qualitative methods, such as various forms of observation, have been used by trust researchers to establish precisely what people are actually doing rather than what they claim to be doing (Tillmar, 2012) in relation to trusting behaviors. Zahra (2011), for example, combined observation (in which her role as researcher was revealed) with interviews, focus groups and documentary analysis to examine the governance of New Zealand regional tourism organizations. She argued that these observations helped her to understand the rich and complex nature of the interrelations and politics associated with regional tourism organizations.

While interviewing and, to a lesser extent, observation have dominated much qualitative research, it is important to note the wide range of other methods available to the trust in tourism development and planning researcher. A good selection of these – including repertory grids, critical incident technique, using historical records and diary techniques – are outlined in our handbook (Lyon *et al.*, 2012a).

For researchers of trust in tourism development and planning, both Yin and Zhao's (2006) and Zahra's (2011) studies highlight aspects that need to be considered before and during qualitative data collection. These and others have been recognized within trust research more generally (Lyon *et al.*, 2012b) and relate to participants' sensitivity about trust situations and the associated need to build rapport, the potential impact of the researcher upon what is being researched and the need to recognize the complexity of trust situations. They also illustrate the utility of combining data from different sources in multimethod qualitative designs and mixed-methods designs, an aspect we discuss in the next section.

Problems associated with participants' sensitivity and the researcher's need to obtain useful data are widespread in research. For example, even where physical access to research trust has been granted, and (perhaps) people have been instructed to take part, it is still necessary to build a relationship with participants. Until rapport is built and cognitive access gained, participants are often unwilling to discuss topics such as trust where they feel embarrassed, threatened or that their response might be incriminating (Jehn and Jonsen, 2010). Consequently, they may give responses that protect themselves from potential harm or embarrassment, present themselves in a positive light or please the researcher. This has the potential to threaten the accuracy or utility of data collected (Dalton *et al.*, 1997). Not surprisingly, this problem is recognized widely; most research methods textbooks emphasise the need to minimise such problems by ensuring saliency of the topic and emphasising privacy and confidentiality (Saunders *et al.*, 2012). Saunders (2012) argues such advice is equally valid for those researching trust. While using a card-sort approach, he highlights the importance of building rapport with participants during interviews while taking care not to influence their responses. These types of techniques can be used during interviews to allow data to be collected on trust situations that might be considered initially to be embarrassing or unusual. In relation to undertaking observations, Zahra (2011) illustrates the importance of being clear as to whether the researcher is formally involved in the phenomenon being observed while also emphasising the importance of understanding and being immersed in the wider context. The latter, she argues, along with reflection, also aids the integration of data from a variety of sources. Such processes invariably take time.

The complexity of trust situations affects the way in which qualitative data collection techniques need to be operationalised. Semi-structured and in-depth interviews allow for aspects to be followed up with probing questions. Hornby *et al.* (2008) report, briefly, on their use of semi-structured interviews with tourism operators using an interview protocol comprising open-ended questions to direct the interview focus. Yin and Zhao (2006: 17) adopt a similar process, including as an appendix their "discussion guide" for interviewers comprising 13 initial open questions that are used with follow-up prompts. In this guide, the initial open question, "Please describe the trust-building process with other partners affiliated with the same RTAs [regional tourism authorities]," highlights again the importance of trust referents within the research, in this case 'other partners'. This would need to have been established explicitly through further questioning had the participants not made it clear. Subsequent prompts for this question remind the interviewer to "follow up on trust-building stages if they are unclear, but avoid too much trust-related detail."

This illustrates the complexity of the trust situation and emphasises the importance of not leading the participant to a particular answer. Zahra (2011: 542) makes an equally important point regarding the utility of qualitative methods in complex trust situations, commenting that through observation and reflection, she "was able to unify the fragmented data gathered from other sources." Tourism researchers also have to decide whether to refer explicitly to the word *trust* or to probe on issues of collaboration and expectation, allowing the interviewee to express trust-related concepts in his or her own words. The English word *trust* may not translate easily in other languages, so qualitative research (especially constructivist designs) offers the potential to explore the different meanings and interpretations.

For researchers of tourism development and planning intending to research trust qualitatively, our discussion highlights three additional concerns to be addressed prior to data collection:

- The appropriateness of the proposed data collection technique (or techniques) to be used, recognizing the wide range of techniques available in addition to interviews and observation.
- The need for suitable ways of building rapport and developing cognitive access, allowing for the sensitivity of trust as a topic to many.
- Ways of questioning without influencing participants' responses while still recognizing the complexity of trust issues.

Multi- and mixed-methods designs

We have already hinted at the possibility of combining of methods within trust research and the potential utility of doing this. Methods can be combined either within a purely quantitative or within a purely qualitative multimethod design or, alternatively, using both quantitative and quantitative within a mixed-methods design (Tashakkori and Teddlie, 2010). Using multimethod, and, in particular, mixed-methods research, has been argued to provide additional complementary data and increase interpretive power (Edmondson and McManus, 2007). Where research questions require rich detailed data, as is often the case in understanding trust, qualitative methods have often been prioritised or emphasised, and quantitative methods have been complementary. In contrast, where research questions require statistical representation, quantitative methods are likely to be prioritised (Teddlie and Tashakkori, 2010). The decision regarding whether to use a mixed-methods rather than multimethod design is, however, dependent upon the researcher's epistemological and ontological viewpoint. For some researchers, quantitative and qualitative traditions are considered completely different in their epistemological and ontological assumptions and therefore are incompatible. For others, the quantitative/qualitative distinction is ambiguous.

Despite these potential epistemological and ontological concerns, both multimethod and mixed-methods designs are used to support understanding of the complexities of trust (Norman *et al.*, 2010), multiple data sources and, in particular, qualitative data being argued to offer additional explanatory capability (Möllering, 2006; Saunders *et al.*, 2010). Research by Yin and Zhao (2006), outlined earlier, adopted a multimethod qualitative design combining a range of data sources, including records of board meetings and publicly available information such as annual reports. However, research adopting a mixed-methods design appears more usual.

Zahra (2011) adopted a mixed-methods design, her qualitative methods including observation, interviews and focus groups alongside secondary data and a (quantitative) questionnaire to obtain a rich understanding of New Zealand's Waikato Regional Tourism Organization. In this design, qualitative research methods dominated. In contrast, a quantitative method dominated Pesämaa and Hair's (2008) mixed-methods design in their study of cooperative strategies for improving the tourism industry in remote regions. In this research, the design of a questionnaire, which included a researcher-developed scale of six trust items, was informed by qualitative research comprising observation, interviews and analysis of documents. Similarly, Etzinger and Wiedemann's (2008) research on trust and distrust in the management of safety management of tourist destinations used 71 interviews to reveal 15 measures and conditions thought to increase tourists' trust. These were incorporated subsequently in an online questionnaire as separate trust and distrust items, the questionnaire receiving 640 responses.

For researchers of tourism development and planning considering using multimethod or mixed-methods designs, this discussion highlights two research design concerns that the researcher needs to consider prior to data collection:

• The compatibility between the proposed multimethod or mixed-methods research design and the researcher's epistemological and ontological beliefs.
• If compatible, the extent to which the adoption of multimethod or mixed methods rather than using a single (mono) method will provide additional insights and increase interpretive power.

Summary

Choice of method or methods when researching trust in tourism development and planning is influenced by the researcher's epistemological and ontological beliefs. These beliefs invariably affect the decision regarding the use of quantitative or qualitative methods, whether a mono-method, multimethod or mixed-methods design is adopted and whether the research is cross-sectional or longitudinal. Other aspects of design that require clarification, because they will influence subsequent choice and use of method, include the cultural context in which the research is being undertaken and how trust will be conceptualised. In particular, it is important to establish whether the research is concerned with trustors' intentions, trustees' trustworthiness, the trusting act or the process of trust development as well as clarifying the referent of each trustor's trust. Where an existing trust instrument is being considered, it is crucial that it measures trust in the same way as it has been conceptualised within the research. Consequently, it is important to establish a trust scale's derivation, including whether adaptations have been made and whether it has been validated for the intended research context and referent group. Qualitative methods also offer a wide range of data collection techniques that need to be assessed for their appropriateness to the specific research question, their success in understanding trust being dependent upon developing cognitive access. However, considering these issues and addressing these practical concerns is of little use if the choice of method and how it is operationalised do not enable the research question to be answered or research problem to be addressed.

References

Altinay L., Saunders, M.N.K. and Wang, C. (2014). The influence of culture on trust judgments in customer relationship development by ethnic minority small businesses. *Journal of Small Business Management,* 52(1), 59–78.

Bachmann, R. and Zaheer, A. (2006). *Handbook of Trust Research.* Cheltenham: Edward Elgar.

Berg, J., Dickhaut, J. and McCabe, K. (1995). Trust, reciprocity and social history. *Games and Economic Behavior*, 10, 122–142.

Bigley, G. A. and Pearce, J. L. (1998). Straining for shared meaning in organizational science: Problems of trust and distrust. *Academy of Management Review,* 23(3), 405–421.

Dalton, D. R., Daily, C. M. and Wimbush, J. C. (1997). Collecting sensitive data in business ethics research: A case for the unmatched count technique. *Journal of Business Ethics,* 16, 1049–1057.

Deutsch, M. (1958). Trust and suspicion. *Journal of Conflict Resolution*, 2, 265–279.

Dietz, G., N. Gillespie and G. T. Chao (2010). Unravelling the complexities of trust and culture. In M.N.K. Saunders, D. Skinner, G. Dietz, N. Gillespie and R. J. Lewicki (eds) *Organizational Trust: A Cultural Perspective*, Cambridge: Cambridge University Press, 3–41.

Dietz, G. and Den Hartog, D. (2006). Measuring trust inside organizations. *Personnel Review*, 35(5), 557–588.

Edmondson, A. C. and McManus, S. E. (2007). Methodological fit in management field research. *Academy of Management Review,* 32, 1155–1179.

Etzinger, C. and Wiedermann, P. M. (2008). Trust in the safety of tourist destinations: Hard to gain, easy to lose? New insights on the asymmetry principle. *Risk Analysis*, 28(4), 843–853.

Ferrin, D. and Gillespie, N. (2010). Trust differences across national-societal cultures: Much to do, or much ado about nothing? In M.N.K. Saunders, D. Skinner, N. Gillespie, G. Dietz and R. J. Lewicki (eds) *Organizational Trust: A Cultural Perspective,* Cambridge, Cambridge University Press, 42–86.

Gezelius, S. (2007). Can norms account for strategic action? Information management in fishing as a game of legitimate strategy. *Sociology,* 41(2), 201–218.

Gillespie, N. (2012). Measuring trust in organizational contexts: An overview of survey-based measures. In F. Lyon, G. Möllering and M.N.K. Saunders (eds) *Handbook of Research Methods on Trust*, Cheltenham: Edward Elgar, 175–188.

Hornby, G., Brunetto, Y. and Jennings, G. (2008). The role of inter-organizational relationships in tourism operators' participation in destination marketing systems. *Journal of Hospitality and Leisure Marketing,* 17(1–2), 184–215.

Jehn, K. A. and Jonsen, K. (2010). A multimethod approach to the study of sensitive organizational issues. *Journal of Mixed Methods Research,* 4, 313–341.

Kim, M-J., Chung , J. and Lee, C-K., (2010). The effect of perceived trust on electronic commerce: Shopping online for tourism products and services in South Korea. *Tourism Management,* 32, 256–265.

Kramer, R. M. and Lewicki, R. J. (2010). Repairing and enhancing trust: Approaches to reducing organizational trust deficits. *Academy of Management Annals*, 4, 245–277.

Lewicki R. J. and Brinsfield C. (2012). Measuring trust beliefs and behaviors. In F. Lyon, G. Möllering and M.N.K .Saunders (eds) *Handbook of Research Methods on Trust*, Cheltenham: Edward Elgar, 29–39.

Lewicki, R. J., McAllister, D. J. and Bies, R. J. (1998). Trust and distrust: New relationships and realities. *Academy of Management Review,* 23(3), 438–458.

Lewicki, R. J., Tomlinson, E. C. and Gillespie, N. (2006). Models of interpersonal trust development: Theoretical approaches, empirical evidence, and future directions. *Journal of Management*, 32(6), 991–1022.

Lyon F., Möllering G. and Saunders M.N.K. (eds) (2012a). *Handbook of Research Methods on Trust*. Cheltenham: Edward Elgar.

Lyon, F., Möllering, G. and Saunders M.N.K. (2012b). Introduction: The variety of methods for the multi-faceted phenomenon of trust. In F. Lyon, G. Möllering and M.N.K. Saunders (eds) *Handbook of Research Methods on Trust,* Cheltenham: Edward Elgar, 1–15.

Mayer, R. C. and Davis, J. H. (1999). The effect of the performance appraisal system on trust for management: A field quasi-experiment. *Journal of Applied Psychology*, 84(1), 123–136.

Mayer, R. C., Davis, J. H. and Schoorman, F. D. (1995). An integrative model of organizational trust. *Academy of Management Review,* 20(3), 709–734.

McEvily, B. and Tortoriello, M. (2011). Measuring trust in organizational research: Review and recommendations. *Journal of Trust Research*, 1(1), 23–63.

Moliner, M. A., Sánchez, J., Rodríguez, R. M. and Callarisa, L. (2007) Relationship quality with a travel agency: The influence of the postpurchase perceived value of a tourism package. *Tourism and Hospitality Research*, 7(3/4), 194–211.

Möllering, G. (2006). *Trust: Reason, Routine, Reflexivity*. Oxford: Elsevier.

Möllering, G. (2013). Process views of trusting and crises. In R. Bachmann and A. Zaheer (eds) *Handbook of Advances in Trust Research,* Cheltenham: Edward Elgar, 285–306.

Möllering, G., Bachmann, R. and Lee, S. H. (2004). Understanding organizational trust: Foundations, constellations, and issues of operationalisation. *Journal of Managerial Psychology,* 19(6), 556–570.

Münscher, R. and Kühlmann, T. M. (2012). Cross-cultural comparative case studies: A means of uncovering dimensions of trust. In F. Lyon, G. Möllering and M.N.K. Saunders (eds) *Handbook of Research Methods on Trust,* Cheltenham: Edward Elgar, 161–172.

Norman, S. M., Avolio, B. J. and Luthans, F. (2010). The impact of positivity and transparency on trust in leaders and their perceived effectiveness. *Leadership Quarterly,* 21(3), 350–364.

Nunkoo, R., Ramkissoon, H. and Gusoy, G. (2012). Public trust in tourism institutions. *Annals of Tourism Research*, 39(3), 1538–1564.

Nunkoo, R. and Smith, S.L.J. (2013). Political economy of tourism: Trust in government actors, political support, and their determinants. *Tourism Management*, 36, 120–132.

Pesämaa, O. and Hair, J. F. Jr. (2008). Cooperative strategies for improving the tourism industry in remote geographic regions. *Scandinavian Journal of Hospitality and Tourism*, 8(1), 48–61.

Redman, T., Dietz, G., Snape, E. and van der Borg, W. (2011). Trust in the workplace: A multiple constituencies approach. *International Journal of Human Resource Management,* 22(11), 2384–2402.

Rousseau, D. M., Sitkin, S. B., Burt, R. S. and Carmerer, C. (1998). Not so different after all: A cross-discipline view of trust. *Academy of Management Review,* 23(3), 393–404.

Saunders, M.N.K. (2012). Combining card sorts and in-depth interviews. In F. Lyon, G. Möllering and M.N.K. Saunders (eds) *Handbook of Research Methods on Trust,* Cheltenham: Edward Elgar, 110–120.

Saunders, M.N.K., Lewis, P. and Thornhill, A. (2012). *Research Methods for Business Students* (6th edn). Harlow: Pearson.

Saunders, M.N.K., Skinner, D., Gillespie N., Dietz, G. and Lewicki, R.J. (eds) (2010). *Organizational Trust: A Cultural Perspective.* Cambridge: Cambridge University Press.

Saunders, M.N.K., Ditez, G. and Thornhill, A. (2014). Trust and distrust: Polar opposites or independent but co-existing? *Human Relations,* 67(6), 639–665.

Seppanen, R., Blomqvist, K. and Sundqvist, S. (2007). Measuring inter-organizational trust – a critical review of the empirical research in 1990–2003. *Industrial Marketing Management,* 36(2), 249–265.

Tashakkori, A. and Teddlie, C. (eds) (2010). *The Sage Handbook of Mixed Methods in Social and Behavioral Research* (2nd edn). Thousand Oaks, CA: Sage.

Tillmar, M. (2012). Cross-cultural comparative case studies: A means of uncovering dimensions of trust. In F. Lyon, G. Möllering and M.N.K. Saunders (eds) *Handbook of Research Methods on Trust,* Cheltenham: Edward Elgar, 102–109.

Weibel, A. (2003). Book review – Trust within and between organizations by Lane and Bachmann. *Personnel Review,* 32(5), 667–671.

Whitener, E. (1997). The impact of human resource management activities on employee trust. *Human Resource Management Review,* 7, 389–404.

Yasamorn, N. and Ussahawanitchakit, P. (2011). Strategic collaborative capability, business growth and organizational sustainability: Evidence from tourism businesses in Thailand. *International Journal of Business Strategy,* 11(3), 1–27.

Yin, M. and Zhao, S-Z. (2006). Research on a dynamic model of trust building within regional tourism alliances: Evidence from China. *The Chinese Economy,* 9(6), 5–18.

Zahra, A. L. (2011). Rethinking regional tourism governance: The principle of subsidiarity. *Journal of Sustainable Tourism,* 19(4/5), 535–552.

Index